# RICHARD III

## AND THE DEATH OF CHIVALRY

# RICHARD III
## AND THE DEATH OF CHIVALRY

DAVID HIPSHON

First published 2009

The History Press
The Mill, Brimscombe Port
Stroud, Gloucestershire, GL5 2QG
www.thehistorypress.co.uk

British Library Cataloguing in Publication Data.
A catalogue record for this book is available from the British Library.

ISBN 978 0 7509 5074 9

Typesetting and origination by The History Press
Printed in Great Britain

# CONTENTS

# ACKNOWLEDGEMENTS

I owe a debt of gratitude to far more people than I could possibly mention here, but hope I may be able to repay some of that debt in the course of time. Meanwhile, space allows me to mention but a few. I would especially like to thank Rosemary Horrox for her kindness, understanding and willingness to help when I despatched random plaintive emails. She unwittingly sowed the seeds for this book by bringing the Stanley-Harrington feud to my attention during a supervision in my MPhil year at Cambridge. I apologise to Rosemary for the anguish she may suffer when she glances at the result. I would also like to thank Martin Lubikowski for his ever-optimistic encouragement and help in the early days. My colleagues and pupils at St James all deserve medals for having to put up with me in general, but I would particularly like to thank David Marshal and Peter Crompton for reading and commenting on some of the early chapters. I would also like to thank my good-humoured and enthusiastic sixth-formers for their interest and support, particularly in making suggestions for these acknowledgements. My eldest daughter Emma was ever-willing to read drafts and give sound advice. I would like to thank her and the rest of the family, and especially my wife Sarah Jane for her unfailing presence. Finally, my father brought home a copy of Paul Murray Kendall's book on Richard III when I was a boy. I still have that book: it was the first history book I read from cover to cover. It sparked a life-long interest in Richard III and the search for truth in history. This book is dedicated to the memory of my father and his quest for truth, not only in history, but in life itself.

# ONE

# THE SHADOW OF AGINCOURT

On 22 August 1485 Richard III, by the Grace of God King of England and of France and lord of Ireland, wearing a specially-made golden crown fitted around his helmet, spurred his horse and charged into battle. By his side were his knights of the Body, his friends and loyal servants who had worked with him, lived with him and fought with him over many years. As the trumpets and drums were sounded and the stocky war-horses began to canter, the royal standard was unfurled and held aloft for all to see. It bore the cross of St George, patron saint of England and of soldiers, the white rose encircled by the rays of the sun representing the house of York and the white boar of Richard himself. Woven into the design was the royal motto, *Dieu et Mon Droit*, 'For God and My Right'. The man entrusted with the honour of bearing into battle this heraldic symbol of majesty was James Harrington, friend, counsellor and retainer of the king. Around them were Harrington's kinsmen and associates, colleagues and comrades, the Dacres, Parrs, Middletons, Huddlestons and Pilkingtons. These men were bound together by ties of family, history, culture and aspiration. They were intensely loyal to their lord and master, Richard III, and were willing to fight for him even unto death.

As their horses began to gallop down the slope, with armour and swords glinting and ringing in the dank dawn air hanging over the Leicestershire fields, the lives of these men rose up from the mundane to the sublime, entering a sphere in which the heroic deeds of legend, myth and history could be emulated in a reality that they had each striven to realise. They were to be tested in battle and with their education and training behind them, their true characters would now be revealed. In this moment lived the hope of everlasting glory, fame and honour. Wedded to the service of their lord by oaths of fealty, and to each other through their shared values and kinship, this troop of the royal household, the knights of the Body, armed with swords, flails, hammers, axes and lances, presented a spectacle of power, courage and unity which would never be seen again on English soil. As the hooves of several hundred horses thundered across the battlefield, an ancient code of ethics and loyalty, of honour exemplified in action through religious and physical sacrifice, was charging to an impelling convulsion. This last charge of knights in English history was more than the last throw of the dice for a beleaguered king: it was also the end of an era and the death of chivalry.

As the king and his knights, several hundred strong, swept in a panoply of power past the vanguard of the duke of Norfolk to their right, they may have known already that the loyal duke had been killed, and that the royal men-at-arms in the marshy ground were being pushed back and were on the point of breaking. To their left stood the troops of Cheshire and Lancashire under the command of Thomas lord Stanley and his brother William. Ahead lay the isolated and vulnerable target presented by the rebel earl of Richmond, Henry Tudor, and his contingent of Lancastrians, exiles and French mercenaries. He had been moving towards the Stanley forces to encourage them to abandon King Richard and join him in his attempt to gain the throne. The tidal surge of horse and man pouring across the valley prevented that meeting and separated the untrustworthy Stanley brothers from the Tudor's troops. Before the king lay his prey, the inexperienced Henry Tudor with a group of knights uncertain and untested in quality. Richard's household troops crashed into the Tudor's guard and began to force their way forward towards him through a melee of flashing maces, axes and swords. At that moment when all hung in the balance and the life of Henry Tudor lay at the mercy of the last Plantagenet king of England, William Stanley made his move. In an act of calculated treachery he threw his men into the fray and hurled them at the backs of the royal knights. Within feet of his quarry, Richard, having killed Henry Tudor's standard bearer with his own hand, was surrounded and hacked to death, crying, 'Treason! Treason!'

Richard's death after a short reign of just over two years ushered in the Tudor era and, with it, the inevitable vilification of Richard and the destruction of his reputation. Richard was the most controversial king in English history even without the work of the Tudor propagandists. When his brother, Edward IV, had died in 1483, he had left his eldest son, twelve-year-old Edward V, as his successor. Within weeks the boy, with his younger brother, Richard, had been taken to the Tower of London from whence they never emerged. These two boys, the famous Princes in the Tower, were believed to have been murdered on the orders of Richard III, their uncle, so that he could become king instead. In a shocking and swift coup, Richard had seized power against all expectations, sweeping aside political opponents, ancient conventions and formal legalities. It is hardly surprising that the Tudor historians, keen to shore up the shaky credentials of Henry Tudor, should have had such an easy time in blackening Richard's name and thereby justifying the accession of Henry VII.

The mystery and continuing controversy surrounding the usurpation of Richard and the fate of the Princes in the Tower, has led many to assume that what happened at the battle of Bosworth Field was a direct consequence of those events. They argue that Richard's criminal actions in disposing so wantonly and callously of his nephews and taking the throne for himself, backfired in a reaction which brought him retribution and death. He received his just deserts, they say, and was killed at Bosworth because he could not rely on the loyalty of key men who had qualms about his stealing the crown, were shocked by the horrendous extinction of two innocent boys and felt morally obliged to rise up and oppose him. As we examine these events a little more closely, however, we will see that what happened at that battle had less to do with Richard's usurpation and the disappearance of the princes than it had to do with the threat his kingship posed to the Stanley family and to the earl of Northumberland. When William Stanley betrayed Richard at Bosworth he could not have cared less about the legalities of the usurpation or the whereabouts of Richard's nephews. What mattered to him was the wonderful opportunity presented by that magnificent charge of knights. By Richard's side was James Harrington, a constant thorn in the side of Stanley ambitions in the north-west, along with his kinsmen and supporters, many of whom shared Harrington's enmity of the Stanleys. Richard's rule seriously threatened the expansion of Stanley power because he supported these men and disliked the Stanleys. If Richard made a mistake it was to alienate such powerful men and to invest so heavily in the goodwill and friendship of the northern gentry that formed his affinity. Bosworth was important because it was the beginning of the end of such factionalism. The Tudor dynasty monopolised power and destroyed the medieval regional and personal bonds upon which it had been founded. That Richard was unable to rise above the partisan loyalties and conflicts which led to his betrayal had much to do with his character, his beliefs and the events that shaped them in the years before he took the throne.

Historians have struggled to free British history from the shackles of 1485. It was not the battle of Bosworth Field that brought the end of an era, they argue, but events and shifting cultural currents on a broader sea. The medieval world, which we associate with damsels in distress being rescued from picturesque castles by knights in shining armour, had already been brought to an ignominious conclusion by the advent of gunpowder and artillery. The world of illuminated manuscripts, village pageants and monasteries was approaching its denouement as the twin forces of the Renaissance and the Reformation swept all before them. The printing press and improvements in navigation were changing the world in ways that could scarcely have been imagined a generation earlier. The true end of the Middle Ages, they argue, was 1453 when the Ottoman Turks finally took Constantinople and the Byzantine Empire came to an end. Or, they suggest, perhaps it was 1492 when Columbus set sail for the New World. Either way, it had little to do with a muddy spat on the border between Leicestershire and Warwickshire in 1485.

The extraordinary events at Bosworth, however, cannot be so lightly dismissed. It was unusual enough for a king to die in battle. This event itself was sufficiently rare to expose 1485 to the glare of historical scrutiny. The only other occasion in English history in which a king was killed fighting for his throne and dynastic ambitions was in 1066. In that year two kings met their deaths on English soil: Harald Hardrada of Norway and Harold II of England. Other kings had died in the pursuit of martial exploits – William the Conqueror had been thrown from his horse while on campaign in Normandy and Richard the Lionheart had died from wounds received at a siege – but none had actually died in battle. It was a rare and unusual event. Before the Conquest in 1066 Edmund Ironside had died shortly after the battle of Ashingdon in 1016 but we have to go into the murky depths of the Anglo-Saxon past, before England emerged as a political entity, to find similarly dramatic ends to the reign of kings. In those days, when kings were expected to lead troops in battle, violent death was something of an occupational hazard. Ethelfrith of Northumbria, killed in 616, set a trend in the northern kingdom and was followed in similar style by his three successors, Edwin, Oswald and Oswy, all duly killed fighting their neighbours. Penda of Mercia met his death in battle and Edmund of East Anglia was killed by the Vikings in 868. All these kings were expected to fight and to face death if necessary. With so many kingdoms jostling for position on such a small island, casualties were inevitable. The Viking invasions made the situation worse, of course, but they also cleared away several kingdoms and reduced the number of rivals to a manageable level. By the time William the Conqueror had arrived, much of the business of kingship could be accomplished in councils and banquets. For Richard to die in battle was unusual enough, but to die at the head of his household knights in a flurry of sword strokes after a thunderous charge, four hundred years after the battle of Hastings, was positively anachronistic.

It certainly never happened again. Two years later at the battle of Stoke, Henry VII kept a safe distance from the action and was never in danger. Henry VIII in the sixteenth century toyed with the idea of war but had learnt from his father the benefits of profitable posturing and diplomatic grand-standing. War was expensive and rather risky. Kings became adept at delegation when it came to these tricky matters. Elizabeth famously braved her own body in war against the Spanish, but only as far as reviewing her own troops at Tilbury before sitting back to receive news of the defeat of the Spanish Armada. Charles I found himself with plenty of fighting to do in the English Civil War of the seventeenth century but left it largely to his nephew, Prince Rupert. James II was present at the battle of the Boyne in Ireland but had enough good sense to allow himself room to escape when things got nasty. William III was brave enough but also fortunate to win over John Churchill, the first duke of Marlborough. With the greatest commander on the planet at one's disposal it is safer to spend one's time dodging mole hills at Hampton Court and letting the professionals fight it out on the battlefields of Europe. The last king of England to be present at a battle was George II, at Dettingen in 1743, but he was kept safely in the background while he displayed his warrior credentials to his own grandiloquent satisfaction, marching his horse about in fine style.

After the twelfth century hereditary succession had become well established and this meant that the military skills were not an essential qualification for the job of monarch. The lottery of birth would determine the martial abilities of the king, and this could hardly be relied upon. There were easier and more conventional ways of solving disputes. If fighting war was necessary then it should be left to those whose business it was. It was not in a king's best inter- ests to place himself in unnecessary danger and present an easy target for his enemies. Only in extreme circumstances would he do so. He might, however, place himself at the head of his army and invoke an ancient royal obligation to conquer enemies and lead his warriors to fame, wealth and victory, but in order to do so he would have to be the sort of man who bought into that concept and had the ability to sustain it. There were such men, and their reigns were lauded by the people in songs, chronicles and folklore. The ideal was still very much alive in Richard's day in the memory of the great English conquests in France under Henry V. His victory at Agincourt in 1415 was still bright in the memory of many of those who fought at Bosworth, kindled and kept alight by the knowledge of their own family traditions and their forebears who were there on that glorious day.

As it happens, Richard would dearly have loved to be fighting another Agincourt, with the flower of French chivalry arrayed before him, rather than Henry Tudor with his motley collection of rebels, disaffected Lancastrians and international mercenaries. Ten years earlier, on the sixtieth anniversary of Agincourt, Richard, as duke of Gloucester, had been at that very place in France where the battle had taken place. Leading his men to battle he had eagerly anticipated invoking the spirit of Henry V and crushing the perfidious French beneath the heroic onslaught of English arms. Unfortunately for Richard, and to the disappointment and disbelief of a considerable number of his men, King Edward had other ideas. He had led the expedition to France, but was only too keen to be paid off by the French king and to return home again. Two years later their sister, Margaret, duchess of Burgundy, had appealed to them for help as Louis XI of France ravaged her dowager lands. Richard was desperately keen to help but was again thwarted by his more pragmatic and circumspect brother.[1] Now that he was king himself it would only be a matter of time before Richard turned his attention to reviving hostilities against France. Indeed it was this very fact that had enabled Henry Tudor to receive the backing of the French king. Richard's father, the duke of York, had been the last Englishman to achieve military success in France and everyone knew how keen his son was to emulate him.

The duke of York, also called Richard, had his own reasons for wanting to keep the flame of Agincourt alive. His own father, Richard earl of Cambridge, the grandfather of Richard III, had been executed by Henry V for his treasonable involvement in the Southampton Plot, on the eve of the expedition to France. This had left the four-year-old Richard in a difficult situation. As his mother had died giving birth to him he had become an orphan. His uncle, Edward, duke of York, went on to fight with Henry V at Agincourt and was killed, leaving no children. In view of this praiseworthy service, and out of pity for the small boy, Henry adopted Richard and gave him his uncle's title and lands. The fortunes of the house of York were rescued by the great king and Richard, duke of York, began his life-long obsession with retaining, defending and finally retrieving Henry's conquests in France. He had died, ironically, on English soil fighting against Henry V's son. His own son, Richard III, was now king of England and was well aware how much his house owed to Henry V. As Richard faced Henry Tudor's forces at Bosworth Field he, like Henry V before him, wore a crown of gold around his helmet.

There were other echoes of Agincourt at Bosworth. In his final hours, as he readied himself for battle, Richard was surrounded by a close-knit band of men whose ancestors had won renown at Agincourt. These men had been his indentured retainers when he had been duke of Gloucester and had found him to be a good lord. Thomas Dacre was ready to fight for the king in the same way that his grandfather had rendered service to Henry V at Agincourt. His cousins, the Harrington brothers, owed much to Richard and were with him as he charged to his death. Their grandfather had borne Henry V's banner at Agincourt. Thomas Pilkington, related by marriage to the Harringtons, survived the battle of Bosworth but died fighting Tudor nonetheless, at the battle of Stoke. His uncle and great-uncle were at Agincourt. Another cousin of the Harringtons, John Huddleston, was also with them. Incredibly enough, his father had fought at Agincourt. Seventy years might not seem so far distant to these men, about to risk everything for their anointed sovereign.

There was one huge difference, however. Richard may have been surrounded by fiercely loyal knights, but he was not so fortunate in his magnates. John Howard, the duke of Norfolk, was heroically killed fighting with his troops at the front of Richard's army, but the other two magnates present on Richard's side did not share his loyal spirit. There is something immensely admirable about Howard's faithful and mortal service. It provides a stark contrast to the dissembling, self-interested treason of Thomas lord Stanley, his brother William and the earl of Northumberland, Henry Percy. These three were to cost Richard his life and his throne. At least two out of the three had previous convictions. The Stanleys were past masters in the art of fence-sitting at battles. They usually ended up on the winning side. Their rise, through calculated acts of betrayal and disloyalty, is almost a paradigm of the age. Their grandfather, like the Harringtons, had fought for Henry V.[2] Through carefully and adroitly shifting their loyalties according to the prevailing political wind, his grandsons had learnt to profit from England's internecine warfare while their rivals, particularly the Harringtons, had remained loyal to the Yorkist cause and gained far less. It was Richard's championing of the Harringtons and their friends, and his determination to reward their loyalty and service, which provides the most significant backdrop to the battle of Bosworth. Richard disliked the Stanleys, and they knew it. The hidden story at Bosworth is the tale of how, seventy years after the glorious triumph of a close-knit band of staunchly patriotic men, bound in fidelity to their king, their descendants were punished for their loyalty. Treachery, cunning, dissembling and ploy won the day at Bosworth, and trampled the older virtues into the mud. As our story unfolds we will see that Richard must take a portion of the blame for what befell him and his supporters at Bosworth. His promotion and support of his northern retainers was a considerable threat to the Stanley interests, and was intended to be so. Richard, unlike his brother Edward, and also Henry Tudor, found it difficult, if not impossible, to forgive disloyalty.

In a strange and perverse way it is a disservice to Richard to compare his behaviour at Bosworth with that of Henry V at Agincourt. Henry may have become the archetypal chivalric warrior-king, but he won that reputation while huddled behind his archers. He did not lead a charge of knights in the way Richard did. The famous longbow defeated the French, cutting them down in droves as they attempted to reach their enemy and fight it out in the traditional manner.[3] The lesson of the Hundred Years War was that superior technology invariably wins battles. Henry V didn't even want to fight the French at that stage. He was cornered like a bedraggled rat. He didn't meet his death in battle either; he died of dysentery, leaving the colossal task of holding on to his conquests to his infant son, who made the task impossible by turning out to be an imbecile. Even Henry V's motives for reviving the conflict with France raise questions. He was able to conveniently bury the shaky foundations of his own legitimacy, his father having usurped the English throne, by turning everyone's attention elsewhere and claiming the French one. Let us not be too churlish and cynical, however, lest we deafen our ears to the clamour of adulation Henry inspired in his own day. What people loved about him, apart from the wonderful opportunities he provided to build a reputation, gain honours and make a fortune, was his kingliness. Kings conquered people, won battles, distributed largesse and behaved in a transcendent, royal way. There was something extraordinary about Henry, whether it was his self-belief, his imperial ambition, his ability to inspire others, or just his determination to be a great king. Above all else he was a unifier. All ranks knew where they stood with him and responded with hope and endeavour.

When Richard arrived at Bosworth, he could not dream of bringing such a reputation with him. It was not just his own usurpation that had muddied the waters of royal governance; the disastrous reign of Henry VI had damaged sovereign power immeasurably. What was needed was a king who could unite factions and stand above the partisan squabbles of lesser mortals. Richard was quite unable to do this. It says a great deal about his elder brother Edward, that despite some ghastly mistakes, particularly his potentially ruinous marriage to Elizabeth Woodville, he was able to put aside sentiment and act in the best interests of the greatest number. He usually had his eye on the bigger picture. Richard brought baggage with him to Bosworth and in the end it fell on top of him.

One bundle he carried with him was an antique, old-fashioned, somewhat romantic concept of chivalry. Take that charge of knights, with Richard at the head, galloping towards the enemy and an early grave. If Henry V, seventy years earlier, had found conquering France best accomplished by bows and sieges, what on earth was Richard doing? Even the great victories of Edward III, at Crecy and Poitiers, were gained by the longbow. English archers had consistently destroyed knightly formations throughout the Hundred Years War. Charges of knights were not only a thing of the past but also had a pretty poor historical track record. Richard must have been crazy or suicidal to launch one in 1485. There are certainly those who believe he was one of these or both, but the evidence shows that Richard's mounted strike was a viable option at the time and almost paid off. It had been used to considerable effect by King Ferdinand of Castile at the battle of Toro as recently as 1476, and Richard may have heard about this.[4] He certainly didn't have to worry about the longbow. That remarkable weapon had already been superseded.

The French had turned their fortunes around by learning how to overcome the longbow and by inheriting a couple of good kings. When Charles VI had been their king, Henry V had been able to exploit the political turmoil caused by his insanity. What goes around comes around, or vice versa. By marrying Katherine Valois, daughter of Charles VI, Henry conveyed the mental instability of the French monarchy to the English. His own son, Henry VI, the son of that union, had calamitous bouts of insanity. The great medievalist, K.B. McFarlane, said of him 'second childhood succeeded first without the usual interval and under him the medieval kingship was in abeyance.'[5] His misrule, not surprisingly, coincided with a French revival. Charles VII was more competent than his predecessor in France while comparisons between Henry V and Henry VI are simply unkind. But all this change in fortune caused by the lottery of hereditary succession would have counted for little if it had not been for the French ability to overcome the threat posed by the longbow. Its English users, incidentally, never called it a longbow. It did not receive this appellation until the sixteenth century and was known merely as 'the bow' by contemporaries. The French called it 'the bent stick', when they were being polite about it. At Formigny in 1450 they had shown that it was possible to neutralise the threat posed by this formidable weapon by outflanking the archers. Archers could only be effective if their firepower was concentrated, and preferably against a concentrated enemy. Surrounded and facing different directions they were a liability. If the writing was on the wall by then, and plate armour worn by dismounted knights had already reduced its impact, then the game was well and truly up three years later at the battle of Castillon in 1453.

At Castillon the French built a palisade behind a massive ditch. It stretched seven hundred yards long and was an enormous two hundred yards across. If the attacking archers found the defenders beyond their range, that was nothing compared to the onslaught they faced themselves. The French blasted them to pieces with three hundred guns. They not only used cannon, with a range of four hundred yards, but also hand-guns. John Talbot, earl of Shrewsbury, had led the combined Gascon-English army with courage and skill but became trapped under his horse when it was hit by one of the diabolical new projectiles, and was beheaded with an axe.

The bow, French import in any case, was finished. Archers had probably priced themselves out of the market anyway. An ordinance of 1285 had decreed that one archer was owed by all those in possession of property valued at 40 – 100 shillings per annum. This was not an aristocratic holding and hit the pockets of the rising class of gentry landholders. When it was also decreed that the landholder could hire the archer himself, rather than rendering the service personally, it became just another expense to resist in the long and noble tradition of tax avoidance. At sixpence a day the archer could earn the equivalent of a skilled artisan's annual salary in just twenty weeks; he was very expensive. He may have had a remarkable influence on events for almost four hundred years but his number was up. Oddly enough, this was not the case for the mounted soldier. This was partly because guns were difficult to manoeuvre and took so long to become reliable. Mobile artillery does not appear until Gustavus Adolphus of Sweden wheeled it from success to success across Europe in the early seventeenth century.

A charge of mounted knights in 1485, therefore, was not as foolhardy as one might at first think. Without archers to shoot him down and little or no manoeuvrable artillery as yet, Richard was actually deploying a formidable and legitimate battle tactic. It came remarkably close to success. Its failure may owe something to another French import, again developed to counter English battle tactics in France: the pike. The French had discovered that a sharp piece of metal fixed on to the end of an eighteen foot long spear was not attractive to rapidly approaching cavalry. The horses disliked them, they tended to avoid them, and they became discouraged and dispirited when driven towards them. When deployed in three ranks, the lower pointing upwards and the other two above them, in hedgehog style, horses found themselves confronting a bristling wall of sharp spikes. Horses cannot be trained to commit suicide: a method had been found for stopping them in their tracks. Historians are not certain whether pikes were deployed at Bosworth or not, but their presence, even in relatively small numbers, might account for the survival of Henry Tudor. They would have necessitated the dismounting of Richard and his household troops, if this had not been their intention in the first place. Dismounted, the knight was less formidable than he was charging into foot soldiers.[6] Richard, however, faced an altogether different threat at Bosworth. He faced a weapon so lethal that, at the crucial moment when he was at his most vulnerable, dismounted and in the midst of the enemy, it caused him to be surrounded, overwhelmed and hacked to death. Richard was betrayed.

The betrayal of Richard at Bosworth caused his death and changed the course of English history. He was not defeated by superior weaponry or tactics, or by a more formidable opponent. Thomas lord Stanley and his brother William decided the outcome of the battle by joining Henry Tudor's side just as Richard's charge passed in front of them. They had done exactly the same thing – influencing the outcome of a battle by changing sides at the last minute – on previous occasions. It made perfect sense because it not only ensured that they survived but it also gained them rewards of gratitude from the victor. Minimising risk and maximising profit was the family business so successfully run by the Stanleys throughout the Wars of the Roses. Who can blame them? Their defenders point out that if we expected them to behave according to an aristocratic code of honour and fidelity, we expected too much. They argue that such a code, call it chivalry if you will, never truly existed. At the heart of all human activity is self-interest. If there ever was a chivalric code it had been invented by an aristocratic elite to defend its status and provide a gloss for its oppression. This may be so, but educating self-interest and investing it with a religious idealism can create a culture with the power to influence thinking, conduct, aspiration and ambition. The code of chivalry which still haunted the massive great halls in the castles inhabited by Richard in his youth may have been irrevocably eroded during his own lifetime but it could nevertheless find a resonance in his heart. It was based on the power of a relationship which might transcend kin. At its centre was an ancient concept of loyalty and lordship which has always existed in some form in most societies. It pre-dates the Norman Conquest and has always had two sides to it: the ideal and the reality.

The Venerable Bede tells us about a thane called Lilla who, in the early seventh century, flung his body in front of the king to take the blow from an assassin's blade. He died in order to save King Edwin's life.[7] The same society produced a royal thane who stabbed King Edward to death. While King Alfred the Great was burning cakes in Somerset and the Vikings were burning his towns and villages, ealdorman Wulfhere surrendered to the enemy while ealdorman Odda, without even knowing whether King Alfred was still alive, defeated the Vikings in Devon and captured their famous raven banner.[8] No doubt it would have been difficult to predict their behaviour in advance. Would their friends and acquaintances have been able to predict that Odda would behave heroically and faithfully while Wulfhere would take the road to infamy and disgrace? At the Battle of Maldon in 991, ealdorman Brihtnoth died fighting in defence of his country.[9] His king, Ethelred the Unready, was too incompetent and cowardly to do any fighting himself, but that's another story.[10] The poet who left us a dramatic and evocative account of the battle, and may have been present himself, was struck by the contrast between the thanes of ealdorman Brihtnoth who surrounded his dead body on the battlefield and continued to defend it until they too had been killed, and the thanes who simply ran away. There seemed to him no accounting for the difference.[11] He thought it marked the end of an era and perhaps he was right, but it is just as likely that the disparity between advantage and service had become too great. The ethical code always worked best when advantages both material and immaterial were close at hand.

Such a code existed in medieval times and was called chivalry. The term was adopted from the French *chevalier* in the late twelfth century, meaning simply a horseman. At its heart was an oath of fealty, binding a man in service to a lord and placing him under both subjection and protection. When he took his oath he performed homage and became a vassal. He devoted himself to his lord even unto death. His lord swore also, to protect him and to be his 'good lord'. The ceremony was conducted in a church and had significant religious implications. The system worked to the mutual advantage of both. Good service from the vassal might be rewarded in innumerable ways: money, land, titles, offices, opportunities. The lord would gain labour, support, local influence and expertise. The relationship was essentially based on land tenure. With it went rank, class and the whole raft of inherited values and customs so essential for the self-definition of an aristocratic elite. It enshrined within the boundaries of service and patronage the unvoiced assumption that human society was a vehicle for the fulfilment of God's will on earth. A few might set their sights higher still and, through emulation and inclination, seek to realise in themselves those Christian virtues that defined civilization.

From the time of the First Crusade in 1095 the Church had endeavoured to channel the energies of the warrior class into activities that would promote Christian virtues and benefit the Church at the same time. Knights going off to fight in crusades were called *milites Christi*, the soldiers of Christ. The military orders from which were recruited the knights needed to garrison the castles in the Holy Land were part monk, part knight. The Templars, the Hospitallers and the Teutonic Knights were highly-trained military divisions in the service of Christ. The Knights Hospitaller, for instance, took vows of celibacy, poverty and obedience exactly as they would if they were monks living in monasteries. They served God and their communities, guarding the pilgrim routes and providing state-of-the-art medical facilities in the great hospital of St John in Jerusalem. [12] When the English became as enthusiastic about crusading as their continental counterparts, under Richard I at the end of the twelfth century, ordinary knighthood was transformed into a profession of arms with a strict code of ethics attached to it. The bonds of allegiance that had previously had a purely mercenary and military imperative now encompassed a culture of obligation and moral conduct which transformed them into honourable and elevating ties. [13] Knights on crusade were offered the hope of salvation simply by undertaking the difficult journey to the Holy Land, before they had even lifted a sword against the enemies of the Church. Knighthood could reap eternal rewards. [14]

While all this was happening the physical world around them was being transformed as well. The Norman cathedrals, rather like their castles, built to demonstrate power and strength, with their characteristic semi-circular arches known as 'Romanesque', were being rebuilt with the new Gothic pointed arch. Open spaces and greater elevation provided soaring naves and sublime vistas; brute force was replaced by a more restrained strength. The flying buttress which concealed the support for bold and dramatic structures mirrored the training and austerity of the new knight as he conquered his barbaric tendencies and reached towards the aristocratic ideal.[15] Beauty of form, created out of correct forms adhering to aesthetic values, was reflected in the premium now placed on beauty of conduct.

The process was informed by a growing body of literature celebrating the virtues of chivalric behaviour. The Romanesque language of the aristocracy exposed the island of Britain to the continental world of romance, minstrelsy and ballads. When Geoffrey of Monmouth produced his version of the *Morte d'Arthur* it was an instant hit. Arthur and his knights of the Round Table may have become the staple of the courtly entertainments provided in continental Europe, but he was, after all, a very local hero. English kings with military aspirations and ability were quick to adopt him as their own. Edward I had the putative bodies of Arthur and his queen, Guinevere, re-interred at Glastonbury in 1278 and held 'round table' pageants. His grandson Edward III instituted the Most Noble Order of the Garter in 1348 to unite the great men of the day in honourable service to the king. Arthur himself was the pattern of chivalry: noble, courteous, magnanimous and just.

These heroic ideals were still alive in Richard's day. His brother had built St George's chapel at Windsor to provide the knights of the Garter with their own sanctuary, both royal and sacred. Thomas Mallory's prose version of the Arthurian epic was written in the 1470s and first printed by Caxton during Richard's reign. Caxton dedicated his edition of the *Order of Chivalry* to Richard himself.[16] Richard's concern for justice for the common man was a feature of Arthurian conduct, along with an unyielding loyalty to his faithful servants.

At a more mundane level the system provided the means to advance, to 'get on'. A vassal would expect to receive a grant of land, his fee, in return for the future service he would render. In the fifteenth century, as they had done in the eleventh, contracts based on rent and wages got business done at grass-roots level. If the business was fighting, then a tenant rendering service to a lord might contract that service out by hiring 'indentured retainers'. These men formed the bulk of the armies slogging it out in the civil wars of the fifteenth century. They might enjoy chivalric tales and expect a certain standard from their lords, but then again they might not. The major crack appearing in the structure of this polity in the fifteenth century began to emerge as the tectonic plates of gentry influence and magnate power clashed. It was the rising class of powerful and influential knights, known as the gentry, who might serve the king directly and see him as their lord, rather than an aristocratic intermediary, that challenged, and ultimately changed, the feudal structure. It was at Bosworth that the rumbling earthquake finally struck. Stanley betrayed his king because that close-knit band of household troops around Richard, charging with him to share his destiny, was not a chivalric aristocratic elite, but a group of knights whose ambitions directly threatened Stanley. The gentry had, in a sense, arrived. Unfortunately they suffered a serious setback at Bosworth, but the main reason the battle must be seen as a turning-point is because it showed that the king could no longer rely on the medieval structure of allegiance and service. If members of the gentry could serve him directly, and become powerful in doing so, magnates could still trump him by leading their own retainers against him. A new structure was needed and the one that was to emerge would enable a new 'middle class' to flourish.

In the meantime William Stanley got his calculations absolutely right. His timing was impeccable, his intervention decisive. Seeing Richard and his cavalry charging towards Henry Tudor's standard, he flung his troops into the fray and ambushed the dangerously isolated king. Richard surely knew that Stanley might spoil the party in this way. In fact he was so distrustful of him that he held his son, the mysteriously named Lord Strange, as a hostage in his camp. Stanley was actually married to Henry Tudor's mother, Margaret Beaufort. His defection was perfectly judged. When Henry became king he rewarded Stanley with an earldom. It seems inconceivable that Richard failed to recognise that Stanley's impressive record of treachery was likely to be extended at Bosworth. Either Richard was guilty of a serious misjudgement of character or a catastrophic military miscalculation – perhaps both.

There is another possibility, although it by no means precludes elements of the above: that Richard, already aware that Norfolk was losing the main battle and that Henry Percy, earl of Northumberland, was unreliable and unlikely to commit his troops, made a decision which only he could have made. To understand it we will have to hear the whole story, but let it suffice to say for the moment that footling concerns about Stanley's credibility were not one of his major preoccupations at this hour of need. Whether Richard made a misjudgement or not, in the end he was entirely true to himself. His brother had fled from a potential battle when he had seen that he would lose, and eventually returned from exile to reclaim his throne. This is something Richard had never done, and never would do. He trusted in his own ability, he trusted in his own destiny, and perhaps he trusted Stanley too much. While he had begun to exert pressure on Stanley's power in the northwest, as we shall see, their old rivalry had been between magnates. Now that Richard was king, Stanley owed him allegiance.

Stanley's supporters, few though they be, and Richard's detractors, too many to number, are keen to exculpate Stanley from the charge of treason. His action, they argue, was amply justified by the crimes committed by Richard. Stanley's soul, they say, has been vindicated in the court of history and enjoys the delights of the blessed. All he did was look after his own interests and who can condemn a man for that? Did Richard take such great care to avoid breaking an oath of allegiance when he imprisoned his nephews? Was not one of those nephews a king? For Richard to expect one of his magnates to keep faith when he himself had betrayed the trust of his brother, Edward IV, by ignoring his will, and then committed regicide by causing his nephew, Edward V, to 'disappear', for such a man to take the moral high ground against Stanley would be a bit rich.

Richard had usurped the throne, of that there can be no doubt. His nephew Edward V had sufficient right to inherit the throne from his father and it required swift action, violence and hastily-crafted counter-claims to dislodge him. We shall return to those dramatic events in due course, but for the present consideration it should be noted that Edward V, for all his assumption of regality, had not been crowned. Richard had broken his oath to young Edward, having initially accepted him as king and sworn to be his Protector, but he had not sworn an oath of allegiance to Edward as a crowned king. Indeed he had been determined to avoid that eventuality. The difference lay in the belief that the coronation service, and particularly the anointing of the king with holy oil, set that man apart. He was no longer what he had been. God now had a hand in his destiny. The oath taken by his magnates on that day, and Stanley had been one of the first to swear to King Richard, was sacred and inviolate. Whatever crimes Richard committed in order to displace his nephew, the accusation that he broke his oath to the anointed king could not be levelled at him. He, though, had been anointed. What is more, Richard had evidence to suggest that Stanley might remain loyal. During the storm created by Buckingham's rebellion in 1483, Stanley, remarkably, did not join the rebels, one of whom was Henry Tudor. Certainly on the spur of the moment, in the heat of battle, it might be presumed that Stanley would hesitate sufficiently for Richard to get the job done. What did not help Richard at Bosworth was the resilience of Henry Tudor's defences. Those pikes perhaps? Even then he was within feet of achieving his objective. He personally killed Henry's standard bearer, William Brandon, according to Polydore Vergil, the historian of choice for the Tudors. It must have been frightfully close from Henry's point of view. Richard having lost that decisive initiative, the Stanleys did the rest. It would be going too far to suggest that Richard misread the Stanleys and did not expect them to betray him, but he probably thought that the speed of his action would render them impotent. Stanley's intervention turned out to be critical. Richard had staked everything on disposing of Tudor before Stanley made a hostile move. He failed. There was a huge element of risk in what he set out to do and in the end the gamble did not pay off.

Richard was just thirty-two when he was savagely cut down in the mire, and had reigned for less than two years and two months, yet his untimely end ensured that his reputation would forever be tarnished by the dark rumours of the fate of the Princes in the Tower. Like the dirt sticking to his bleeding and mutilated corpse, he had not had time to wash away the manner of his throne-taking. Bosworth ensured that Richard's reign would always be remembered for the disappearance of two innocent little boys, and not much else. They certainly provided enough scandal to last over five hundred years, and will no doubt continue to invoke the sympathy of generations to come. What we have to be careful to avoid is concluding that Richard's fate at Bosworth was a verdict on his reign. It was not, and we do not know how history would have remembered Richard if he had been given time to prove himself a good king. Previous usurpations had pretty much been accepted at the bar of history, having been followed by reigns more competent than those they supplanted. Henry IV had had Richard II murdered in prison in Pontefract. He may have spent the rest of his reign looking over his shoulder for 'new broils commenced in strands afar remote' and have left the impression of being 'shaken' and 'wan with care', but he at least ruled competently, whereas Richard II had not. Edward II met a gruesome end, despite the attempts by a recent historian to suggest that he escaped.[17] His successor, Edward III, was not only a reasonably good king, but also the son and heir of the deceased Edward II. Young though Edward III was, he came as a blessed relief after the pathetically partisan incompetence of his father and his father's historians.

Richard III's case, however, was rather different. His nephew Edward V, aged twelve, had not had time to prove himself deficient. It could not be argued that he had forfeited his right to rule by his lack of ability. Nor did age bar him. The rule of a minor, though somewhat fraught and undesirable, was a constitutional option for which there were several precedents. One historian has pointed out that it worked 'perfectly well' in the cases of Henry III, Richard II and Henry VI, while conveniently ignoring the fact that these three had calamitous reigns that ended in civil war, rebellion and the murder of two of them. If one was going to use the argument that minority rule had been tried and tested then one would also have to ignore the fact that it had somehow managed to produce the worst possible kings. Why that should be is anybody's guess. The same thing happened later when Edward VI succeeded Henry

VIII. How many people lost their heads in order for that errant youth to sit uncomfortably on the throne? Minority rule was an option, but not, it has to be admitted, a perfect solution. That still does not exonerate Richard from the charge of illegally and brutally disinheriting his nephew in order to reign himself. We will consider that dark and sinister episode later, but for the time being we must be careful not to assume that the participants at Bosworth were passing judgement on the legitimacy of Richard's rule. Many historians have fallen into this trap. Richard lost, they say, because his followers were reluctant to support him. They either stayed away from the battlefield in droves or, being present, they switched allegiance. They were shocked and affronted by Richard's usurpation and unenthusiastic about fighting for him. Some argue that his short reign had been sufficiently partisan and discomforting for many of his subjects, and that they voted with their feet at Bosworth.

These arguments are founded on false premises. Support for the king was not overwhelming and perhaps, from Richard's point of view, a little disappointing, but he had the wherewithal at Bosworth to get the job done. Henry Tudor's support across the country was pathetic and certainly should not have caused regime change in 1485. His claim to the throne was risible. Bosworth was not the product of a groundswell of revulsion against Richard; on the contrary, it was a shock defeat, an unexpected result, an unlikely outcome. Everything hinged on the behaviour of the Stanleys; their defection changed the course of the battle and brought Richard an early death.

Nor can it be argued that the Stanley betrayal was symptomatic of a general malaise. Of course the fighting between the houses of York and Lancaster in the thirty years preceding Bosworth had weakened the bonds between lords and kings, between kings and subjects, but Stanley was no product of this weakening; rather, he was one of its chief causes. As a protagonist in the civil strife of a generation he had refined the art of disloyalty. Stanley killed Richard not because he felt that Richard needed replacing because his claim to the throne was weak or unjustified, not because he felt that Richard's rule had not benefited the people of England, not because he feared the future consequences of that reign for the people, not because he disliked Richard's foreign policy, domestic policy or religious policy. He killed Richard because he stood to gain far more from his death than he ever would from his continued reign. This was intensely personal. Richard, in part, brought this upon himself, as we shall see, by conducting himself in such a way as to alienate Stanley. We shall also see that he did this, not so much as a matter of misguided policy or an underestimation of the consequences of that policy, but as a matter of character. As we discover more about Richard's character, his death at Stanley's hands will make more sense.

Richard was not alone when he died. One man died with him whose story has never been fully told. James Harrington, knight of the Body, faithful servant of the Yorkists in general, and Richard in particular, mortal enemy of Thomas lord Stanley, was killed with his master. Richard had threatened Stanley's local interests and paid a heavy price for it. The man whose cause he championed in the region was James Harrington, and the man who took James Harrington's estates when he died was Thomas lord Stanley. To have both within his grasp in the melee at Bosworth must have presented an irresistible temptation to Stanley, and William did not hesitate. All talk of Richard's past crimes, of his lack of support, of his panicky and suicidal final charge, must fade into the background while the story of James Harrington is told. His feud with Stanley, evolving as it did into a struggle for hegemony in the north-west, cost Richard his throne and his reputation – now almost impossible to salvage from the carnage of Bosworth.

None of the chronicles mentions James Harrington at Bosworth. One account of the battle, possibly based on an eyewitness account, *The Most Pleasant Song of Lady Bessie*, describes the heroic behaviour of 'Sir William Harrington', undoubtedly a mistake for either James or Robert. As with all accounts of the battle it is full of invention, supposition, rumour and error. The earliest transcription of the song dates from 1600 and had no doubt acquired some popular embellishments by then. Ironically enough it describes Harrington saving the life of Stanley's son, the hostage Lord Strange. The ballad states that Richard ordered George Stanley, son of Thomas lord Stanley, to be beheaded but that Harrington made an excuse to avoid doing the deed, without Richard ever knowing.[18] Given that Edward Stanley, George's younger brother, is said to have poisoned James Harrington's illegitimate son, John, in order to grab his property, and was also to disinherit Robert Harrington's children, we can but hope that a Harrington had not intervened to save a Stanley at Bosworth. The other accounts of the battle do not give sufficient detail for Harrington to warrant a mention.

Naturally they describe Richard's death. John Rous, currying favour with the new Tudor dynasty by portraying Richard as the Antichrist, suspends his vitriol for a space in order to report what everyone knew: Richard died bravely:

> For all that, let me say the truth to his credit: that he bore himself like a gallant knight and, despite his little body and feeble strength, honourably defended himself to his last breath, shouting again and again that he had been betrayed, and crying 'Treason! Treason!'[19]

Jean de Molinet, a contemporary French chronicler, disliking Richard and delighting in the fact that he had ended his murderous days 'iniquitously and filthily in the dirt and mire', cannot fail to admit that Richard 'bore himself valiantly'.[20] Polydore Vergil, an Italian humanist and Renaissance scholar, doing his best to write proper history, using sources unrelentingly hostile to Richard, described him deserted on the battlefield and, 'alone was killed fighting manfully in the thickest press of his enemies.'[21] The *Croyland Chronicle*, probably written within a year of the battle by a well-informed cleric, and once again notably critical of Richard, joins in the universal admiration for the manner of his death:

> As for King Richard, he received many mortal wounds, and like a spirited and most courageous prince, fell in the battle and not in flight.[22]

The chroniclers also agree that his naked and mutilated body was exposed for all to see. The *Croyland Chronicle* tells us that Richard's body 'having been discovered among the dead ... many other insults were offered'. The detail of what these insults might have been is supplied by others. Jean de Molinet tells us that his body was put on a horse and carried, 'hair hanging as one would bear a sheep', to the entrance to a village church where it was 'displayed to the people naked and without any clothing'. The *Great Chronicle of London*, another Tudor product, probably that of Robert Fabyan, sheriff of London in 1493–4, gossipy and full of contradictions but containing some first-hand knowledge, delights in Richard's ignominious end:

> And Richard late king, his body despoiled to the skin and nought being left about him so much as would cover his privy member, was trussed behind a pursuivant called Norroy as a hog or other vile beast, and so, all bespattered with mire and filth, was brought to a church in Leicester for all men to wonder upon, and there lastly irreverently buried.[23]

The chronicler is either being deliberately disingenuous in his reference to the hog, or has fortuitously hit upon a very apt similitude. Richard's emblem, the white boar, was known colloquially as the hog. Richard had chosen this because it symbolised the city of York, known in Roman times as Eboravicum. The boar, as it happened, was reputed to be a noble creature that, despite its ferocity and fearsome demeanour, only attacked in order to defend itself or its dependants. To be described in death as a hog may not have dismayed Richard's soul as much as Fabian might have hoped.

Polydore Vergil has his pennyworth too:

> The body of King Richard, naked of all clothing, and laid upon a horse's back, with the arms and legs hanging down on both sides, was brought to the abbey of Franciscan monks at Leicester, a miserable spectacle in good truth, but not unworthy for the man's life, and there was buried two days after without any pomp or solemn funeral.

This display, and probably the authentic accounts of his death also, were both necessary for Henry to expunge any hope Richard's supporters may have entertained of reviving his cause. Richard has no known burial site. Whatever we think of him, his body warranted a burial. Even if one takes the view that he was a monstrously bad man, he had worn the crown of England. King John, almost a caricature of a bad king, is buried in splendour in Worcester Cathedral; Edward II, similarly bad, at Gloucester. When Richard II was murdered, Henry IV, his murderer, so like Henry VII in many ways, neglected his body but when Henry V became king almost the first thing he did was to bring that body from Pontefract to Westminster Abbey where it rests to this day. Even if one believes the king to have reigned unjustly, his proper burial is still necessary to protect the sanctity of his office. The monks at Worcester were keen to get John's body because he had been an anointed king and therefore his remains would bring honour and prestige upon their house. William Rufus was an atheist who terrorised the Church but his body lies in the middle of Winchester Cathedral.

So where is Richard? Henry paid £10 1s in 1495 to have a tomb built for the body, in Leicester. A dispute between contractors then seems to have ensued and whether it was built or not is not known. If it was, Henry VIII destroyed its likely resting place, Grey Friars, Leicester, in the dissolution of the monasteries. Richard is thus unique in the annals of English history in possessing no grave, no tomb, no earthly resting place, certainly since poor old Harold lost everything at Hastings. Even Harold was sufficiently honoured by William the Conqueror, despite William considering him a usurper, to have the high altar of Battle Abbey built on the spot he died. It stood in that place until, inevitably, Henry VIII had his way. A plaque commemorates the spot.

Richard has an unlikely epitaph, however, in the poignant and unvarnished entry written by a secretary recording the minutes of the York City council meeting on the day after the battle:

> Were assembled in the council chamber, where and when it was showed by diverse persons, and especially by John Spooner, sent unto the field of Redemore to bring tidings from the same to the city, that king Richard late mercifully reigning upon us was through great treason … piteously slain and murdered to the great heaviness of this city…[24]

The unfeigned love of that city expressed in those words invites us to consider what it was that they thought they had lost and what the real Richard was like.

# TWO

# CHILDHOOD DANGERS

Richard Plantagenet was born at Fotheringhay on 2 October 1452. He was the youngest son of Richard, duke of York and Cecily Neville. His father was one of the most powerful members of the nobility and had a direct claim to the throne of England. At the time of Richard's birth, the Yorkist line represented by his father was beginning to look like a viable alternative to the incompetence of Henry VI's administration, at least in the eyes of the Yorkists themselves and their not inconsiderable number of supporters. His father, the duke of York, a simple and straightforward man of courage and integrity, was certainly beginning to consider the possibility of pressing his claim to the throne in the early 1450s, but England would be dragged into a violent civil war before this claim could be prosecuted fully. It was far harder to remove an anointed king than he imagined, even a bad one, especially if that king was the son of the great Henry V. In the end the duke of York never became king but he died in the attempt, and two of his sons, Edward and Richard, were to be crowned.

When he was born, however, there would have been universal astonishment at the suggestion that in a little over thirty years Richard, the youngest son of the duke of York, would be king. He had three older brothers who survived to adulthood, each of whom would have a better claim to the throne if such a claim was ever advanced. Their children would all take precedence over Richard, the junior cadet. He was destined for a life of aristocratic privilege in the peripatetic household of a great magnate with titles and honours befitting the status of the youngest son of a man descended from King Edward III.[1] This would, in the normal course of events, have meant the inheriting in due course of a few good estates, the possibility of augmenting them through a good marriage and perhaps the title of marquis, viscount or even earl. He could expect to see royal service of one kind or another, perhaps on the council, and further opportunities for wealth and aggrandisement if he proved astute and competent. Even at the outset of his life the difference between his status and that of his older brothers was made clear by the granting of separate household establishments for Edward and Edmund, with governors and tutors, while Richard and his brother Clarence stayed with their mother at Fotheringhay.

There were worse places to stay. His mother knew her worth and lived the life of a senior ranking aristocratic lady of great taste, piety and refinement. Indeed, she cost her husband a fortune. She had at one time been friendly with the queen herself and did not brook rivals when it came to keeping up appearances. The Duchess Cecily, the daughter of Ralph earl of Westmorland, was herself the great-granddaughter of Edward III through her grandfather John of Gaunt. She was famous for her beauty, known as 'the Rose of Raby', and had married Richard of York when she was fourteen and he eighteen.[2] They did not have children until she was twenty-four but she then produced thirteen in sixteen years, seven of whom survived childhood. She was thirty-seven when she gave birth to Richard and went on to have another child, Ursula, when Richard was three, but this little sister did not survive. Cecily was to live to see her daughter Margaret become duchess of Burgundy and her sons Edward and Richard become kings of England. She outlived her youngest son and not only witnessed the dramatic events of his usurpation and short reign, but also played some indiscernible part in shaping his destiny. In the end the fate of her male relatives provides a stark illustration of the turbulent times through which she lived: her husband and two of her sons were killed in battle and the third executed.

The world that Richard inhabited as a small child was an idyllic oasis of opulent calm. His eldest sister Anne had already left the nest to marry the duke of Exeter but Elizabeth was eight years old, Margaret six and George four when Richard was born. His two older brothers, Edward and Edmund would provide Richard with glimpses of adolescent knighthood at the great religious feasts and family celebrations he was allowed to witness in his early years. When Richard was six his eldest brother Edward reached the age of knighthood, and the following year Edmund followed suit. Those seven years, the gathering storm clouds of dynastic conflict and bloody violence darkening the end of the decade, gave Richard the rudimentary elements of the aristocratic beliefs, values, education and skills of his class in a relatively peaceful environment. All took place under the protective shadow of his grand but distant father.

Fotheringhay itself was a bustling community of soldiers, courtiers, stewards, officials, traders, servants, guests, musicians and priests. The castle possessed a great hall and apartments, kitchens, storerooms and recreation areas all in the shadow and protection of the great stone keep. One of Richard's earliest memories would have been the view from the nursery across the winding River Nene and the gently undulating landscape of the woods and green pastures of Northamptonshire. The keep itself sat atop a huge earth mound, a Norman motte, and dominated the eastern part of the county. Climbing the staircases to the battlements at the top Richard could see for miles and sense the power and security the fortress still afforded. While the river meandered slowly in snake-like curves below, it was too deep and too wide to be forded by a hostile army. A wide moat allowed the castle grounds to resemble an island with a massive gatehouse barring the entrance.

A short distance away to the north stood the large and impressive collegiate church which Richard's great-uncle Edward had founded for twelve priests. They had living accommodation, a library, cloisters and a refectory. The main purpose of such a college, apart from the training of priests and the advancement of learning, was to provide continual prayers for the souls of the founder and his dependants. Edward, the second duke of York, killed at Agincourt, was buried there. Richard's father, the third duke, enlarged it and paid for its restoration and renovation while Richard's brother, when he became King Edward IV, had the church almost completely rebuilt in grand style. The impressive nave and the beautiful octagonal tower still survive. The colourful medieval pulpit with the royal coat of arms on the back, was a gift from the same king. Supporting the royal shield are symbols representing his two brothers: the black bull of Clarence and, on the right, the white boar of Richard. This church meant a great deal to the Yorkists, and to Richard in particular. It was here that Richard stood as chief mourner at the delayed and emotionally charged reburial of his father in 1476.

When Henry VIII disbanded the college at the Reformation, the church, like so many subject to the wanton vandalism of that period, fell into disrepair. When Henry VIII's daughter, Elizabeth I, paid a visit to Fotheringhay she was shocked by what she saw and paid for its restoration. Thanks to her, the memorials to Richard's ancestors still stand on either side of the altar. She was well aware that these were her ancestors too. Henry VIII's mother was Elizabeth, the daughter of Edward IV and the niece of Richard. He may not have cared much about it but Henry VIII was fifty per cent Yorkist. His daughter knew how important her Yorkist blood had been in shoring up the shaky credentials of the Tudor dynasty. The tombs of two dukes of York and of Cecily were restored.

The castle was not so fortunate and little now remains of it apart from the base of the keep, the sweep of the moat and the level ground where the great hall stood. The castle was deliberately destroyed, ironically enough, by

Elizabeth's successor James I. It was at Fotheringhay in 1587 that Elizabeth's cousin, Mary Queen of Scots, was beheaded for treason. Mary was James' mother and he had the castle 'slighted' for its part in her death. In the seventeenth century such impressive symbols of medieval power were worth more for the dressed stone they afforded than for any security they offered. Cannon balls had made them obsolete and peace had done the rest. The stone of Fotheringhay was eagerly snapped up by enterprising locals in the reign of Charles I. The Talbot Inn at nearby Oundle boasts a quantity of that once proud rock. It is perhaps fitting, but certainly not surprising, that Richard, with no known burial site, should share the windswept, forlorn ruins of his birth place with the Mary Stuart Society's memorial to a queen whose head was severed from her body in the same place. Perhaps the spot was cursed. At least the local pub, where Ricardians can ruminate while drowning their sorrows, is named after a symbol of the dukes of York, the Falcon.

Richard was born in an archetypal medieval castle and died almost thirty-three years later in a classic charge of medieval knights, but the world into which he was born was changing rapidly. Richard was the last medieval king of England and something in him, aware perhaps of the shifting sands of time, longed for a return to the reassuring certainties of the age of chivalry. The changes that would sweep that world away were well advanced beyond the English horizon. In the same year of his birth Leonardo da Vinci was born in Florence. Italy was bursting with artistic talent, imagination and creativity. While Cosimo de Medici tightened his control over the republic of Florence, the Renaissance was being fostered by the profits from his bank. At the time Richard was born, the great sculptor Donatello, the first to produce a freestanding bronze statue since classical times, was producing his late masterpieces. Filippo Lippi was at the height of his powers while a young Botticelli was dazzling with his precocious talent.

While Richard was trying his first sword for size in the castle courtyard, Henry the Navigator was introducing sugar and coarse pepper to Europe: valuable preservatives. The Portuguese ruler, a grandson as it happens of John of Gaunt through the marriage of his daughter Philippa to John the Great of Portugal, had sent expeditions as far down the eastern coast of Africa as Sierra Leone. At his community in Sagres on the southern coast of Portugal mathematicians, astronomers, chart makers, shipmasters and translators were poring over Greek, Latin and Arabic texts while experimenting with ship design. The new caravel Henry produced, a synthesis of Classical and Arabic ideas, was especially suited to long voyages. The first set of latitudinal tables was produced there and improvements made to astronomical and navigational instruments. The New World awaited and while Spain and Portugal were dividing it between them England exported sheep's wool to the Netherlands.

While Richard was learning to get to grips with a mace and trying to shoot rabbits with a bow and arrow, Ming dynasty China was putting the finishing touches to the reconstruction of Beijing. Ghengis Khan had destroyed the old one, as was his wont, and despite the efforts of his grandson Kublai, work was needed. The Temple of Heaven, the great avenue known as the Spirit Way with its sculptures of warriors and exotic beasts, and the blue, gold and silver imperial palace in the Forbidden City all survive today as reminders of a highly sophisticated fifteenth-century urban culture. The Ming emperors also promoted a somewhat puritanical absolutism and a distrust of outsiders which has always lingered over Chinese culture, but they were trading in tea, silk and porcelain while the English were bargaining over fleeces. They were also reading novels and newspapers a few hundred years before the rest of us.

Closer to home a colossal struggle was being waged between the Ottoman Turks and the Christian world. Sultan Mehmed I, appropriately known as 'the Conqueror', brought the Roman Empire finally to an end by taking Constantinople from the Byzantines a year after Richard was born. It was to be the new capital of the Ottoman Empire. The Sultan's ambitions were not satisfied with this dramatic conquest and he turned his attention and military might on eastern Europe. As Richard, at the age of four, was learning the Lord's Prayer and his father was grappling with Henry VI's unsteady administration, John Hunyadi of Hungary was leading resistance to Sultan Mehmed at the siege of Belgrade. The Turks' advance was halted. While a dynastic conflict between the supporters of the Lancastrian Henry VI and the Yorkist duke Richard was brewing in England, a head-on collision was taking place in eastern Europe between two great powers with opposing religions, histories, cultures and traditions. Matthias Corvinus, son of John Hunyadi, and a hero, autocrat, humanist and nation-builder, was defending European civilisation from the Turks while the young Richard was play-fighting with his brother George. Matthias founded the brilliant international university of Buda in his spare time while the English were seizing each other's property.

As Richard looked in fascination at the brightly-coloured, illuminated initial letters painted on to the parchment of his mother's bible, Johan Gutenberg was printing a bible in Mainz. Printing reached Paris in 1470 and England in 1476 when William Caxton printed Chaucer's *Canterbury Tales* at his workshop in Westminster. The changing world was beginning to reach the court of Edward IV but Richard always seemed keen to hold on to the old. The year after he was born the English had been blasted out of France by new-fangled artillery and Richard's father built his political career on claiming that the war had been conducted incompetently. His ultimate goal was a restoration by arms of English conquests on the Continent. His youngest son, Richard, growing up listening to tales of his father's successful campaigns, hearing the daily prayers sung for his great-uncle Edward who died fighting in France, and possibly even hearing his father in person grumble about the incompetence, cowardice and lack of martial vigour now in England, developed a distinctly conservative attitude towards the French. It was an attitude steeped in the past, nurtured at Fotheringhay and owing much to his father.

While Cecily was giving birth to Richard, his father was in the midst of a grave political crisis. In the two years preceding his birth the polarisation of the political class into what might loosely be called Lancastrian and Yorkist had begun. Failure abroad and disorder at home created the dry tinder of discontent and faction. The king's inability to deal effectively with his problems not only exacerbated the very real grievances of those suffering injustice, but also provided opportunities for the unscrupulous, or the lucky, to make gains. The king's favourite, Edmund Beaufort, duke of Somerset, had returned from France having lost Anjou, Maine and Normandy. Only the fortress of Calais remained in English hands in the north and Gascony was under threat in the south, and yet the king would not hear criticism of Beaufort. There was considerable discontent and disturbance in England, fuelled by high taxation and the disgruntled returning soldiery. At the same time Somerset was waging his own political war against York.[3]

A serious rebellion in Kent in 1450, led by Jack Cade, was being blamed on York. The duke was worried that he might be indicted for treason and that the presence of Somerset by the king's side was dangerous both to himself and to the country at large. York had presented the king with a bill for reform, 'after the Comouns desyre' in 1451. The king prevaricated, declining to give York authority to establish order and promising a settlement of his grievances 'in schort tyme'. All York could get the king to agree to, was to give him a place on the council. He left London, a year before Richard's birth, to gather support.[4]

York paid a visit to the holy shrine at Walsingham and then travelled to Norwich to converse with the duke of Norfolk. There were only four adult dukes in England and with Somerset and Exeter against him York needed Norfolk. He then went to visit the shrine of St Edmund at Bury St Edmunds in Suffolk before raising support in the Midlands and the Welsh marches. Advancing on London he was determined to have a greater say in events. He coordinated his entry into the capital with Norfolk who followed the next day. As York entered, surrounded by a considerable retinue of armed guards, he had his ducal sword borne upright before him, a gesture of profound, almost regal, significance.

During the course of the next few months the duke was outmanoeuvred by Somerset. The king began to rely once again on his household rather than a council and this meant York was excluded from the king's company. So averse was the king to the presence of the duke of York that he went from the capital into Kent with the duke of Somerset and 3,000 men to restore order there. York was helpless and isolated. Popular though he no doubt was he was not astute enough when it came to political machination. He could not get the ear of the king and he could not win over a majority of the lords. Even his eldest daughter's husband, the duke of Exeter, was more interested in getting his hands on the duchy of Lancaster and befriending the Percys in the north. The Percys were in almost continuous conflict over their northern interests with the Nevilles, who were York's chief supporters. Weakness at the centre and misgovernance of the realm at large provided opportunities for men like Exeter. York, with his programme of 'reform' was a nuisance, not to say a threat. This was another legacy the young Richard was to inherit from his father: impatience with opposition, self-righteousness and an inability to calculate the self-interest of the leading magnates.

While he was in Kent the king was arresting trouble-makers and discovering to his increasing anger that they were largely the supporters of York. No doubt goaded on by Somerset he had men executed for talking against the king and 'havyinge more favyr unto the Duke of Yorke thenne unto the kynge'. The king became convinced that rebellion was afoot and that York lay behind it. He was determined to discipline the duke and to neutralise him. York was forced into a humiliating climb-down at Dartford, having to beg for pardon and swear his allegiance to King Henry. With Somerset in the ascendant York retreated to his estates to lick his wounds.

In a letter to the city of Shrewsbury, written a few months before Richard was born, his father explained that he was in danger from the duke of Somerset who 'laboreth continually about the King's highness for my undoing, and to corrupt my blood, and to disinherit me and my heirs, and such persons as be about me'.[5] Another inherited characteristic can here be detected; the duke of York was not only proud of his high birth and conscious of his noble inheritance, but also keen to ensure that his blood was not corrupted – that is, his royal blood should not be attainted. Accusations of treason could undo everything and York had only just escaped such an accusation by the skin of his teeth. With Somerset determined to strengthen his grip on power at York's expense, the storm clouds of civil war were gathering.

Whether, during his troubled sojourn at Fotheringhay in the autumn of 1452, York popped along to the nursery to view the new arrival is not recorded. Whether he thought he was an ugly, scrawny, smelly thing to be avoided at all costs or a delightful, innocent little treasure in whose company solace could be found must remain a matter for speculation. He already had three healthy sons with whom the ducal inheritance might be guaranteed and the influence of the dynasty rescued, cherished and advanced. Richard was a minor insurance policy. Few would have been bold enough to predict that one day Richard would be king of England. A contemporary poet was even unsure whether the baby would survive. A verse rather tersely comments 'Richard liveth yit', having mentioned that a brother born before him, called Thomas, had died. These words could be taken to suggest that Richard was sick in his infancy and not expected to continue long in this world. Six of Cecily's thirteen children did die; the poet was simply being realistic. In the outcome his pessimism was confounded by Richard's survival.[6]

Richard was in his first year when the climactic events of 1453 unfolded. The fall of Constantinople was to have an effect upon England over time. Scholars, escaping from the city as the likelihood of destruction loomed, brought Greek philosophy and literature with them into Europe. The defeat of John Talbot at the battle of Castillon, and the loss of Gascony, had a more immediate impact. York's concerns about the way the war in France was being conducted were vindicated and Somerset's position, certainly in the long term, became untenable. News of the defeat began filtering through in early August, but before then two dramatic events closer to home changed the political landscape profoundly. At the very end of July 1453 Henry VI lapsed into serious mental illness and two months later the queen gave birth to a boy.

The first consequence of Henry's insanity, possibly brought on by the disastrous news from France, would be to force the duke of Somerset to accept a wider consensus. He could no longer pretend to be enforcing the will and policy of the king. York would have to be admitted to the council. The second was to introduce complete uncertainty into the heart of the body politic. The king spent long periods gazing into space and saying nothing. If this was embarrassing at first it was a disaster soon enough. It was not only that the normal functions of the courts, of parliament, of commissions, of domestic and foreign policy, and the whole range of government business required the oversight, the assent, and the physical instrumentality by the use of the royal seals of the person of the king; the whole direction and morale of the country was predicated on a living, acting, purposeful royal human being at its centre.[7] To have a vacuum at the heart of power was to cut off the blood supply to the rest of the body. Even a bad king was better than no king at all. At least you could attempt to secure a better future if the king's will was known. You could work around it, keep a low profile, manipulate it to your advantage or rebel against it. Henry's insanity removed all certainty. No one knew whether it was temporary or permanent. No one was willing to lift a hand against a non-entity. Treason might be justified if the monarch had behaved cruelly or unjustly, but if he merely stared innocently into space there was nothing of which to accuse him. Furthermore he was an anointed king and the son of the great Henry V. In the upshot Henry's insanity was not the main dynastic problem. In the flexible, pragmatic way the English have for dealing with constitutional emergencies a workable solution was found in the creation of a Protectorate. The duke of York, in March 1454, came in from the cold and was proclaimed 'Protector of the Realm and Chief Councillor'.

Margaret's baby was an altogether different matter. With the birth of Edward, Prince of Wales, Henry VI had an heir. The duke of York's claim to be the rightful successor of the king vanished. Furthermore, and far more problematic, the queen herself, as is the way of queen mothers, began to take an active interest in affairs. Not only was she keen to take a greater part in government now that her husband was incapacitated, but she was also resolutely determined to secure the interests and the succession of her son. Her intervention, hatred of York as the perceived threat to the interests of her child and partisan fanaticism for the rights of her infant led, tragically but inevitably, to her son's death in battle. York may have been able, indeed initially had been able, to accommodate the new political reality. He may have been capable of renouncing his ambition to succeed Henry VI and may perhaps have been willing to act as Protector until the new king reached maturity, but all was scuppered by Queen Margaret's distrust of him. She was convinced that the duke of York posed a threat to her son and, as a consequence, peaceful solutions evaporated.[8]

York, it is true, can hardly claim to have acted impartially himself. During his first Protectorate he imprisoned Somerset in the Tower of London and appointed the earl of Salisbury, his own brother-in-law, as chancellor. This was the most important office of state as the chancellor was the keeper of the Great Seal, the instrument by which all government acts were validated. A position of such trust was traditionally given to a leading churchman. Cecily's brother was many things but a notable ecclesiastic he was not. However well or otherwise this may have turned out, another dramatic twist threw everything into confusion again. On Christmas Day 1454, Henry VI recovered his wits. To the astonishment of the whole company he began to recognise those around him and to speak lucidly. Margaret rushed to bring her son to him and presented him with the boy he had not yet acknowledged. He asked its name and when he was told it was called Edward he wept for joy. Edward was the name of his favourite saint, a king only marginally more competent than Henry himself. Another king to revere the memory of Edward the Confessor had been Henry III, a king as dreadful as any, whose reign had ended in civil war. All three left fine buildings: Edward the Confessor built Westminster Abbey, Henry III rebuilt it – the building we see today is largely his recreation – and Henry VI built Eton College and King's College Chapel in Cambridge.

From York's point of view it would have been better if King Henry had remained incapacitated. Whatever it was that caused him to lose his wits, it continued to affect him when he recovered them. His judgement was poor, his mind weak and his personality susceptible to influence: all that was undesirable in a medieval king.[9] There was now the added danger of Queen Margaret. The king was wholly under her control and that of Somerset. This was starkly revealed in March 1455 when Henry dismissed York from the Protectorate, Salisbury from the chancellorship and released Somerset from the Tower. In a Great Council held at Greenwich, Somerset was declared innocent of all charges made against him. No one knew how long the king's fragile sanity would last but all knew that Somerset's position depended on it. He acted swiftly while he could, meeting with his supporters in April and agreeing on a strategy that would ensure his influence could survive another bout of royal debilitation. Confident of support among the nobility, he called a great council to meet at Leicester. York, Salisbury and Salisbury's son, Warwick, were not invited. York knew that if this council met it would be packed with peers hostile to him and would lead to his impeachment. With Salisbury, he retired to his northern estates to raise troops. His aim, as a matter of survival, was to prevent the great council from meeting.

The stage was set for a showdown. As soon as Somerset realised that York was raising troops he sent out summonses far and wide. York and the Nevilles moved south while the king left London to proceed to Leicester. It was only when Somerset was informed that York had passed Leicester that he realised that his enemy was intent on preventing the king from reaching the council. Somerset ordered his supporters and their levies to join him at St Albans where the king would be stopping for the night. Those around the king began to realise that York might actually attack the royal party and they hastily dismissed Somerset from his office of constable, appointed a third party, Buckingham, and attempted to negotiate. The two camps met in the town. Buckingham opened negotiations with York but York wanted Somerset arrested again on charges of conspiring to influence the king against him and this Buckingham could not do; the king had already pardoned Somerset at the Greenwich council. Buckingham stalled for time while more royal troops were arriving. York had to act quickly.

It was the morning of 22 May 1455 and, as it became clear that negotiations had failed, the royal standard was unfurled and set up in the marketplace, next to the king's tent. All those who advanced against it would be guilty of treason. It was the king's battle standard. York and his supporters were all traitors now. They had threatened the king and the least they could now expect was execution and forfeiture. There was no going back and the ensuing murderous débâcle has acquired the dubious honour of being considered the first battle in the Wars of the Roses. It wasn't much of a battle in truth. There were no more than two thousand Lancastrian supporters of the king and slightly more Yorkists. As York and Salisbury attempted to break through the gates of the town, heavily defended by Lord Clifford, Northumberland and Somerset, Warwick crossed over a ditch between the gates and soon found himself in the marketplace with the royal tent in front of him and Lancastrian troops still putting their armour on. An alarm bell sounded to warn that the king was in danger; hurrying to his aid, Northumberland and Somerset abandoned the gates. They were too late and had put themselves in the line of fire. Warwick's troops let fly a volley of arrows, wounding Buckingham's son and killing Clifford and Northumberland. Somerset fled to the Castle Inn where he was cornered. History has a duty to record that Edmund Beaufort, duke of Somerset, realising that he was about to be captured, decided to brave it out and die fighting like a true knight. Tradition says that he killed four men before he himself was hacked to death. He may have brought the country to the very brink of civil war but he died nobly.[10]

There were only about a hundred casualties at the first battle of St Albans but many of them were high-profile lords. As the vicious storm of arrows struck the Lancastrian camp the most high-profile of the lot was also struck. Henry VI, king of England, was hit in the neck and wounded. He was a fraction of an inch away from death. History hinges on such fractions. If Henry had been killed, Richard of York would no doubt have claimed the throne as Richard III. That would not have been the end of the civil war, one suspects, but would have made a difference to the career of his son Richard. As it happened Henry survived. Bleeding from his brush with death, he hid in a tanner's house where he was discovered by York's men. To their credit they attended to his scratch and took him into the nearby abbey where, on bended knee, they professed their allegiance and sought forgiveness.

It would have been easy to finish Henry off and make a new start. We tend to assume that with the crown within their grasp medieval aristocrats with royal blood in them would not hesitate to seize it. At the first battle of St Albans in May 1455 they did precisely the opposite. Respect for royal authority, the importance of legitimacy and the sanctity of the anointed all contributed to the universal abhorrence of regicide. At the subsequent crown-wearing ceremony at St Paul's cathedral on Whit Sunday it was York, at the specific request of the king, who placed the crown on Henry's head, rather than Archbishop Bourchier.[11] A few days after the battle, John Crane wrote to his kinsman John Paston with news of the fighting: 'As for our sovereign lord, thanked be God, he has no great harm.' There was no appetite for dynastic change. Because the legitimacy of Henry was never challenged or questioned, he could not be brushed aside.[12]

York did not even seek to profit from the victory overmuch. The fighting had served its purpose in getting rid of Somerset. The Nevilles, Salisbury and Warwick, who were Cecily's brother and his son, and the Bourchiers who were York's sister Isabel's husband and brothers-in-law, all gained the lion-share and mostly at the expense of the Percys of Northumberland. York called a Parliament where he made a profuse declaration of loyalty to the king and the house of Lancaster. He was content to accept the honorific title of constable of England. His feelings towards the Lancastrian king were rather different five years later when he was quite prepared to do away with Henry and take the throne himself. The reason for the contrast was the behaviour of Margaret of Anjou, Henry's wife, in the intervening period.

Although Somerset was now dead, Margaret resented his demise and allied herself with his son and the sons of the other lords killed at St Albans. She cultivated the friendship of those hostile to York, particularly the earls of Wiltshire and Shrewsbury, and single-mindedly sought to destroy him. He posed a threat, not only to her husband, but also to her beloved son and heir. Given that York could easily have disposed of her husband in a tanner's shop in St Albans, but had refrained from doing so, and given his suppression of violence subsequently and his adherence to constitutional norms, it ought to have been possible to live peaceably with him. If this had been achieved, the first battle of St Albans may have been the last and not the first in a civil war. It might be remembered as a bloody aristocratic affray, if it was remembered at all, rather than the beginning of the Wars of the Roses.

Margaret moved to the Midlands, taking Henry with her, and for the next four years England was governed from Coventry. The routine bureaucratic functions of government were still discharged from Westminster. Royal authority could only be hampered and diminished by this arrangement and York increasingly pushed into opposition. York had briefly exercised a second Protectorate at the end of 1455 when it became clear again that Henry's mental health was deteriorating. If the news of Castillon and the realisation that he had succeeded in losing almost all of his great father's conquests in France had tipped him over the edge in August 1453, then perhaps the stress of the battle of St Albans had a similar impact in the summer of 1455. He was nevertheless well enough in February 1456 to dismiss York, or, more accurately, to accept his resignation. Margaret, replacing Somerset as the power behind the throne, was one headache for the council: John Bocking, writing to John Paston at this time described her as 'a grete and stronge laboured woman' and John Benet, a contemporary chronicler, said that she 'greatly loathed' both York and Warwick, but York's programme of reform was another.[13] The peers were simply not prepared to accept the resumption of their lands by the crown. York knew that Henry had plunged the monarchy into financial crisis by granting too much land to magnates. Retrieving it was a prudent and sensible option but impossible to effect without serious and powerful opposition. It was opposition that Margaret was only too keen to exploit. York was up against forces beyond his control. Because he was not king, everything he tried to do in the king's name could be construed as partisan, as exploiting royal authority, as seeking to pervert the administration of the realm for his own ends. Even his talk of the 'common weal' could be misconstrued. It had connotations associated with the mob, with violence and with lawlessness. The truth was that neither Margaret nor York was ultimately to blame for the descent into civil war; the problem was the king.

It was impossible for the government of England to function for any period of time in the Middle Ages without effective kingship. It is all very well considering Henry VI as a feeble but unfortunate and much-maligned king. His reign was a disaster for everyone. Thousands died because of it, fighting their fellow countrymen, their neighbours and their kinsmen. All they wanted was an authority strong enough to be impartial and careful enough to bind them all together. Instead they were exposed to the dreadful vicissitudes of arbitrary whim: weakness at the centre which could only bring ruin to all. Some consider Henry VI a saint, a man whose birth cost him the religious solitude he craved. Be that as it may, his craven ineptitude damaged England and many of those who had the misfortune to be born during his reign. It might have been better if scruples had not intervened in the tanner's house at St Albans.

Even though an uneasy political truce existed from 1455–1459 between York and Margaret, it is unlikely that Richard saw much of his father at Fotheringhay. York was still the most powerful magnate in England and doing his best to quell widespread disturbances. Feuds and lawless violence, the symptoms of weak kingship, were rife in Devon, Kent, Northumberland and Wales. James II of Scotland had to be seen off too. The primary duties of a king, peace at home and security on the borders, were so badly neglected that minor tensions anywhere could escalate into violence. York spent his time based at Sandal in west Yorkshire when in the north, Ludlow in Shropshire when in the west or Sir John Fastolf's mansion when in London. His London residence, Baynards Castle, had been taken by Margaret in 1453 but he seems to have re-acquired it by 1458. The occasional visit to his family – York always valued Cecily's advice and company – and the news constantly arriving at his household would have been full of the talk of dangerous queens, weak kings, foreign humiliations and the old royal blood of England. If all this meant nothing to Richard as a six-year-old boy, it is possible that it began to mean something to him as he turned seven. At that rather impressionable age his life was turned upside down.

In 1458 it was becoming clear to York that Margaret was gathering her forces to challenge him. He was losing offices such as stewardships and wardenships to her supporters. Government by council and noble cooperation was not in her interests as it sustained York's authority. As her control over the king increased so the role of the council diminished. In March 1458 the council had engineered a display of reconciliation between the Yorkists and the heirs of the Lancastrians killed at St Albans. This so-called 'Loveday' was hijacked by Margaret who turned it into a spectacle in which she and the king paraded with the rival magnates who walked through the streets of London holding hands. The queen herself walked beside York. She, who had no constitutional right to legal authority over the magnates, made herself the equal of York. All this contrived ceremony demonstrated was that two equal factions existed among the nobility, and that the queen controlled the king. Both sides now knew that cooperation in an impartial council was impossible. The king had a beatific smile on his face as he left St Paul's, as if this was the end of all his troubles.[14]

Margaret realised that time was of the essence. Warwick had a powerful garrison at Calais and York's strength was growing. In June 1459 she summoned a great council to meet at Coventry. York, Salisbury, Warwick and the Bourchiers were not invited. It was clear that she was going to have them indicted. York knew he was in danger and gathered his family and retainers at Ludlow. The shadows and swirling mists of intangible forces which had hardly disturbed Cecily's household at Fotheringhay now assumed the rude and noisy forms of hurried packing, galloping horses, glints of steel and barked commands. The duchess and her children made haste across the west Midlands and into Shropshire. Everywhere they went the signs of musters could be seen: groups of infantry, cavalry and archers making their way to their rendezvouses.

At Ludlow Richard would have seen soldiers gathering, messengers racing, defences raised, weapons readied, worried faces and servants bustling everywhere. His father presided gravely but purposefully over all. The two oldest boys, Edward and Edmund, were in their father's counsels and had their own bristling retinues. Ten-year-old George no doubt wished he had the same. He, closer to Richard than the others, would have transmitted his fears, excitement and anticipation to his younger brother. The news was that their uncle, the earl of Salisbury, was making his way towards them from Yorkshire, with his northern retainers armed to the teeth, being shadowed by Lord Audley and a hostile royal army. Their cousin, Warwick, had just arrived with his forces after being pursued all the way across England by the young duke of Somerset, who was no doubt eager to settle a few scores. Warwick had part of his Calais garrison with him, though not as much as the duke of York would have liked, when he arrived unscathed at the end of September. Ludlow was getting crowded.

Not crowded enough as it happened. Margaret was assembling the royal host and determined to get rid of York once and for all. He was badly outnumbered and needed Salisbury to get to him quickly. Salisbury did his best but was unable to slip past Lord Audley and, a few miles west of Market Drayton, he was confronted by a vastly superior force of Cheshire levies under the colours of Margaret's son Edward, Prince of Wales. At Blore Heath the two armies clashed. If St Albans had been a short, sharp affray, Blore Heath was a real battle. Salisbury had 5,000 men and was outnumbered by a Lancastrian force of at least 10,000. The decisive difference between the two armies, however, was not in their numbers but in their commanders. Audley had some experience of fighting in France, but not much, while Salisbury was a seasoned campaigner of great ability and experience. Audley was also hampered by his strange orders from Margaret to take Salisbury prisoner. How he was expected to do this was anyone's guess. In the end the attempt cost him his life. Audley's force was mainly cavalry and Salisbury's archers spent much of the morning shooting their horses from under them. When the Lancastrians dismounted, fierce hand-to-hand fighting ensued which the Yorkist infantry were better equipped to handle. Audley's death saw the remaining Lancastrian cavalry disappear and Salisbury's route to Ludlow open. Unfortunately for the duke of York however, Salisbury's victory had been too hard won. A glance at the casualty figures tells us everything. Salisbury had two thousand men killed while Audley lost only five hundred. It had been a classic pyrrhic victory. So battered were Salisbury's troops that he allowed many of the survivors to return to their homes in the north, including his two sons, Thomas and John Neville.[15]

While the battle had been raging, troops from Lancashire led by Thomas lord Stanley and his brother Sir William Stanley stood idly by. They had been commanded to join Audley by Margaret. They both disobeyed that order. Thomas watched events and then sent a congratulatory letter to Salisbury, while William changed sides and joined the Yorkists. After the battle Salisbury's sons and Thomas Harrington with his own son James were ambushed at Acton Bridge and imprisoned in Chester castle. They had either been pursued on their way back to Yorkshire or, more probably, had themselves been pursuing Lancastrian stragglers and been outnumbered. The fate of the two Stanleys, who profited by betraying their sovereign, and of the Harringtons who suffered because of their fidelity to York, presaged events a quarter of a century later at Bosworth Field. At that battle these two Stanleys would act in exactly the same way once again. Thomas would withhold his forces from the king while William would throw in his lot with the king's enemies. That king would be Richard, now just over a week away from his seventh birthday and waiting for news in Ludlow. James Harrington, faithful to the Yorkist cause and now suffering for it in Chester, would pay the ultimate price for his life-long devotion to the Yorkists and die at Bosworth by Richard's side. His father, Thomas, in Chester castle with him, was to die by the side of the duke of York in a little over a year's time.

As Salisbury arrived at Ludlow with his battered and blood-stained troops, his main concern would have been the fate of his sons and their Harrington companions. Even if Richard had overheard these conversations, their meaning would surely have been lost in the ferment and anxiety all around him. The evidence of danger and alarm was everywhere: the wounded and exhausted soldiery billeted in the town, their captains in the castle, his father's own realisation that his forces were insufficient, Cecily's consternation and fear for the safety of the family, Warwick's concern for the safety of his captured brothers. The names of Stanley and of Harrington would have meant nothing to Richard then but they were to relive the parts they played at Blore Heath with uncanny accuracy and calamitous consequences at Bosworth Field. If Richard had been old enough to understand what had happened at Blore Heath, if he had been able to learn the lessons it taught, he might have saved his life at Bosworth. In the event the seventh anniversary of his birth was spent in spiralling confusion and incomprehensible danger.

If York's aim had been to gather sufficient protection to negotiate from strength, rather as he had done before at St Albans, his plan had miscarried. Margaret was not going to make the same mistake twice. The king would not be caught off-guard this time. For two weeks both sides licked their wounds and waited for the dust to settle. Then, on 9 October, the king summoned Parliament to meet on 21 November at Coventry. The 'St Albans Three', Warwick, Salisbury and York, were not invited. It was clear that the purpose of the Parliament was to impeach the three lords and pass acts of attainder against them. Almost at the same time as the summons was being issued, the bishop of Salisbury arrived at Ludlow offering a royal pardon to the Yorkist lords if they would surrender themselves to the king. Having not been summoned to Parliament, Warwick replied to the bishop that their safety was compromised. If they were in the king's custody and Parliament declared them traitors, as was clearly Margaret's intention, they were doomed. In any case, as York pointed out, for what were they being pardoned? To accept a pardon was to accept their guilt.[16]

As the bishop left Ludlow, York, Salisbury and Warwick led their armies swiftly to Worcester. They had felt trapped at Ludlow and needed to move closer to their Midland estates where reinforcements might be found. As if to illustrate the determination of Margaret to pin them down and prevent them from escaping her clutches, they were met at Worcester by Garter Herald who solemnly declared them traitors. They persuaded the herald to accompany them to Worcester Cathedral where, at the high altar, they declared their allegiance to Henry. They then signed a letter for him to take to the king explaining that their military defiance was simply self-defence. This was any man's prerogative, and few could deny that their lives were in danger. There was no question that the Yorkists were in a battle for survival. York turned south, perhaps hoping to make it to London. In the event he was confronted by a Lancastrian army near Tewkesbury and, knowing he was outnumbered, he returned once again to his stronghold at Ludlow without giving battle.

In a field outside the town, across Ludford Bridge, York established his camp, fortified his position as best he could, and awaited the royal army. The whole family, watching from the castle heights, could see the armies taking up positions in the field. On the horizon the king's forces were arriving. Richard would have been aware that his uncle, cousin, father and eldest brother, Edward, were facing a hostile army which was heading towards the castle and the town of Ludlow. If those pillars of manhood failed to defeat that army then Richard, his brothers George and Edmund, his sister Margaret and their mother Cecily would be in mortal danger. Only his sisters – Elizabeth, married the previous year to John de la Pole at the age of fourteen, and Anne, married to Exeter – would be out of harm's way. His father was outnumbered something like three to one. Catastrophe seemed inevitable.

The armies manoeuvred into position and as dawn broke on the 12 October hurried preparations were made for battle. York had managed to obtain several cannon and they fired intermittently, randomly and to little effect into the Lancastrian lines. Before York were three hefty contingents lead by Humphrey Stafford, duke of Buckingham, whose son had been wounded at St Albans, Henry Percy, earl of Northumberland, whose father had been killed at St Albans, and Henry Beaufort, Duke of Somerset, whose father had also been killed at St Albans. These men were on a mission. They were hell-bent on revenge. Even more worrying from York's point of view was the fact that they were accompanied by fourteen other lords and their retinues. Bringing up the rear, at a safe distance this time, were the king and queen. As the day wore on heralds approached the Yorkist ranks and offered a royal pardon to all those who deserted. The royal standard was once again unfurled, as it had been four years earlier at St Albans. York, Warwick and Salisbury spent the afternoon rallying their troops who showed distinct signs of recalcitrance. They had little enthusiasm for a battle against their own king, especially as no one seemed to know what would happen if the king were to be defeated. York was not claiming to be king. If his problem was the threat to his own life then perhaps it might be better if he rode off into the night and saved everybody else's lives along with his own. In the end this was precisely what he did do.

At some point in the evening, Andrew Trollope accepted the king's offer of a pardon and led his crack Calais troops over to the Lancastrians. Others followed suit. Outnumbered now more than ever, it would have been suicidal for the Yorkists to engage in battle. At about midnight York, Warwick and Salisbury went back to Ludlow castle. There they took their leave and fled. York, with his son Edmund, earl of Rutland, by his side, sped through Wales, destroying every bridge they crossed to evade any pursuit, and took ship for Ireland. Warwick, Salisbury and York's eldest son Edward, now earl of March, fled abroad too and ended up in Calais. Cecily and the three youngest children, George, Margaret and Richard, were abandoned to their fate. One chronicle speaks of Cecily standing in the marketplace at Ludlow, her children beside her, trusting to the mercy of the Lancastrians. For their part, finding on the morning of the 13 October that their opponents had abandoned their battle standards and their troops, the surprised Lancastrians accepted the surrender of their equally bemused opponents and contented themselves with looting, plundering and ransacking Ludlow. The battle, with virtually no casualties, became known as 'the Rout of Ludford Field'.

It is difficult to assess the danger Cecily and her younger children faced. No one lifted a finger against them and she was permitted to remain at Ludlow for the next few weeks. When her husband was duly attainted at the November Parliament in Coventry, known to Yorkists as the Parliament of Devils, she lost everything, including Ludlow itself, and threw herself on the king's mercy. He granted her a pension of 1,000 marks a year and handed her over to the keeping of her sister Anne and her husband, the duke of Buckingham. Cecily, the young Richard still in tow, probably ended up in the not inconsiderable grandeur of the duke's palatial residence at Maxstoke castle in Warwickshire. Due largely to her former friendship with Margaret, Cecily and her little innocents were safe, and York knew as much.

Nevertheless, Margaret was appallingly bad at controlling her troops and the Ludlow riot might well have led to some accidental deaths. It certainly cannot have been pleasant for York's family to have been witness to the violence and the ransacking of their own home. A London writer, William Gregory, heard that

> the king's gallants at Ludlowe, whenn they hadd drokyn i-nowe of wyne that was in tavernys and in othyr placys ... robbyd the towne, and bare awaye bedding, clothe and othyr stuffe, and defoulyd many wymmen.

This writer also describes Cecily going to the king at Coventry where she 'submyttd hyr unto hys grace'. We are told that the king 'fulle humbely grauntyde hyr grace, and to alle hyrs that wolde come with hyr'.[17] The

Coventry Parliament confirmed her grant of a pension for 'the relief of her and her infants who had not offended against the king'. The whole episode can only have been a harrowing experience even if we do not accept William Gregory's view that the duke of Buckingham and his lady, Anne, Cecily's sister, kept her 'fulle strayte and many a grete rebuke'. She had lost pretty much everything. Richard was the youngest son of a traitor who had lost all his lands and possessions, had fled from a battlefield and had abandoned his wife and small children to go into exile.

Cecily and her offspring spent six months with Humphrey, the duke of Buckingham, and the duchess Anne. Humphrey was a Lancastrian in so far as he would not fight against the king. He had been with the king in his tent when Warwick had unleashed his volley of arrows at St Albans, and was wounded in the subsequent melee. His eldest son, also called Humphrey, was also wounded in the battle. This son had died sometime between the battle and the arrival of Cecily, leaving a son named Henry, who was now the heir of the first Humphrey. The duke was an honourable man who did his best in the most difficult of circumstances. Cecily was his sister-in-law and, despite William Gregory's supposition, there is no evidence that he mistreated her or her children. His character was such that it is highly unlikely that he would have tolerated any insult to so high-born a lady and a kinswoman. Even though her husband had fought against him, he was the sort of man Cecily would happily have trusted. He had tried to remain friends with York despite the deteriorating political situation, and was to be killed at the battle of Northampton, defending the king. His heir, his grandson Henry, was just four years old when Richard came to stay. When Henry grew up he was to help Richard take the throne in 1483. Richard placed enormous trust in him then, a trust that proved to be horribly misplaced. Perhaps he trusted Henry Stafford, second duke of Buckingham, so much because Henry's grandfather had been such a rock when Richard's whole world was falling apart after the rout at Ludlow. In a world where treachery, self-interest and duplicity were becoming the armoury of survival, where civilised conduct and civil strife seemed opposed, Humphrey Stafford, duke of Buckingham, stands out as a man of integrity, probity, dignity and honesty. Two decades later his heir proved to be the opposite. Richard was to miscalculate the character of Henry Stafford with disastrous consequences. If he thought he would be like his grandfather he was hoping for too much. Men like Humphrey belonged to a different world, the world of Richard's childhood, the world, perhaps, of his father.

The duke of York spent his time in Ireland gathering men, money and support. He was still technically lieutenant there, despite the fact that Margaret had 'appointed' Wiltshire to that post. He was reasonably safe, with considerable

Anglo-Irish support. The Gaelic Irish were fighting their own civil war in the north and west, but York confined his movements to county Meath and Dublin where he was considered a good lord. Warwick visited him in Dublin and, on returning to Calais to join Edward and Salisbury, he issued a manifesto, in June 1460, setting out all their grievances. The propaganda duly disseminated, with York and the Calais lords claiming to be the saviours of the realm (which York probably believed) the time had come to act.[18]

Warwick and his father Salisbury, with Edward, earl of March, and two thousand troops, landed at Sandwich at the end of June 1460. They pushed on to London which opened its gates to them, to their considerable relief. The mood in England had changed. There was sympathy for York and concern about the arbitrary way Margaret was running affairs. Warwick and Salisbury found it much easier to raise troops than before. The retainers of many of the twenty-six lords in exile with York were about to demonstrate their loyalty. Too many family traditions, ancient and recent favours, personal memories and local interests linked these men to their lords. Margaret's replacements would disrupt their common purpose and carefully-managed local stability. As the Calais lords marched north, the men from their regional affinities flocked to their banners and were joined by a considerable number of their friends. Salisbury remained in London to besiege the Tower, which was still held by the Lancastrians, while Edward and Warwick moved swiftly through the south Midlands.

The king and queen were still at Coventry and taken by surprise at the speed and size of the earls' advance. Reaching Northampton, Margaret had about 10,000 men. Commanding her troops, establishing a strong defensive ditch and placing artillery in position to await the coming Yorkists was none other than Humphrey, duke of Buckingham. Protecting Cecily's three youngest children in his Warwickshire castle, he was about to die fighting her eldest son. His story is a small illustration of the appalling tensions and conflicts caused by civil war. The battle of Northampton on 10 July 1460 exposed many of the ugly vices unleashed by internecine warfare. Fissures in the laboriously-constructed web of courtly and political conventions became crevices and benign blemishes became brutal ruptures. The Yorkists secured an overwhelming victory largely because Lord Grey of Ruthin, leading the Lancastrian right wing, changed sides and joined the Yorkists. The Lancastrians were thrown into complete confusion and the battle lost in thirty minutes. Rain had affected the artillery and casualties amounted to no more than three hundred, mostly Lancastrian. Lord Grey, made earl of Kent in 1465 by a grateful Edward IV, showed how treachery could pay in a civil war. On foreign soil national honour was at stake and faithful service against the king's adversaries and the enemies of the realm could bring the just rewards of virtue and valour. In a civil war all became confused, distorted and indistinct. Fidelity was weighed against injustice, friendship against advantage and sacrifice against security. Against a foreign enemy the chances of the nobility being taken alive and brutally done to death were slight. Ransom was far more valuable than a carcass. At Northampton, the duke of Buckingham, the earl of Shrewsbury, Viscount Beaumont and Lord Egremont were all taken alive; all were executed on the spot. The king was found, as usual, in his tent, where the Yorkist lords, as usual, knelt down before him and paid homage. Margaret escaped with her son, Prince Edward.

Cecily and her three small children were taken by servants of her eldest son, the victorious Edward, earl of March, to London to stay in the large mansion that had belonged to Sir John Fastolf. The moated house, across the Thames from the Tower, was vacant, as the good Sir John had just died, and London was safe in Salisbury's hands. The news was exhilarating, the journey to London triumphant and the relief palpable. Richard was safe, his family alive and expectant, his brother Edward's star rising and the return of his father from Ireland imminent.

In fact nothing was certain. The king was still the king and, feeble though he was, he was no less rightful a monarch than he had been before. Warwick was rather enjoying issuing edicts under the Great Seal and instructing councillors to go about his business. Margaret was still at large, probably in Scotland, and if her husband should be deposed she had the rightful heir to the throne with her. York was coming from Ireland, he landed at Chester on 13 September, but what he would do was not clear to anyone. Had he come to claim the throne? Would he be accepted as king while Henry was still alive? Would there have to be more fighting? As Richard passed his eighth birthday, enjoying the large garden by the river in Southwark and being visited by his warrior brother Edward every day, he could not have suspected that the turmoil of the previous year would seem a distant tremor in comparison to the earthquake that was soon to hit the house of York. Richard's childhood was about to be disturbed again.

# THREE

# THE CLOAK
# OF ROYALTY

The duke of York, arriving from Ireland in September 1460, soon made it abundantly clear that he had come to claim the throne itself. Margaret of Anjou, by dismembering and redistributing his estates, had left him with no alternative. As he progressed through the marches, reassuring his tenants, removing Lancastrian intruders and issuing indentures to swell the ranks of his armed following, he began to behave as though he were already king. He had evidently renounced his allegiance to Henry VI. His commissions made no reference to the king, even omitting the regnal year. At Chester, Ludlow, Shrewsbury and Hereford he was received like a conquering hero with stage-managed petitions begging him to take the throne. He bore the full arms of England before him and his steady advance towards London could not be distinguished from the pageantry and majesty of a royal progress.[1]

At Hereford the duchess Cecily joined her husband, leaving Richard, his brother and his sister in Southwark. At Shrewsbury the earl of Warwick met the duke and conferred with him for four days. Here, as he must have done when visiting the duke in Ireland, Warwick discussed the best strategy for implementing the duke's wishes. Reaching Gloucester in October and moving to Abingdon a few days later York prepared to march on the capital. As he reached Barnet, Warwick, who had gone on ahead, was busy preparing the ground. He had summoned Parliament, announced York's imminent arrival and, in Henry's presence, denounced the king's conduct of government. The next day, with the election of a sympathetic Speaker, both Houses of Parliament assembled to await the arrival of the duke.

Richard knew that his father was approaching because his elder brother Edward, earl of March, kept him informed of the exciting drama now unfolding.[2] They had not seen their father, nor their brother Edmund, earl of Rutland, for a year. He now entered London, trumpets blazing, eight hundred soldiers in his entourage, with the arms of Clarence borne before him. Thomas Langley, duke of Clarence, had been the second son of Edward III. Henry VI was descended from the fourth son. The message was unmistakable: Richard, duke of York, had come to claim the throne as rightful successor to Edward III. The Lancastrian usurpation of Henry IV, by which Richard II had been deposed and murdered, was about to be reversed.

Entering the chamber of the House of Lords with his sword borne upright before him, a royal gesture, York walked slowly and steadily towards the throne. It stood at the end of the chamber under a canopy covered in the cloth of state. All the lords, temporal and spiritual, stood and watched, uncertain of what the duke intended to do. Reaching the throne, York turned to face the tense throng of anxious nobles, and, placing his hand on the arm of the seat of majesty, steadied himself in readiness to sit upon it. He waited a moment, perhaps in order to fully imbibe the significance of the historic occasion, perhaps in nervous expectation of a favourable acclamation from the lords before him, perhaps in an involuntary, instinctive realisation that all was not as he had imagined. In the brief lacuna provided by his hesitation, York heard the sound he had least expected: a sharp intake of breath. It was a gasp of horror which, escaping from the mouths of the mightiest men in the kingdom caused the duke to freeze. There was silence. No one moved and no one spoke. Those present hardly dared breathe. The duke scowled at them in bewildered incomprehension. Then, after an eternity had elapsed, Thomas Bourchier, the archbishop of Canterbury, asked, rather clumsily, if the duke wished to see the king. It was an odd thing to ask but something had to be said and someone had to say it. The duke, baffled and angry at this totally unexpected reaction to the culmination of his plans, replied, 'I know no man in England who aught not rather come to see me than I go to him.' He then strode out of the chamber, marching towards the king's chamber and bellowing to the soldiers running behind him that they should break down the doors if anyone dared to bar his way. The terrified king scurried off to the queen's quarters while the duke took over the royal apartments and sulked, nursing the burning fury of thwarted ambition.[3]

Despite years of misgovernment, civil war and foreign humiliation, the majority of subjects both high and low did not have the stomach to remove a living king. Henry was a simple man, ordained by God to rule and to whom they had all taken oaths of allegiance. York had misread the mood of the people. So near to achieving the ultimate goal, the duke had no 'plan B' and no idea of what to do next. He wanted the throne, believed it was his and was determined to get it, either constitutionally or by force. That moment's hesitation was to prove very costly and, ultimately, fatal to the duke; he was to be killed in battle just two months later.

When the duke's supporters realised the strength of the opposition to a deposition they began to look for other solutions. The first task was to persuade the duke himself to adopt another course of action. The Yorkists were popular because they had promised to reform the government and bring stability, not because they had planned to remove the king. The lords met in conference at Blackfriars the next day and agreed to send the earl of March to try to persuade the duke to take a different approach. They had given assurances, they said, for the king's safety and if they were to renege on their promises the citizens of London would raise havoc. Edward declined to go and a delegation of two bishops, a baron and a citizen of London went instead. York was obdurate and informed them that he would be crowned the following day, 13 October, in Westminster Abbey. It would be a fitting occasion on which to celebrate St Edward's day. A new king would sit on Edward's chair by Edward's shrine in the cathedral Edward had founded, and usher in a new age of true royal government.

Unfortunately for the duke, no one else seemed to share his glorious vision, which, given that the symbolism was fraught with dangerous resonance and subject to misinterpretations, was hardly surprising. St Edward, after all, was said to have borne an uncanny resemblance to Henry VI, the very king which the duke of York was trying to supplant. It was widely known that Henry revered the saint and worshipped him regularly. Invoking the presence of St Edward was bound to cause trouble. The baronial council adjourned overnight and the next morning sent Thomas Neville, his nephew, the brother of Warwick, to try to make the duke see sense. The duke was busy preparing for his coronation but whatever Thomas said must have had the desired effect. The crowds assembling at the abbey were told to disperse. The duke agreed to submit his claim to Parliament, presumably believing that Parliamentary sanction, combined with the undoubted justice of his claims, would put the matter beyond further question. On 16 October the Lords bought themselves a little more time by submitting the matter to lawyers. On 22 October, much to the frustration of the duke, the chancellor declared that the king had required that the lords discuss the matter. At this point the justices among the lords, called upon to deliver an opinion on York's title to the throne, declared that so high a subject was manifestly beyond their competence. 'The matter was so high,' they declared, 'and touched the king's high estate and regality, which is above the law and passed our learning, whereof we durst not enter into any communication thereof.' The lords then referred the matter to the sergeants of the law and the king's attorney but they declared that if the matter was beyond the competence of the justices then it was certainly above the learning of the sergeants.[4]

On 24 October a compromise was reached known as the Act of Accord. By this instrument York's claim to the throne was recognised but Henry was to keep the throne for his lifetime. York, in other words, became the heir of Henry. On Henry's death the crown would pass to York and his heirs. York and his eldest son, Edward, confirmed their agreement to this act before Parliament. Henry, for his part, processed, crowned, through the streets of London to St Paul's cathedral. York's supporters vented their fury at these proceedings by rioting and encouraging York to try to force the dim-witted king to abdicate. It was too late, and York's time had passed. He himself agreed to the arrest of his violent supporters. Two things were clear: there had to be order and peace, and Henry, whatever his mental condition, would never abdicate. York could not claim to be restoring good government on behalf of the common weal if his supporters rioted and caused bloodshed. He was rebuffed precisely because men feared the lawlessness attendant upon a deposition. What of the debts owed by the king? What of his grants? What of the titles and offices he had distributed? What of his acts? There was far too much at stake to risk a change of monarch, however bad at the job the incumbent was. There was also, York began to discover, residual affection for the king who had weathered so many storms and who had never wavered in the belief in his divine destiny to rule.

The stage was now set for the final act in York's tragic story. He had failed to take the throne because the consensus was against him, but he had disinherited Margaret's beloved son, Edward, and that she would not have. War was inevitable; any hope of a peaceful transition of power evaporated in the heat of Margaret's maternal ire. As she massed her forces in the north and began to provoke the duke by systematically pillaging his estates and terrorising his tenants, his youngest son, Richard, saw him leave once more. He would never see his father again. It would be too fanciful to suppose that the little boy, who had been led to expect to see his father crowned and was to have his high hopes cruelly dashed to pieces, had learned a lesson he would never forget. If you are going to take the throne, do it quickly and do it without hesitation, or lose everything.

Margaret's response was surprisingly swift and powerful. Somerset returned from France and proceeded to York. The earl of Devon joined the earl of Northumberland in constructing an army in Yorkshire, centred on Hull. They were joined by the duke of Exeter, lords Clifford and Roos and the senior, disinherited branch of the Nevilles. York's castles at Pontefract and Wressle were taken and his lands in the West Riding were devastated. He marched north, setting out on 2 December, recruiting as he went, with his son Edmund and Salisbury. His eldest son, Edward, was sent to Shrewsbury to deal with the uprising of Jasper

Tudor. It was winter, provisions were low and it was very wet. The duke was harassed en route by a Lancastrian contingent under Andrew Trollope, which he managed to beat off, but he arrived at his castle of Sandal, near Wakefield on 21 December rather the worse for wear. Provisions in the castle were already low but the Lancastrians had made the situation far more difficult for the duke by anticipating his arrival, surrounding the castle and attacking his foraging parties whenever they sallied forth to augment their victuals.

On 30 December one of the foraging parties was attacked, as it returned to the castle, by the forces of Somerset and Devon. York, apparently against the advice of his councillors, decided to sally forth to rescue the party. He may have been influenced by the arrival over Wakefield Bridge of a large force, possibly 8,000 men, which York believed to be for his own relief. This force was led by Lord John Neville, leader of the senior Nevilles, determined to destroy the junior branch represented by Salisbury. How York could be so mistaken is difficult to imagine. It is possible that he had met John Neville earlier in the week and issued him with the requisite authority to raise troops, but how he could believe that these troops would not be used against him when John had already fought a battle against Salisbury at Blore Heath the previous year is a mystery. Andrew Trollope is alleged to have tricked the duke by dressing his troops in the livery of Warwick and pretending to relieve the castle of Sandal itself. One tradition that has the ring of truth about it is that York declared that he would rather fight like a lion, in the open, than be trapped like a dog in a kennel.[5] The situation he was in was itself the result of a series of impetuous miscalculations. An inept naivety clings to all his actions in the weeks, days and hours before his death. He had been lured into a trap by opponents who clearly had the measure of the man. He lacked the cunning, the political guile, the sophisticated calculation required to out-fox his rivals. He was too proud, too predictable and perhaps too honest to survive in the climate of 1460.

The drawbridge of Sandal Castle was lowered and York led his troops out with his banner displayed in front of him. 'Advance', he is reported to have said, 'in the name of God and St George, for surely I will fight with them, though I should fight alone.'[6] This chivalric gesture splashed a glint of colour on to the drab canvass this grim battle presented. There were no exchanges of heraldic messages, no bravura challenges or courteous ripostes, no trumpets and no ceremony. York's men were greeted by a storm of arrows as they charged across Wakefield Green. The enemy appeared to retreat but were merely luring the hapless duke further into the woods where Lancastrian reinforcements lay in wait. Heavily outnumbered and eventually overwhelmed, the duke fought on to the end, refusing to surrender or retreat. He issued one last order, that his son, Edmund, should be led to safety, and then, surrounded by his enemies he prepared to fight to the death. One chronicler, who was there at the time, saw the duke, 'when he was in the plain ground between the castle and the town of Wakefield, environed on every side, like a fish in a net, or a deer in a buck stall.' There were those who wished to spare him and amid the din of battle their cries of, 'Yield, yield thee!' could be heard, but the duke refused, and, lashing out time and time again with his sword, was finally cut down. A later chronicler recalled, 'He manfully fighting was within half hour slain, and his whole army discomforted and with him died his true friends'.[7]

His son, Edmund, never made it to safety. As he fled across Wakefield Bridge with his tutor, Sir Robert Aspall, he was spotted by Lord Clifford who cornered the seventeen-year-old and, drawing a dagger while Edmund knelt in supplication, plunged it into the youth's heart with the words, 'By God's blood, thy father slew mine, and so will I do thee and all thy kin'. Salisbury managed to escape but was captured by Andrew Trollope's men, taken to Pontefract Castle and publicly beheaded the next day. York's head was severed from his corpse and, mocked by a paper crown, stuck on Micklegate Bar, the southern gateway into York, with the head of Salisbury and those of their sons, Edmund and Thomas. It was Margaret herself, apparently, who ordered this grisly tableau, 'So York may look upon York'.[8]

Richard, still at Southwark with his mother Cecily and his siblings George and Margaret, was now fatherless. He bore his father's name and, in many ways, came to bear the burden of his father's legacy. While Edward, the eldest son, inherited his father's cause and successfully prosecuted the claims of the dynasty, his intelligence, good humour, good looks, charm and sophistication were in stark contrast to the career and personality of his father. Richard, on the other hand, bore many striking resemblances to the duke of York, not the least of which was to be the manner of his death. While Edward was to die in his bed, Richard was to die leading his troops into battle, surrounded by his foes, manfully, like his father, fighting to the last breath. It is not the cynical guile, for which Richard III is often accused, which stands out from the record of his early life, but the lack of it. It is not the trimming, the cunning, the plotting and scheming, of which his detractors accused him, that strikes the neutral observer, but the similarity between father and son: both were blunt, direct, loyal and brave. Deception and treachery were the key ingredients in the disaster which almost ended the history of the Yorkist dynasty at Wakefield in 1460. They were to re-emerge over twenty years later at Bosworth and finally destroy it.

In the meantime, the duchess Cecily, having lost her husband, a son and a brother in the battle of Wakefield, now faced the prospect of the victorious Lancastrians, led by Margaret of Anjou, descending on London. Cecily's eldest son Edward, hearing the news of his father's death while at Shrewsbury, had moved towards the family stronghold at Ludlow. He was actively recruiting, planning, watching and waiting. He could look after himself. Although only eighteen years old, Edward was a highly competent soldier and commander and he was soon to rescue his entire dynasty from oblivion. Cecily's concern was for the younger sons, George and Richard, now at her residence in Baynards Castle in London. So dangerous was the situation now, so vicious the blood-letting at Wakefield, that trusting to the mercy of her enemies was no longer an option. The battles of Northampton and Wakefield had removed the last vestiges of civilised discourse and convention upon which Cecily had been able to rely after the rout at Ludlow just over a year ago. Edmund had been murdered at Wakefield and his brothers' lives had suddenly been set adrift on the turbulent sea of bloody feud. She could not risk allowing them to stay in London. Bravely, as ever, she decided to remain herself but sent her boys to the safety of the duke of Burgundy in Utrecht.

While Warwick held London she might have waited for better times, and these were certainly promised by the news from Hereford. On 2 February 1461 her eldest son Edward had defeated Jasper Tudor, earl of Pembroke, who, with his father Owen Tudor and the earl of Wiltshire had been heading for Ludlow. From there they planned to join forces with Margaret. Edward, attempting to reach London himself, had intercepted this large Lancastrian force. Wiltshire had brought Irish, Breton and French forces with him and, combined with the Welsh forces of the Tudors this army would give Margaret insuperable power. The battle of Mortimer's Cross not only reignited Yorkist hopes but also proved that Edward, an eighteen-year-old rookie, was a skilled commander. While accompanied by Sir Walter Devreux and Sir William Herbert, it was Edward himself who led his troops in the centre and pushed Jasper Tudor's line back until it broke. No doubt still smarting from his father's ignominious end at Wakefield, Edward executed the sixty-year-old Owen Tudor in Hereford marketplace. Jasper and Wiltshire escaped but the grandfather of the future king of England, the step-father of Henry VI, the founder of the Tudor dynasty, was put to death by Edward. The Chronicler, Gregory, described the scene:

And Owen Tudor was taken and brought unto Haverfordwest, and he was beheaded at the market place, and his head set upon the grice of the market cross, and a mad woman combed his hair and washed away the blood of his face, and she got candles and set them about him burning, more than a hundred. This Owen Tudor was father unto the Earl of Pembroke, and had wedded Queen Katherine, King Harry the VI's mother, weening and trusting all away that he should not be beheaded till he saw the axe and the block. He trusted on pardon and grace till the collar of his red velvet doublet was ripped off. Then he said, 'That head shall lie on the stock that was wont to lie on Queen Katherine's lap', and put his heart and mind wholly unto God, and fully meekly took his death.[9]

When Owen's grandson Henry Tudor fought at Bosworth it is worth remembering that old scores were being settled that day that reached back to 1461.

Marvellous though the news of this triumph must have been to Cecily and her young brood anxiously waiting in London, their own safety was perilously compromised when Warwick left London to face the advancing Lancastrians under Margaret and was comprehensively defeated at the second battle of St Albans on 17 February. Out-manoeuvred and out-thought, Warwick had not only exposed London to the full weight of Margaret's power, but had also allowed her to gain possession of the king, her feeble-minded husband, whom she found laughing and singing under a tree. London was in panic and, despite Edward's victory and Warwick's escape from the débâcle at St Albans, the capture of the king now gave the Lancastrians the legitimacy the Yorkists had so carefully engineered for themselves. It was at this point that Cecily, no doubt agonising for a short time over the separation she was about to endure, had decided to send George and Richard abroad.

Philip the Good, ruler of the Burgundian Netherlands, presided over a wealthy and fashionable court. A friend of the duke of York, largely through their mutual dislike of France, they shared a love of chivalry, ceremony, pageantry and ostentatious display. Richard, transported across the sea for the first time in his life, found himself far away from the danger and fear of civil war and entering a bustling world of trade and profit adorned by a lavish court where civility and protocol were rigidly observed. Here was an exciting mix of the modern and the antique. Merchants, fabulously rich on the profits of the cloth trade, William Caxton among them, vied with their neighbours to commission works of art with which to decorate their opulent residences. For a brief few months of his young life, Richard was exposed to the heady fragrance of the flowering of the Italian Renaissance as it wafted northwards across the Alps. The English Channel, and the Wars of the Roses, seemed to present impenetrable barriers to the reception in England of the cultural changes sweeping across Europe, for the time being at least.

For two months the two boys in Utrecht were kept at a diplomatic distance by the duke of Burgundy. Their journey had been dangerous and cloaked in secrecy with a small, low-key escort and no comforts to betray their noble origins. While safer in the Low Countries they were nevertheless the scions of a house with uncertain prospects. Richard, still only eight, had George aged eleven for company but his father was dead, his mother a long way off, and no news of his brother Edward could be gleaned from any source. There were books and tutors aplenty, with many friends of the erstwhile duke of York to wish the brothers well, but with such a doubtful future and with so many foreign and unfamiliar sights and sounds, it is more than likely that distraction, confusion, fear and despondency filled the thoughts of the young exiles.[10]

Back in England their brother Edward was marching towards London. The city had been bracing itself for the arrival of Margaret and the king, dreading the destruction that her northern troops might wreak. The magistrates had sent high-ranking envoys with impeccable Lancastrian credentials to ask Margaret to make her intentions known. On 20 February they returned and reported that, 'The king and queen had no mind to pillage the chief city and chamber of their realm, and so they promised; but at the same time they did not mean that they would not punish the evil doers.'[11] A curfew was declared and the citizens prepared themselves for trouble. The whole exchange reveals Margaret's problem. Not only did the Londoners not trust her, nor she them, but she could not bring herself to give them the assurances they needed. Her haughty disdain of the 'rabble', who happened to be the leading merchants and citizens of one of the greatest cities in Europe, and her refusal to guarantee their safety, was a gross miscalculation. Who could tell what she meant by 'evil doers'? No one was safe. The citizens, in an uproar, began to arm themselves. Further negotiations ensued by which it was agreed that the queen's party could enter the city but that the bulk of the army would remain outside. Even so, 400 of her finest soldiers, marching from the seat of the negotiations in Barnet to the gates of the city at Aldgate, were refused entry by the aldermen and sheriff's militia. The city waited with baited breath as its own armed citizens held the gates against a hungry and victorious Lancastrian force. Rumours began to sweep through the town that Edward, now the duke of York, had joined up with Warwick at Burford in the Cotswolds and was marching towards them from the west. Whether Margaret had the same information is not known, but on 25 February she withdrew all her forces to Dunstable. The Londoners had set themselves against her and her cause was lost. In many ways they had taken the most decisive step in the Wars of the Roses and chosen in favour of York. They prided themselves on their liberty and here took it to unprecedented lengths. The Milanese ambassador to the court of France, Prospero di Camulio, writing from Brussels to Francesco Sforza on 15 March, recognised what the Londoners had done and commented rather cynically that they were careful, 'never to let things go so far that they cannot turn.' More importantly, however, he observed that as London, 'is very rich and the most wealthy city of Christendom, this enormously increases the chances of the side that it favours.'[12]

On 27 February Edward and Warwick reached London which immediately flung open its gates. As Anthony Rivers commented to Camulio, 'the Lancastrian cause was lost irredeemably.' Robert Fabyan, author of the contemporary *Great Chronicle of London*, saw Edward enter the city, 'the which was of the citizens joyously received'. He then describes how Warwick mustered his people in St John's Field:

where unto that host were proclaimed and shewed certain articles and points that King Henry had offended in, whereupon it was demanded of the said people whether the said Henry were worthy to reign as king any longer or no. Whereunto the people cried hugely and said, Nay, Nay. And after it was asked of them whether they would have the earl of March for their king and they cried with one voice, Yea, Yea. [13]

A petition was taken to Baynards Castle and presented to Edward. He declined to accept because, 'he was insufficient to occupy that great charge for sundry considerations by him then shewed'. He was, nevertheless, prevailed upon by the bishop of Exeter and the archbishop of Canterbury, 'and other noble men then present', and 'took upon himself that charge.' As Fabyan relates, Edward was, 'elected and admitted for king.'

It was just five months since Edward's father had effectively been refused the throne. Where now were the parliamentary procedures, the legal niceties, the lengthy constitutional debates and the cloud of reservations? What had become of the biggest stumbling block of them all: the popularity of Henry VI? How, in such a short space of time and to such unanimous acclaim, had the fortunes of the house of York so completely reversed? The proceedings at St John's Field have all the hallmarks of the hustings for a democratic nomination of a popular candidate in an election. Certainly public opinion had played its part. York had been too presumptuous, too arrogant and too curmudgeonly to win support. Like Margaret, he didn't believe he needed the approbation of the lower classes. Edward was popular and Warwick knew precisely how to utilise this asset. It may be that he would have shared the view of another Italian in London at the time, named Coppini, that, 'My lord of Warwick has come off the best and has made a new king of the son of the duke of York'.

Of course water had flowed under the bridge, even in the space of five months. The duke of York had taken matters to the very brink and prepared the way for the 'election' of his son. Parliament and the king had agreed to make Edward the heir to the throne. Since then Edward had won the sympathy vote. Although the duke of York was not popular, in the modern sense, few wished to see him so comprehensively destroyed as he had been at Wakefield. Then there was Margaret. It was now clear to the entire realm that Margaret intended to rule in her husband's name. It was also clear that Henry VI was incapable of exercising any authority. While Margaret had been defeating York at Wakefield the king had been in London with Warwick. When Margaret had defeated Warwick at St Albans the king had started the battle with Warwick and ended it with Margaret. He was a cipher. If it was necessary for royal power to be exercised for him then it was perhaps time to vest it in a man who could exercise that power himself. There was also now another dimension: Edward had been victorious in battle:

he was a decisive and effective man of action who offered the best prospects for peace. In less than a year there had been four battles: at Northampton, Wakefield, Mortimer's Cross and St Albans. The violence was affecting everyone, in all corners of the realm. Edward seemed to be the best hope for the future.

After his strange 'election' on 3 March, Edward spent 4 March racing through the formalities. He processed to St Paul's with all the necessary pomp and circumstance and heard the singing of a *Te Deum* before riding to Westminster and a hastily arranged ceremony of inauguration. In Westminster Hall he was placed on the marble royal bench and given the royal sceptre:

> Where he so being set and his lords spiritual and temporal standing about him and the hall being full of people, anon after that silence was commanded, it was showed the rightful inheritance of this prince.[14]

What was shown was that Edward had a rightful claim to the throne through the title of his father duke of York, and that Henry, by breaking the agreement with the duke of York, killing him being considered to represent the requisite breach of faith, had forfeited the throne. Once again the crowd was manipulated into shouting their assent. It worked wonderfully well the day before so why not make the most of this new-found people power? Across the road and into the Abbey for the solemnisation of the proceedings: the golden staff of office presented to the enthroned king, offerings to the shrine of St Edward, another *Te Deum*, and also a *Laudes Regiae*, then back by water down the Thames to St Paul's for a quiet evening in the bishop of London's residence. No triumphalism. There was much to be done. There were, after all, now two monarchs in England; there was going to have to be another battle. Throughout all the carefully staged rituals and ancient royal ceremonies, some of which had not been used for over a century, Edward had not received unction and had not actually been crowned. This would have to wait until the other king had been dealt with.[15] The Croyland chronicler noted that

> 'He would not at present allow himself to be crowned, but immediately, like unto Gideon or another of the judges, acting faithfully in the Lord, girded himself with the sword of battle'.

While attending to the constitutional minutiae Edward, like a skilled politician, had made a very good impression. Camulio wrote of the 'good opinion of the temper and moderation of Edward'.[16] If popularity had allowed Henry to hold on to the throne at the expense of Edward's father, then Edward had won that popularity, removed the residual vestiges of Henry's claim to legitimacy, and overthrown him at last.

The duke of York had stalled in London. Queen Margaret had been repulsed by it and retreated from it. Edward had made it his own. He worked it, used it and won it, and in doing so he had become king. London was too important, historically, economically, numerically and militarily, to be threatened, scorned and abandoned. Margaret had made her greatest mistake and Edward had capitalised on it in brilliant style. Perhaps, too, after almost forty years in which a dangerous vacuity had slept at the heart of power, there was a sense of relief. Riding on the crest of a wave of enthusiasm and goodwill, on 11 March Edward marched north to confront Margaret and allow the god of battles to decide between the two kings.

It is a little ironic that the Lancastrians were camped in Yorkshire, mainly around York itself. Margaret's chief supporters, the disinherited Nevilles, the Percys of Northumberland, the lords Clifford and Roos, had their estates and retainers in York's old dukedom. Edward, on the other hand, drew the main body of his support from Kent, East Anglia, the Welsh Marches and the Midlands. As his brother was to discover in due course, the age-old mistrust between north and south was a powerful factor in the politics of fifteenth-century England. Richard's love affair with the city of York would, in the decades that followed, provide a contrast with Edward's secure investment in London. Edward, urbane and cosmopolitan, had learned from his father's mistakes. Richard seems to have been too young to have witnessed and understood those flaws; as it was, he became more like his father than Edward ever did.

Edward made slow progress through the Midlands in order to recruit men in Warwick's heartlands. Eventually, on 27 March, he reached Pontefract Castle. The Lancastrians, led by the duke of Somerset, had taken up a defensive position fifteen miles south-west of York, across the River Wharf near the village of Towton. Between the village and Edward's army lay the River Aire, full with spring rain and impossible to cross, except by the bridge where the A1 still crosses it at Ferrybridge. Edward sent the duke of Suffolk ahead to seize the wooden bridge but they found that the Lancastrians had already destroyed it. The advance party set about rebuilding it and had almost finished when night fell. They guarded the bridge overnight but as dawn broke on 28 March they were taken by surprise by a Lancastrian cavalry force led by Lord Clifford. In the sudden clash many of Edward's men, including their commander, Lord Fitzwalter, were killed. Edward threw his army forwards to try to rescue the advance party and force a crossing of the Aire. Clifford, however, held his ground and Edward's casualties mounted. He decided to attempt to outflank Clifford by sending Lord Fauconberg, Warwick's uncle, with Sir Walter Blount and a force of Kentishmen, three miles upstream to Castleford where there was a crossing. Such a strong force, however, was impossible to conceal and Clifford, realising the danger he now faced, began to pull his troops back towards the safety of Towton. Fauconberg, having crossed the river, galloped as fast as he could with his mounted archers to attempt to cut Clifford off before he reached the safety of Somerset's army. As dusk fell Fauconberg's men intercepted Clifford along with John Neville and killed them quickly, fearing that they too might be caught by a relieving force from Towton. In the event Somerset did not come to Clifford's rescue. As Edward brought his army across the makeshift structure at Ferrybridge, he had the satisfaction of knowing that Clifford, who had murdered his brother Edmund at Wakefield, and Neville, who had betrayed his father in the same battle, had received their just desserts.[17]

Edward advanced towards the Lancastrians and reached Saxton village, just south of Towton, as darkness was falling. Conditions could not have been worse. It was the end of March, but Yorkshire can hold on to some bitter winter weather well into spring. It was very cold and snow began to fall. Edward's men had not eaten; the baggage train with all their provisions was having difficulty keeping up over mud – churned up by the boots of over twenty thousand men and the hooves of thousands of horses – which was now freezing over. They endured a freezing night with empty stomachs.

As dawn broke the armies approached each other across Towton Vale. It was Palm Sunday, 29 March 1461, and the biggest, bloodiest battle ever fought on English soil was about to begin. Over fifty thousand men were to engage in horrendous slaughter and many thousands would not live to see the rest of Holy Week. As they fought, Henry VI was celebrating Mass in the safety of York. While he reflected on Christ's entry into Jerusalem, over thirty thousand of his supporters attempted to shore up his ailing regime.

The appalling conditions actually favoured Edward. The wind was blowing north into the faces of the Lancastrians and, as they faced each other across a small valley, the Yorkist archers could fire further than their adversaries. The Lancastrians, with the snow blinding them, found that their arrows were falling short and being picked up and sent back by the Yorkists. On the Lancastrian right flank the duke of Somerset, alarmed by his mounting casualties, ordered his force to advance. He made good progress but the Yorkist line held. On the other wing the earl of Northumberland was slow to see what was going on and made no move to advance. He was held in a ferocious and prolonged melee which, towards the middle of the afternoon, cost him his life. The duke of Norfolk then arrived. He was elderly and had been delayed by sickness but as soon as he reached the battle he threw his forces against Northumberland's crumbling wing and broke the Lancastrian left. Throughout the day the killing had been so intense that each army had had to stop from time to time in order to clear away the huge number of bodies. Now, as the Lancastrians turned to seek safety, a terrible and deadly pursuit began.

There was no escape. A small stream to the Lancastrian right, the Cock Beck, and the River Wharf behind them, created a trap. The bridge at Tadcaster might have enabled some to escape, but the Lancastrians themselves had destroyed it. Archaeologists have been astonished by the number of skeletons they have found at Towton, many of which show massive trauma at the back of the skull. These catastrophic injuries were caused by heavy weapons striking men who were obviously facing away from their assailants. In battle, fleeing men have only a slight chance of survival. One curious finding has been the number of skeletons showing previous injuries, some serious enough to have been disabling and disfiguring. Many of the participants at Towton were veterans and had the scars to prove it.

Unfortunately for Edward, and despite his decisive victory, Henry and Margaret were able to make good their escape and fled to Scotland. Somerset and Exeter also escaped, as did Lord Roos. Edward was now the undoubted king but Lancastrian resistance lingered on and was to flare up dramatically at the end of the decade. The battle had gone on all day and did not end until ten o'clock at night. As soon as he was able, Edward rode to York: he had some unfinished business to attend to. When he reached Micklegate Bar he ordered the heads of his father, brother and kinsmen to be taken down. It was three months to the day since they had been so cruelly exhibited for the political edification of the inhabitants. Edward had what remained of them reunited with their bodies in Pontefract and interred with as much decency and dignity as was possible given the exigencies of the turmoil around him. It was the least Edward could do. It was to be Richard, his younger brother, who was to see the duke of York properly buried at Fotheringhay, sixteen years later. Perhaps Richard cared more about such things.

News of the battle of Towton spread quickly. No one seemed too clear about what had happened to the king and queen, many believing them to have been captured, but it was clear that they had been soundly defeated and that the young Edward was now the king of England. There was a mood of rejoicing in London from where an anonymous Italian wrote on 14 April:

> King Edward has become master and governor of the whole realm. Words fail me to relate how well the commons love and adore him, as if he were their God. The entire kingdom keeps holiday for the event, which seems a boon from above. Thus far he appears to be a just prince who intends to amend and organise matters otherwise than has been done hitherto, so all comfort themselves with hopes of future well-being.[18]

The news reached Sluys, where George and his brother Richard were lodged in relatively modest circumstances, on about 12 April. Their fortunes were rapidly transformed. No longer disinherited fugitives causing inconvenience to an embarrassed benefactor, they had become royal brothers of enormous diplomatic importance. Philip of Burgundy needed an alliance with England to resist the ever-hostile ambitions of France, and his preferred clients had been the Yorkists. Now that Edward was king, the grand duke of the West could cast caution aside and show him the courtesy and hospitality for which he was famous. On 17 April the duke's emissaries arrived at their lodgings, paid deference to them and waited upon them to escort them to the ducal palace at Bruges. The visitors that day were among the highest ranking noblemen in Burgundy, including the papal legate, and their gallant civility gave the boys a taste of what was to come.

Curiously, the duke should have been a keen supporter of the Lancastrians in so much as he was related to them by marriage. His wife Isabella of Portugal was the daughter of John I of Portugal and Philippa of Lancaster. Philippa was the daughter of John of Gaunt and the brother of the first Lancastrian king, Henry IV. If those Lancastrian connections were not strong enough, Philip's sister Anne had married John, duke of Bedford, the brother of Henry V. Philip himself had aided the Lancastrian regime in many ways. He had been a staunch ally of Henry V and had famously captured Joan of Arc and handed her over to the English for burning. Why, we might ask, was he so keen to demonstrate his support for the Yorkists?

The answer lay with France. Margaret of Anjou was herself French and had caused the duke, out of sheer hatred for Charles VII, to shift towards her opponents. In 1419 at Montereau, Philip's father John the Fearless had been betrayed and murdered. He had come to a bridge between his dukedom and the kingdom of France for a meeting with Charles, then the dauphin or heir to the throne, and had been set upon by Charles' escort, not suspecting any treachery at all. This breach of diplomatic protocol shocked the whole of Europe, thrust the twenty-three year-old Philip onto the ducal throne and gave birth to the deep enmity he nursed against Charles. When Charles, shortly after, became Charles VII of France he faced the implacable hatred of Philip. By Philip's side was none other than the dauphin of France, Louis, the son of Charles, living in exile having been disowned by his father. The two plotted at every turn to thwart Charles' ambitions. What is more, these two Yorkist boys who had washed up on his doorstep were the sons of the most ardent champion of the anti-French policy for which so much English and Burgundian blood had been spilt. He was delighted to be able to welcome them so openly now that their brother had become king of England.

At Bruges the duke visited Richard and George, feasted them and provided them with lavish entertainments. Philip was a true Renaissance prince, patron of goldsmiths, jewellers, artists and music. His special love was for fine tapestries woven with silk and gold, and for illuminated manuscripts. He commissioned these jewel-encrusted delicate treasures to add lustre to his library. In all he bought six hundred of them, setting the standard for the whole of Europe, creating the market and shaping the trends. In his magnificent library, the envy of Europe, the medieval monastic tradition of illustrating texts met the artistic talent and creativity of a new generation. It was under his patronage that the Flemish school of art began and it was with his money that the greatest masters in northern Europe, Hugo van der Goes, Rogier van der Weyden and Jan van Eyck developed their skills. The duke, the epitome of noble courtesy, paid his respects to the two small boys as a duke towards princes. The eight year-old Richard was, for the first time in his life, greeted as a prince of the blood royal.

Philip's friendship was never forgotten by Richard. In the darkness of his unhappy exile a light had shone upon him. Philip was an extraordinary man by any reckoning. The prosperity and prestige which had grown under his leadership and had made his court the artistic and commercial centre which set the tastes and fashions for the rest of northern Europe, sprang as much from his personality and determination as from the favourable economic and political conditions latent in his inheritance. Above all he was a lover of honour, of chivalry and of virtue. He had been offered a knighthood by Henry VI. A grateful court had wished to enrol him in the most prestigious order of knighthood in England, the Order of the Garter, for his services against their enemy Charles VII. Philip had found it impossible to accept because, he said, it would compromise his feudal obligation to the king of France. As he was at war with the king of France one might have thought that this legal detail could be quietly set aside, but it is symptomatic of Philip's personality that he would not countenance it. Charles had committed the wrongs which had led to war; Philip would not allow himself to breach an ancient code, even if his overlord had done so. Instead he established his own order, the Order of the Golden Fleece, based, as was the Order of the Garter, on the stories of the knights of the Round Table. Philip loved chivalry and sponsored some of the most spectacular tournaments in history. He burned with crusading ardour; the Ottoman Empire was his real target, and the unity of a Christian brotherhood in arms against the infidel was the vision he fostered. It was not to be, of course, but it tells us much about him. This was the man Richard now met.

We do not know what impact Philip had on Richard in the two months they spent together; we do not even know how much time they spent in each other's company. It goes beyond the hard evidence available to speak of a vulnerable and impressionable boy being deeply affected by a man who seemed to embody all the ancient heroic virtues, a man devoted to chivalry, manners, display, and civility; a man of sense, of taste, of loyalty. It goes further than the historian can suggest to speak of the similarities between Philip's character and that of Richard's dead father. What we can note, however, is how the future was to reveal in Richard an unwavering hostility to France, an unequivocal adherence to Burgundy and a love of courtly display and chivalric tales.

Camulio, reporting to his master in Milan, witnessed Philip's treatment of the boys. 'The duke, who is most kind in everything,' he wrote, 'showed them great reverence.'[19] In early June the duke escorted them from Bruges to Calais. Surrounded by the ducal guards and feted as they went, they arrived at the English garrison to prepare for the return to England. The contrast between this journey and the outward-bound one could not have been greater. The duke took his leave and handed the boys over to the custody of their brother's officers. Richard and George now out-ranked every one of them. The skulking and fearful fugitives had become cherished regal presences. As the elderly Philip – he was sixty-four – offered his blessings and bade the princes farewell, a new world opened up before them.

On or about 12 June 1461 Richard and George landed in Kent and proceeded to Canterbury. They attended a banquet in their honour given by the city fathers and, perhaps still in awe at their elevation and newly acquired celebrity status, headed for London. The city prepared to greet them in the most fitting style. The Common Council and 'the most worthy citizens of the guilds' were instructed to turn out in their liveries and join the mayor and the aldermen, dressed in crimson, at Billingsgate to welcome the nearest kinsmen of the new monarch. After an enthusiastic entry through cheering crowds the two boys were escorted into the presence of the king. They knelt before him and paid homage. He was their brother whom they had not seen for seven months but he was also King Edward IV.

The young king was famous for his good looks and high living; no one enjoyed a good party quite as much as Edward, but he was also self-assured, resolute, confident and relaxed. Foreign commentators might believe that Warwick was in charge, indeed Warwick probably believed the same, but his putative protégé had been victorious in every battle he had fought; the same could not be said of his thirty-two year-old cousin. That aura of victory placed him on a plane to which Warwick could aspire but would never attain. Edward had not been made king by Warwick; Warwick had been defeated at the second battle of St Albans and ignominiously fled to Edward. The new king had been victorious at Northampton, rescuing his father's ruined hopes, at Mortimer's Cross which saved Warwick and damaged Margaret, and at Towton where Heaven itself had seemed to endorse his rule. Edward was his own man despite appearances, and his style of kingship breathed new life into that troubled institution.

On 26 June, two days before the most elaborate coronation the realm could devise, Richard was among twenty-eight knights of the Order of the Bath created in preparation for the great state occasion. He was inducted into the order in an elaborate ceremony followed by a vigil in the Chapel Royal which ended at dawn with the celebration of Mass. Afterwards he was presented to the king by the marshal of arms while two knights fixed his spurs to his ankles. The king himself then girded his brother with a sword and belt, dubbed him and gave him the kiss of peace. Richard then returned to his chamber in the royal apartments of the Tower where he was dressed in a blue robe with a white hood. The following day, the day of the coronation itself, Richard rode before his brother Edward, with the other newly-created knights, from the Tower to Westminster. George had been made duke of Clarence and a knight of the Garter that very day and therefore, as was fitting for the heir presumptive, rode with the king himself. The coronation, for which the elaborate but hasty rituals performed in March had been mere preparation, was the most solemn and splendid national celebration witnessed in over fifty years. There was a palpable sense of euphoria in the air. The people dared to believe that the dark days of civil bloodshed were finally over and a new era of peace and prosperity was dawning.[20]

There was also some unease. Despite the slaughter at Towton, leading Lancastrians had escaped and everyone knew they would cause trouble. There was also the matter of King Henry. Not only was he still alive but he was also the last person to have been crowned in Westminster Abbey. The sanctity of the proceedings could only be tarnished by this reflection. Henry V's chantry overlooked Edward's throne as he received the sacraments and the holy oil of anointing. The great warrior king, whose tomb was inches away from Edward as he received St Edward's crown, was the father of the very king now being so demonstrably displaced. These were uncomfortable thoughts for those with the reflective capacity to indulge them during the drama of ancient rites accompanied by singing, incense, trumpets and the tumultuous shout of, 'God Save the King! Long Live the King! God Save the King!'

It is unlikely that these sombre meditations afflicted the young Richard. If the court of Philip the Good had introduced him to the fabulous world of chivalry, ritual and courtly display, 28 June 1461 drenched him in its sights and sounds. All was meaningful, proper, hallowed and sanctified. The being of the participants was transported above the ordinary world of transitory existence and into a timeless realm of tradition, certainty, value and right. The horrors and the vagaries of a capricious world could be forgotten in an eternal space. This solemn peace with all its colours, smells and sounds, had a reality which the wheel of fortune could never overturn. One day a troubled man would place himself at the very heart of this ancient rite and no doubt hope that the blessings and succour it offered would protect him from the storms of life. For the moment he watched in awe as his brother, orb and sceptre in his hands, head anointed and bearing the Cap of Maintenance, dressed in white silk, gold, red velvet and ermine, enthroned in majesty, received the jewel-encrusted gold crown from the Archbishop of Canterbury and heard, as the choir burst into song, what seemed to be a crowd of angels echoing through the gothic splendour of the Abbey.

Not long afterwards Richard, like his brother George, received a dukedom and became duke of Gloucester. Shortly after this he was admitted into the Order of the Garter in St George's Chapel, Windsor. He was now nine years old. Shortly after his tenth birthday he was created admiral of England, Ireland and Aquitaine. While Clarence, as George was now called, was always preferred on account of his superior years, Richard was showered with gifts and titles. These were both marks of affection and fitting offices for a prince of the royal blood. He needed the endowments and the honours commensurate with his rank. Every mark of distinction, every step of advancement, was occasioned by the elaborate courtly ceremonial it warranted. Edward, who rebuilt and refurbished the chapel at Windsor dedicated to St George, was, as it turned out, a lover of chivalry. He revived the Order of the Garter in almost conscious imitation of Philip the Good. Of course ideal and reality rarely coincide but to have those ideals was the first step towards shaping a vision of reality.

For the rest of the decade Richard, as best we can tell, received the conventional education of an aristocratic youth. At first he probably spent much of the time with his mother Cecily, brother Clarence and sister Margaret in the royal establishments in and around London. These included Windsor, Greenwich, Sheen and the Tower. There is not much evidence for his whereabouts or his activities from the age of ten to thirteen. All we have is the evidence that can be gleaned by records in the royal household accounts relating to the money, clothes and transport needed for the royal siblings, and in the accounts of others who spent money on their behalf. The archbishop of Canterbury, their kinsman Thomas Bourchier, was the host of the two royal dukes in 1463 in Canterbury, and they may have spent some time with him. Apparently George, duke of Clarence, misbehaved on this trip and showed an arrogant disregard for the men of the cloth. Clarence was to develop many unhelpful traits. There is no evidence that Richard behaved in any other way than that which was entirely proper and fitting.

As he entered adolescence, in about 1465, Richard was handed over to his cousin Warwick to be educated in an aristocratic household. This was the customary practice at the time: boys were sent off to be tutored in the households of noble kinsmen where they were to be schooled in the arts of knighthood and the conventions pertaining to it. Reading and writing were necessary but not considered of primary importance. Richard did learn to read and write, as it happened, but many aristocratic men paid secretaries to perform such menial tasks. More important was learning court etiquette, dancing, playing a musical instrument and languages: Latin, French or Italian. The real business, however, was learning to handle weapons and horses. Attending tournaments and following hunting expeditions were essential training for war, and war was never very far away. Warwick was the foremost magnate in the land, effectively in charge of foreign affairs and with a grip on all the avenues of royal power. Richard would have spent some time in the great seats of Warwick's power, the formidable castles of Middleham and Sheriff Hutton, both in Yorkshire, and there developed the skills required to participate in the life of the court. He also began his life-long love of the north.[21]

At Warwick's castle at Middleham in Wensleydale, Richard was surrounded by the austere beauty of the Yorkshire moors; the dales, crags, pikes and scars whose very names had a strength and vigour of a robust past, and the haunting echoes of a Viking conquest. Here were Coverdale, Swaledale and Arkengarthdale, Spennithorne, Agglethorpe and Carthorpe, Ellingstring, Warthemaske and Theakston, Baldersby, Kirklington and Wath. There were Tarns and Fells, Ings and Gills, craggy outcrops of limestone amidst the misty lakes. Here a fiercely independent class of gentry, retainers to the great earl of Warwick, managed their forests and quarries, sheep farms and mills, fish garths and granges. Among the notable visitors to the great castle, whether an earl, a viscount, a legate or an ambassador, these men provided the escorts, the guides, the safe-conducts and the essential services that might be required. It was with these men that Richard came into close contact as they came and went on Warwick's affairs; constables, castellans, sheriffs and stewards, foresters, bailiffs, justices and receivers. It was with these men, the Scropes, Huddlestons, Pilkingtons and Harringtons, the Dacres, Greystokes, Fitzhughs and Ratcliffes that Richard was to meet most frequently. It was with these men that he was to grow to manhood and it was with these men that he, in due course, was to place his greatest trust.

These were years of comparative peace and safety for the young duke. There was still the threat from the Lancastrians in the north and the hint of rebellion simmering in the Percy lands, but Warwick's power, embodied in the mighty stone keep and thick curtain walls at Middleham, provided ample security for a growing youth. His martial education and physical exercise were given pointed focus by the knowledge that they might one day be needed in battle, but for the time being Richard's family were in power and secure. It would have astonished him to know that by his seventeenth year, just as he himself was approaching an age when he might take a more active role in affairs, those closest to him, the earl of Warwick and the duke of Clarence, would rebel against his brother Edward. The house of York was about to be turned upside down again.

# FOUR

# ADOLESCENCE AND UNCERTAINTY

The peaceful stability Richard enjoyed at Middleham from 1465 to 1469, during his early teens, was deceptive. As a young boy he had experienced both the disasters and the triumphs of his family; he had felt the pain of the loss of a father and brother, killed at the battle of Wakefield, and suffered the ignominy and danger of flight and exile. He had returned to England as the brother of a king and enjoyed the fruits of Edward's military victories at Mortimer's Cross and Towton. Yorkist rule was gradually being established and the restoration of royal authority seemed to be recreating a natural order many had feared they would never see again. The forest fire of war had destroyed the hopes and aspirations of a generation. Edward's reign heralded the cooling rains of order and peace which promised growth, prosperity and security. Yet, having been king for seven years, Edward was to be defeated, imprisoned, released, betrayed and forced to flee abroad. Richard was once again to feel the pain of fear and exile, to become a fugitive, *persona non grata*, a traitor with a price on his head.

It seems incredible that Edward and his family should sink so low again, and from such lofty heights. After the appalling brutality and loss of life, beginning at St Albans in 1455 and culminating at Towton in 1461, very few prophets of doom would have dared suggest that the Wars of the Roses had three more bloody battles to deliver before Edward was finally able to rule securely. It would have required a perversely cynical character to be able to predict so much turmoil and bloodshed after seven years of young and energetic kingship. Nevertheless, with the historian's gift of hindsight, it is possible to read the runes and interpret the warning signs. Edward undoubtedly made mistakes.

The first serious mistake for which he might be culpable was his tendency to be lenient towards his enemies. The chief and most surprising beneficiary of Edward's generosity was Henry Beaufort, duke of Somerset. He was a diehard Lancastrian and was never going to be anything else. His father had been killed fighting the duke of York at St Albans and he himself had led the Lancastrian forces at both Wakefield and Towton. Edward not only allowed him to live, but restored him to his title and lands. Similarly, Ralph Percy, brother of the earl of Northumberland, was treated far too kindly. He was in an almost constant state of rebellion against Edward in the early years of the reign but allowed to keep the border castle of Dunstanburh and trusted to help the king against the Scots.

Edward only issued fourteen attainders against nobles at the beginning of the reign and all of these were against men who had either already died fighting for the Lancastrians or who were still in arms for their cause.[1] Even those who had been killed often left heirs who were treated well. The most notable recipients of this largesse were the duke of Buckingham and the earl of Shrewsbury. The property of the duke of Buckingham, killed at Northampton, was not confiscated but preserved for his heir. In exactly the same way, the twelve-year-old heir to the earl of Shrewsbury, whose father, John Talbot, had been killed at Northampton, was able to inherit his father's title and lands. It is true that it would have been vindictive in the extreme to have punished the heirs to two honourable and famous men. Humphrey Stafford, the duke of Buckingham, had been a blameless follower of his king, simply attempting to do the right thing in an impossible situation. John Talbot, earl of Shrewsbury, was the son of the last English hero of the Hundred Years War, who had died fighting for the legacy of Henry V at the battle of Castillon. Nevertheless there were many men in the fifteenth century who, in Edward's situation, would have had no compunction in dispatching potential threats.

Much of this attempt at benign even-handedness backfired. Somerset's survival was so unpopular that the earl had to be spirited away to Wales for his own safety. He still managed to escape to the north, join up with Ralph Percy, and conjure up a serious rebellion in favour of Margaret and Henry VI who were still in Scotland. By March 1464 this had become a massive insurrection, with dangerous riots in many counties including Gloucestershire, Cambridgeshire, Lancashire and Cheshire. The day was saved by Warwick's younger brother, John Neville, Lord Montagu, who defeated the rebels in two battles. The first, at Hedgeley Moor in April 1464, saw Ralph Percy finally slain. The second, three weeks later at Hexham, saw Somerset captured and beheaded along with thirty other Lancastrians. It took John Neville, rather than Edward himself, to sort the mess out, for which he was rewarded with the earldom of Northumberland.

These events effectively extinguished the Lancastrian cause, at least for the next five years. The big problem was that inveterate Lancastrians, and other disaffected chancers, always had another king to whom they could adhere. Even after the battle of Hexham, Henry VI managed to escape and wander around for another year before being captured. If Edward's first mistake was leniency towards rebels, his second was not to have their figurehead executed when he could. The bedraggled and pathetic former king was led to the Tower instead of being quietly put out of his misery. This always gave men with a grievance the justification and alternative they needed. England was not big enough for the two of them, as events were to prove. There is no place for a redundant monarch in the kingdom of his supplanter.

When Ralph Percy was finally cut down at Hedgeley Moor, apparently after an enormous leap which failed to take him out of the clutches of John Neville's men, he consoled himself, as he lay dying, with the knowledge that at least he had 'saved the bird in my bosom'. The bird was his loyalty to his former king.[2] He may have betrayed the new king, who had done more than could be expected to reconcile the discontented knight with the new regime, but he died for the old one. This shows not only how some men had remained staunchly loyal to the erstwhile king, but also how entrenched these feelings had become after so many family members had shed their blood for one side or the other. A tall and impressive stone cross provides a fitting memorial to Ralph in the bleak northern landscape in which he chose to fight to the death. The cause for which he died so bravely was, as it turned out, to live on and erupt dramatically in 1470.

Edward was young, just nineteen at his coronation, inexperienced and short of options. Royal authority had taken a pounding in the absence of direction and the lack of purpose that had characterised the rule of Henry VI. Mismanagement and bankruptcy had left the monarchy in tatters. Henry VI had failed in pursuing English hopes and ambitions abroad and in maintaining order at home. His kingdom was riven with faction and bleeding heavily from the wounds caused by lawlessness, injustice and lack of due process. It was a Herculean task to restore the fabric of the rule of law, and Edward was always treading a fine line: trying to balance the need to appear impartial with the need to extinguish threats. He had to be seen transcending factionalism and offering satisfaction in a royal government in which all could benefit. This meant hoping that men like Ralph Percy could tidily put away the years of bitter conflict and settle their differences with their mortal foes.

In the end Edward's handling of former enemies, his willingness to forgive them and to offer them suitable roles in government, was vindicated in his second reign but it contributed to his near demise in 1469. Of course there were one or two people who would never accept his authority. In the end the only solution was elimination. It was a policy Edward did not wish to promote but was finally forced to adopt. At first he was able to get away with a more conciliatory strategy. There can be no doubt that this was risky and Edward rode his luck early on. He was rather fortunate, for example, that the rebels in the north had had such poor support from the Scots, and, for that matter, the French. Both countries had lost their rulers shortly after Edward's accession in bizarre circumstances. James II of Scotland, ever active and hostile towards England, had actually embarked on an invasion months after Edward's accession. He had crossed the border in support of Margaret and Henry VI and was besieging Roxburgh Castle when he decided to surprise his wife and show off his new artillery. Mary of Guelders arrived at the scene of the siege to be greeted by a cannon salute. Unfortunately one of the cannon exploded; a piece of the barrel smashed into the thigh of the proud monarch and killed him. His son and heir, James III, was only eight years old and Scotland divided into factions. Helping English rebels dropped down the Scottish agenda for a while.[3]

Edward was similarly lucky with the French. On 22 July 1461, just a few weeks after Edward's coronation, Charles VII of France died at the hands of his dentist. To give the medieval profession of dentistry its due, he actually died from complications following the removal of a diseased tooth; visits to the dentist in an era before antibiotics and anaesthetics were always extremely perilous. This unfortunate incident temporarily put paid to French hopes of profiting from the unstable situation across the Channel. Louis XI was, as it turned out, a formidable successor to Charles VII and was to become a thorn in Edward's side in the coming years, but for the moment his attention was concentrated on recovering the Somme towns from Burgundy which France had ceded in 1435. Louis needed Edward's help and actually signed an Anglo-French convention in August 1463, which included a year's truce.

Both these accidents gave Edward much-needed breathing space at the onset of the reign, but there were two problems that smouldered in the background and finally exploded in 1469. The first was Edward's marriage to Elizabeth Woodville in 1464, and the second, quite closely related to it, was Warwick. If we are cataloguing Edward's errors we would have to add his curious choice of bride to the list. Warwick's disaffection is another matter; the likelihood is that conflict with the 'Kingmaker' was all but inevitable. The Woodville marriage did, however, provide Warwick with grist to the mill of his perceived grievances.

Edward's marriage to Elizabeth Woodville baffled contemporaries; she was a Lancastrian, a widow with two children of her own and the daughter of a low-born knight. Kings were supposed to marry into the aristocracy at least:

preferably royalty and usually into a foreign royal family which might bring diplomatic and material gains with it. No English king had married an English woman since the Norman Conquest four hundred years earlier, and no king of England had ever married so far beneath him. Edward appeared to have spurned the opportunity to use his status to forge an alliance abroad at a time when this might have been most useful. The substantial dowry a foreign prin- cess would be expected to bring with her would also have been very handy. It is difficult to fathom what Edward was playing at.

As the northern rebellion was reaching its climax, Edward was, rather typically as it turned out, meandering about in a rather complacent fashion somewhere in the Midlands. From what scant information we have it would seem that he was out hunting in Whittlebury Forest when an extremely attrac- tive twenty-seven-year-old lady leapt out from behind a tree and flung herself at his feet. Elizabeth Woodville was keen to use the opportunity presented by the proximity of the royal hunting party to get personal access to the king. She either wished him to endorse an arrangement she had just made with William, Lord Hastings, Edward's friend and chamberlain, or she wanted to improve the offer Hastings had made. She had been trying to get Hastings, the most influ- ential man at court, to help her to secure her late husband's lands for herself and her sons. Hastings appears to have driven a hard bargain and forced her to share fifty per cent of the income derived from the rent of these lands with him. A complicated marriage arrangement was also involved which would have committed her eldest son, Thomas, to marrying a daughter of Hastings, even though he had not yet got one. Elizabeth might have been satisfied with these arrangements since her husband had died fighting for the Lancastrians at the second battle of St Albans and would therefore have expected to have had his lands confiscated by attainder. It would seem, however, that she was not, and wanted to see the king in person to get a better deal.[4] It is even possible, given Hastings' later track-record, that he deliberately gave Elizabeth access to the king because he thought the king might like the attractive widow. He seems to have taken it upon himself to provide the king with attractive ladies of relaxed virtue. If that was his intention he considerably underestimated Elizabeth and must have been as surprised as any at the outcome. Elizabeth Woodville was not the stuff of which mistresses were made. Less than three weeks later, on 1 May 1464, Edward secretly married her at Grafton as he marched north to deal with the northern rebellion.

With hindsight it seems hardly surprising that he left John Neville to deal with the rebellion, given that his own mind was on other things. The battle of Hexham, which finally put paid to Somerset, was only two weeks after the hasty and clandestine marriage ceremony. John Neville was doing such a good job in those northern parts it probably seemed a shame to trouble him with a royal visit. Historians, just as much as contemporaries, have found it difficult to explain Edward's extraordinary marriage. The likelihood is that Edward, an impetuous twenty-two year-old, put considerations of state aside and allowed his hormones to set the agenda. As it happens it is possible to put a gloss on these events and credit Edward with a bold attempt to create a new independent affinity, entirely beholden to him, which would enable him to demonstrate his freedom from the powerful influence of Warwick. The thought that Edward could cock a snook at Warwick and scupper his very advanced plans for a marriage between the English king and a French princess, may have crossed Edward's mind. Elizabeth Woodville's prospects could only have been enhanced by the opportunity presented to the young king to take his lordly and all-important older cousin down a peg or two.

It is far more likely, however, that he simply fell in love. The contemporary chronicler, William Gregory, was in no doubt about the matter and saw fit to warn his readers, 'Now take heed what love may do.' Gregory was aware of the problems the marriage created, not least of which was the baggage the new queen brought with her: a horde of grasping relatives on the make. Elizabeth had five brothers and no fewer than seven unmarried sisters, not to mention a father, two sons, an aunt and a cousin. All these were to be provided for, and the daughters alone pretty much cornered the aristocratic marriage market that was so vital to the interests of noble dynasties.

The marriage could not have come at a worse time for Warwick. He was busy forging an alliance between France and England and was in the later stages of arranging a marriage between Edward and the French king's sister-in-law, Bona of Savoy. The deal was all but in the bag and all that was needed was Edward's consent. In September 1464, at a council held in Reading, Warwick triumphantly reported the success of his negotiations and the opening of a new era of friendship with France which would enable England to put the Hundred Years War behind her and move on in peace and prosperity. Unfortunately we have no eyewitness reports of the eerie silence that must have greeted Edward's forced admission that he was already married. We have no account of the spluttering incomprehension with which the earl of Warwick may have greeted the news. We can only guess at the dumbfounded incredulity of the assembled councillors. It is possible even at this late stage, five months after the nuptials, that only Hastings among them was aware of the truth.

Hastings, at thirty-three, was only three years younger than Warwick himself but he had already become the boon companion of the king. Their relationship was one of trust and friendship which Hastings never blatantly exploited. All access to the king was usually controlled by the chamberlain and this naturally gave him enormous power and influence. It is notable that given his access to royal favours and his pre-eminence at court, not even his enemies ever accused him of corruption. He was staunchly loyal to Edward, dying for him in the end, and, if Edward married Elizabeth because he fell in love with her, he also trusted Hastings because they were genuine friends. Edward's character is but faintly discernible across the half-millennium that separates him from us, but his warmth and likeability permeate across the years. Although he was a medieval king, he was also human. In the end Hastings was accused of pandering too readily to the king's baser instincts – they famously shared a mistress in Jane Shore – and even of contributing to Edward's early death through licentious indulgence, but in an age abounding with stories of corruption, intrigue, deception and betrayal there is something attractive in Edward's faith in Hastings. It contrasts rather markedly with Edward's relationship with Warwick.

That relationship never recovered from the blow it received at Reading. Warwick had already negotiated a truce with France and was about to seal it with the marriage proposal when Edward dropped his bombshell. The French king, Louis XI, had cleverly massaged Warwick's ego and treated him as if he were the real ruler of England. Most European commentators believed he was, for all intents and purposes. The French chronicler, Philippe de Commynes, said that Warwick 'could almost be called the king's father as a result of the services and education he had given him'.[5] A French alliance made so much sense to the great arbiter of English affairs; the Yorkist dynasty was still in its infancy and the peace and security that would come with a treaty between such powerful neighbours could not be underestimated. There were many residual benefits, not the least of which was the exclusion of Margaret of Anjou and her Lancastrian friends from the succour of France.

Edward had his own views and Warwick had not been very assiduous in gleaning what they were. Edward was gradually moving towards the view that an alliance with Burgundy, a big trading partner and old friend, would not only be more advantageous, but also more popular. Edward was not the cipher Henry VI had been, as Warwick was to learn to his cost. One gets the sense that Edward did not place much confidence in Warwick; after all, Warwick had lost the second battle of St Albans, and that defeat would have destroyed the house of York if Edward's own martial prowess had not rescued them all. He had no cause to trust or value his pompous and self-important cousin. Of course, personal antipathy aside, Warwick was head of the Neville clan, the most powerful family in the kingdom, and Edward needed their resources and support. Edward was intelligent enough to be able to set aside his feelings when royal authority was at issue; Warwick was not. It is not surprising, having been so publicly slighted, that Warwick's resentment began to smoulder.

Elizabeth Woodville was only the first of Warwick's annoyances. Her family came to fill so many places at court that Warwick began to feel himself a stranger. These were 'new men' whom the old nobility detested. Edward seemed to be surrounded by them. Hastings, with a finger in every pie, was the most egregious, but then there was William Herbert, soon to be earl of Pembroke, who had not only risen from nowhere but was actually challenging Neville power and expansion in south Wales.[6] Of course one of those now closest to the king was the queen herself. Edward had surrounded himself with his own choice of companions, none of whom had much time for Warwick. Elizabeth was not the type to take kindly to the suggestion that Edward had married beneath him. She had plenty of pride herself and not a little influence over her husband. Warwick's star was on the wane and a clash between the proud earl and his young protégé was inevitable.

Warwick's underestimation of Elizabeth Woodville was commonplace at the time and has persisted to this day, but she was by no means a low-born woman. Her mother, Jacquetta, was the daughter of Pierre de Luxembourg, Count of St Pol. Jacquetta's first husband had been none other than John, duke of Bedford, the brother of King Henry V of England. When her husband died in 1435 she became the dowager duchess of Bedford. This gave her a third share in Bedford's extensive English properties, worth over £4,000 a year: a huge sum in those days. She also inherited his French estates but these suffered the fate of all English possessions in France at the end of the Hundred Years War and disappointingly reverted to their rightful owners. Jacquetta was a wealthy member of the European aristocracy. Her sister, Isabel, was married to Charles, Comte du Maine, who just so happened to be Margaret of Anjou's uncle. The irony was that Jacquetta, shortly after her first husband's death, married beneath her. She was still only twenty years of age when she married Sir Richard Woodville who was no more than a member of the Northamptonshire gentry. She had to pay £1,000 to the king as a fine for marrying so far beneath her station. Richard's father had served as an esquire of the Body to Henry V and had risen to become Bedford's chamberlain. Richard served in Bedford's household too and no doubt caught the eye of the young Jacquetta. Her marriage to the middle-aged Bedford had been a diplomatic tool in an alliance between England and Burgundy. Her marriage to Richard seems to have been the result of the intervention of the same god, Eros, who was to change the life of her daughter. There is a strange symmetry to Elizabeth Woodville's marriage to Edward IV, if one considers her mother's marriage to Richard Woodville.

Elizabeth's father served under both Somerset and York in France, with some distinction. He was chosen, with Jacquetta, to escort Margaret of Anjou to England to marry Henry VI in 1444. He was elevated to the peerage as Baron Rivers in 1448. After helping suppress Jack Cade's rebellion in 1450 he was admitted into the noble Order of the Garter. Despite her mother's nobility and her father's acquisition of a lordship, Elizabeth herself was only able to marry a knight, Sir John Grey. She was very young at the time, possibly only thirteen, but this was not uncommon. She may well have felt, ironically, that she had married beneath her. They had two sons, Thomas and Richard, before Elizabeth suffered the loss of her husband at the second battle of St Albans in 1461. She was still only twenty-three and already a widow with two children to support. Her husband had been fighting for the Lancastrians against the earl of Warwick. Her meeting with Edward, three years later, by a tree beginning to sprout its spring foliage, would have been interesting to watch. Something occurred between them which transcended the regal niceties which had begun to encompass the king. He, it must be remembered, had not been born to kingship. He did not feel constrained by the strictures a royal upbringing may have imposed. Elizabeth may have been vulnerable and appealing but she was also intrepid, proud, independent and canny. While few doubt that she and Edward enjoyed each other's company, she became every inch a queen.

Queen she might be but another Margaret she was not. The imputation that the dissension between Warwick and Edward was fuelled by Elizabeth does not bear scrutiny. Warwick had far too many other grievances to select from to need to accuse the queen of poisoning relations between them. Nevertheless, Warwick's introduction to the new queen would have been one of those excruciating occasions for which tickets would not have been difficult to obtain. Courtiers must have been volunteering for other duties in droves on that particular day. The general view was that Warwick rebelled against the king because of Edward's ridiculous choice of bride. The Croyland chronicler known as the First Continuator, the prior of Croyland Abbey in the Lincolnshire Fens, writing not long afterwards, reported that the disagreement between Warwick and Edward stemmed from the influence of Elizabeth Woodville:

> The reason of this was the fact that the king, being too greatly influenced by the urgent suggestions of the queen, admitted to his especial favour all the relations of the said queen, as well as those who were in any way connected with her blood, enriching them with boundless presents and always promoting them to the most dignified offices about his person; while at the same time he banished from his presence his own brethren, and his kinsmen sprung from the royal blood, together with the earl of Warwick himself, and the other nobles of the realm who had always proved faithful to him.[7]

Shortly after the 'disagreement' had blown up into full-scale rebellion, the monk of Croyland laid down his quill without even reporting on the outcome. He apologised for the deficiencies in his Chronicle, explaining that he had been so busy in his office of prior that the Chronicle did not receive the attention he would have liked to devote to it. It was composed 'on occasions snatched by stealth at intervals, and frequently at hurried moments' he moaned. Seventeen years later, in 1486, a second Continuator decided to advance the narrative and bring the Chronicle up to date. This writer was an altogether different character from his predecessor. He was urbane, well-informed, well-connected and evincing an air of courtly experience which suggests he had been a senior official in Edward's administration. He began his task by endorsing the apologies of his predecessor and explaining that the scribe had been so full of 'zeal for the interests of holy religion' that he did not 'generally care to be fully acquainted with secular matters.' This damning indictment of the former prior is followed by a more detailed account of the events his predecessor described, with a different interpretation cast upon them, based on the vastly superior worldly knowledge of our new guide. The Second Continuator was in no doubt that the real cause of the dissension between Warwick and King Edward was not the marriage between Edward and Elizabeth Woodville, but a wholly different marriage.

In March 1468 Edward signed the treaty by which his sister Margaret would marry Charles, the new duke of Burgundy, and in July of the same year the marriage was solemnised in a ceremony of unparalleled splendour. England and Burgundy were allies and all Warwick's efforts to forge a new relationship with France were ruined. The new Croyland chronicler was keen, for some unknown reason, to exonerate Elizabeth Woodville from any culpability in the breakdown of the ties between Warwick and Edward. Warwick had got over that earlier business of the king's marriage, we are told. When Edward married Elizabeth Woodville, Warwick had been keen for him to marry Mary of Guelders, the widow of the incendiary James II, not a French princess. He soon got over the disappointment of the king marrying Elizabeth. It wasn't her fault that Warwick fell out with his cousin; it was 'her relatives and connections' who were promoting the Burgundian marriage 'contrary to his wishes'. It is important to note at this juncture that our new and more knowledgeable guide through these events, the Second Continuator, having traduced the reputation of his predecessor, displays little of the former chronicler's lack of prejudice. Like the well-placed courtier and diplomat he had formerly been, he had views which were quietly but inadequately concealed, and they were not open to negotiation. He always favours Elizabeth and, in due course we will see that he always thinks the worst about Richard duke of Gloucester.

The First Continuator had explained that the events he recorded which had occurred in his own time had been read about 'in the book of experience'. Our better informed Second Continuator can supply us with valuable detail but not the same objectivity. His 'book of experience' is somewhat tainted for being written in the reign of Henry Tudor.

Robert Fabyan, a prominent London draper, reported that in January 1468 'many murmerous tales ran in the cite atwene the erle of Warwick and the Quenys blood'. Even though Elizabeth Woodville was not the main cause of Warwick's disaffection, relations between Edward and his cousin were soured by the marriage; nor was the Burgundian marriage between Margaret and Charles the main cause, but it did little to help matters. In fact even a year earlier there were distinct signs that all was not well between Warwick and Edward. At the beginning of 1467 Warwick had been stunned to receive the news that the king was going to prohibit the projected marriage between Warwick's elder daughter, Isabel, and the king's brother, Clarence. Warwick had no sons and it was imperative for him that his two daughters married into the royal family. There was no other way to preserve the Neville inheritance in the manner which it deserved. Warwick was instrumental in the triumph of the house of York; his father had died for it and Warwick and all his house had fought for it, bringing their considerable resources to bear at critical times and in crucial places. Surely the marriage of Warwick's daughters would be treated as a matter of great circumstance and moment by a grateful king? It was the least that could be expected in recompense for such manifold and conspicuous service.

Edward, however, thought differently. It seems to have taken Warwick completely by surprise that Edward thought at all. Thinking was Warwick's job. He had just about got over the aberration which had brought the problem of the Woodvilles, and now the king had the effrontery to intervene in the marriage arrangements of Warwick's own daughter. It was not just that Warwick found it hard to swallow the fact that his influence was waning; it was the pain of thwarted ambition and the fear of loss. Gradually the discontented earl found common cause with another powerful ego destined forever to be second best: Clarence.

George Plantagenet, duke of Clarence, cuts a sorry figure in the annals of restless younger sons who can never come to terms with the proximity of the absolute power wielded by a sibling. They feel cheated, patronised, forever near to the summit but never allowed to ascend and enjoy the view. Neither Clarence nor Warwick could quietly accept the fact that Edward was, after all, his own man. Neither could accept the fact that Edward's coronation had placed him in a sphere beyond their reach. While Edward was carefully gathering to himself the royal authority that had seeped from the crown since Henry

V's death in 1422, Warwick and Clarence began to work together to prevent him doing it. They would not be marginalised.

It does not seem to have occurred to Edward that such a powerful combination would form and act against him. Clarence was still heir presumptive and his marriage was far too important to be determined by anyone but the king. Edward had, perhaps unwittingly, underestimated the dangers of causing such dangerous men to lose face. He blithely continued to admit Warwick into his intimate counsels and to shower him with honours. But by the middle of 1467 he was also pursuing his own agenda, regardless of Warwick's views. What most upset Warwick was that it all seemed to be happening behind his back and to his utmost discomfort. While the earl was busy in France still pursuing his grand design of an alliance with Louis XI, Edward was entertaining a Burgundian party led by a scion of the ducal house who rejoiced in the name Bastard of Burgundy. He was a famous knight trained at the Burgundian court which so prided itself on its espousal of the chivalric arts. The whole of London buzzed in anticipation as the Bastard challenged Anthony Woodville, the queen's brother and champion, to a joust. The tournament was the hottest ticket in town and news of Anthony's victory spread far and wide. It even reached the ears of an incredulous Warwick. At the same time George Neville, Warwick's brother, who was Archbishop of York, was summarily dismissed as Chancellor. Edward arrived in person, with a formidable escort, to deprive the astonished prelate of the Great Seal. This act seemed to have no other purpose but to demonstrate that the Nevilles were no longer the power behind the throne.[8]

Coincidently, at the same time as the celebrated tournament was taking place, Duke Philip the Good died and his son Charles became duke of Burgundy. He was far less cautious than his father had been and was keen to prevent the French from reclaiming his duchy. Swiftly Edward's pro-Burgundy inclinations became an open policy. Robert Stillington, the new Chancellor, promptly announced to Parliament that Edward needed money for a planned invasion of France. Perhaps the removal of Warwick's brother from his office was the essential prerequisite for this announcement. George Neville could not have so publicly refuted his brother's pro-French policy. Warwick was left high and dry.

In July 1467 a French embassy left dissatisfied and complaining of a cold reception. Edward, it so transpired, had been too busy to see them. A Burgundian embassy then arrived and got down to business. A commercial treaty between England and Burgundy was signed in November.[9] The Croyland chronicler tells us that Warwick found the Woodvilles were favouring designs 'to which he was strongly opposed'. The most serious of these was the proposed marriage of Margaret, the king's sister, to Charles of Burgundy. Apparently it wasn't just that Charles was Burgundian which upset Warwick. 'The fact is,' wrote the chronicler, 'that he pursued that man with a most deadly hatred.'[10] In January 1468 Warwick had had enough and refused to obey a summons from the king. He declared that he would not attend the king as long as Herbert, Rivers and Scales were also there. This was, of course, a completely unacceptable ultimatum. The offended earl, having made his point, agreed to attend a great council at Coventry where Edward managed to patch up an accord mediated by George Neville and Lord Scales. Warwick was clearly demonstrating that he felt excluded from the counsels of the king by the queen's family and by the 'new men'.

All may yet have been well if the earl had been able to accept that, while he was still the greatest magnate in England, policy would be henceforth decided by the king and whomsoever he chose to be his councillors. As the year 1468 proceeded, however, it became evident that he could not settle for anything less than his former prominence. The marriage alliance was duly signed in March and solemnised in July. Both events were bitter blows to Warwick who was increasingly turning to Clarence and treasonous thoughts.

Clarence too had his grievances and these provided fertile ground in which Warwick could plant his treachery. The proposed marriage between Clarence and Warwick's daughter, Isabel, made perfect sense to the king's brother. No other bride in England was more suitable. Isabel, the same age as Clarence, was the wealthiest and most highly ranked prospect available. The marriage could have no dynastic implications that might threaten Edward's throne. If Clarence married a foreign princess this might be interpreted as regal behaviour, especially as Edward had singularly failed to do so himself, but Isabel was simply the obvious match for the brother of the king. In fact, after the project was scuppered by Edward, Warwick continued to seek papal dispensation for the marriage, which was required because the protagonists were first cousins. Edward may have thought this verged on open defiance but most people believed that Warwick was within his rights to continue negotiating. Of course he should attempt to change the king's mind, or at least assume that Edward would be persuaded to allow the marriage in due course. Why Edward was so reluctant to countenance the match is something of a mystery, unless he already distrusted a Warwick–Clarence combination.

Clarence had other grumbles fuelling his growing resentment. Edward was moving towards a restoration of the Percys in Northumberland and Clarence was bound to lose the lands there that had come to him from confiscations. The three chief beneficiaries of the dispersal of the Percy estates were none other than Warwick, his brother, John, and Clarence. Three Percys had been killed in the recent war: Thomas Percy at Northampton in 1460, his brother Henry Percy, the earl of Northumberland, at Towton in 1461 and the younger brother, Ralph Percy, at Hedgeley Moor in 1464. Clarence had picked up substantial estates in Yorkshire and Lincolnshire as a result of their demise. What Clarence would never be able to understand was why his brother would want to give all this back to Henry Percy, the fourth to bear that name and the heir to the Percy earldom, now languishing in the Tower of London. Neither Clarence nor Warwick would ever accept such a loss of wealth and influence. They could not see, as the king could, that the people of Northumberland considered the Percys to be their rightful lords, and no one else. Edward's policy of reconciliation was about to backfire in spectacular fashion.

Clarence, eighteen years old in 1468, would already have felt his importance waning. He had been steward of England at Elizabeth's coronation in 1465, and sole heir to the throne. The following year, with the birth of the Princess Elizabeth, Edward's first child, Clarence shared his precedence with the new arrival. In 1467, just a year later, Mary was born. It was only a matter of time before the queen would give birth to a son and Clarence's eminence would further diminish. The boy was duly delivered in 1470. By then Clarence was already engaged in a full-scale rebellion with Warwick.

While Warwick was negotiating for a French alliance he let Clarence believe that Louis' first priority would be to dismember the anachronism called Burgundy and that Clarence would become lord of Holland, Zeeland and Brabant after the French had invaded.[11] Clarence could expect to rule over his own dominions, with a nominal overlord in the king of France, free from the jurisdiction of his brother. By the end of 1468 the designs of the two great malcontents certainly included defying Edward by going ahead with the marriage of Clarence and Isabel and they probably encompassed armed rebellion in order to bring the king to heel. They may even have gone further. If Warwick could no longer exercise hegemony over Edward then perhaps it was time to replace him with a more compliant monarch: George I. Clarence, the George in question, would no doubt show more gratitude than Edward had towards the Kingmaker. As it happened Warwick was two hundred and fifty years ahead of his time; England was not yet ready for a George.

The rebellion began with a series of uprisings in Yorkshire in April 1469. The rebels seem to have been supporters of the Percys at first but Neville adherents soon began to emerge, most notably Sir John Conyers who was Warwick's steward at Middleham Castle. The members of the minor nobility connected to Warwick raised their tenants and marched in open defiance of the king. Initially the revolt was crushed by the stalwart efforts of none other than John Neville, Warwick's own brother. One of Edward's ablest commanders, he remained steadfastly loyal to the king. The revolt was, after all, in his own earldom; the very earldom Edward had given him for his success against the Lancastrians and the Scots at the beginning of the reign. The stress and tensions experienced by John can hardly be imagined. He must have known that his elder brother was behind the insurgency but he continued, for the time being, to behave with exemplary rectitude. Then matters began to get out of hand. In June the rebellion took off again, this time fuelled by a substantial popular uprising. The general discontent Warwick was able to manipulate stemmed from the latest heavy bout of taxation Edward had imposed to fund his projected French campaign. At Newark in Nottinghamshire Edward learned of the size of the rebel army heading south towards him. He retreated to Nottingham to await reinforcements. Warwick's *coup d'etat* had begun.[12]

It was at Nottingham that Edward heard that on 11 July Clarence and Isabel had been married in Calais by George Neville, the archbishop of York. From Calais Warwick issued a manifesto of his grievances which catalogued Edward's inadequacies: royal finances were in a mess, taxation was unjust and too high, foreign policy was a fiasco, law and order in the localities had not improved and, above all, Edward had 'estranged the grete lordes of his blood'.[13] Edward had surrounded himself with favourites, such as Herbert and Hastings, and had not paid enough attention to the counsels of the true nobility, that is, Warwick, George Neville and Clarence. Detached observers may have experienced a certain *déjà vu* on reading this. Was not this last complaint precisely the accusation made against Henry VI by the duke of York? Just to emphasise the point the manifesto likened the favourites to those of Edward II and Richard II. Both these kings had been deposed and met rather nasty ends. These were dangerous insinuations.

Warwick and Clarence set sail from Calais, after only two days of wedding festivities, and marched to London while Edward continued to wait at Nottingham. His chief lieutenants, William Herbert and Humphrey Stafford, the earls of Pembroke and Devon respectively, were marching to join him and Edward could be reasonably confident that the three of them would put paid to Warwick's crazy escapade. Warwick, for his part, did not stay in London for very long but headed for the Midlands to cut off Edward's reinforcements. The people of Kent had given Warwick a good reception, perhaps still smarting from Edward's punitive raid on the county in 1461, and the people of London, while being a little more equivocal, had given the earl a loan of £1,000. Buoyed up by this support Warwick, too, was feeling confident. Edward continued to wait. The army approaching from the north, under a captain calling himself Robin of Redesdale, probably Sir William Conyers, bypassed Nottingham in order to join up with Warwick and cut Edward off from London. This manoeuvre took the rebels west and directly into the path of the earls of Pembroke and Devon. On 26 July 1469 at Edgecote the Wars of the Roses began again after five years of peace. There would be three more bloody pitched battles before they finally came to an exhausted end.

ﺤﻟﺞ ﺤﻟﺞ ﺤﻟﺞ

The battle at Edgecote, between Banbury and Chipping Warden near the Oxfordshire border with Northamptonshire, was a disaster for Edward. He had stipulated that Devon's men should consist of archers and Pembroke's levies should be men-at-arms and cavalry. The two armies were designed to act together, and indeed they succeeded in joining at their rendezvous in Banbury. Unfortunately the two earls promptly had a blazing row over trifles. Ignoring the imminent danger to their king, they argued about lodgings, precedence and, most bizarrely, about who had the right to a local serving-woman. In high dudgeon Devon marched off to Deddington Castle, ten miles to the south, taking his archers with him. Pembroke, for his part, may have won the right to a charming girl from Banbury, but he was left to fight the rebels on his own. At first he did well and got the better of 'Robin of Redesdale', but the next day the advance contingents of Warwick's army arrived. William Herbert and his younger brother, Richard, fought valiantly but their Welshmen were overwhelmed and slaughtered in droves. The two Herberts were surrounded and taken prisoner. The earl of Devon deemed it politic to slink away and, making it back to the safety of his earldom, was murdered by a mob in Bridgewater. Perhaps the natives of that place didn't appreciate a man who could not win the right to female intimacy in Banbury. Sadly, neither of the two Herberts was alive to hear of the summary justice meted out to their erstwhile colleague whose fit of pique had cost them the battle. They were taken by Warwick to Northampton and executed the next day. William Herbert, rather poignantly, asked Warwick to spare his valiant younger brother, but Warwick, in no mood for mercy, put them both to death. Warwick had only just begun the purge his vengeance craved.

Shortly after the battle Richard, Earl Rivers, the father of Elizabeth Woodville, and his second son, John, were discovered at the town of Chepstow, arrested and marched off to the earl of Warwick who was waiting in Coventry. They were both immediately executed. Meanwhile Edward's own troops had melted away when they heard about the calamity at Edgecote. No one could guarantee the king's safety with Warwick in this mood. Edward himself was found a few days after the battle with just a few followers. He was taken captive and sent to Warwick castle, and later to Middleham, for safe keeping. There were now two kings in England under lock and key. Henry VI was in the Tower and Edward IV in the Yorkshire Dales. This was a unique moment in English history but few felt the urge to celebrate. Warwick was undoubtedly in charge now and exercising the power over kings in which he specialised. His only difficulty was that no government in England could function without a living monarch. No commission, no writ, no summons and no order, could be issued without a king's authority. The Croyland chronicler explained that when the Lancastrians far in the north took advantage of the topsy-turvy situation:

> The earl of Warwick found himself unable to offer an effectual resistance to these, without first making public proclamation in the king's name that all liege subjects must rise to defend him against the rebels. For the people, seeing their king detained as a prisoner, refused to take any notice of proclamations to this effect.[14]

Disorder in the northern counties forced Warwick to accept that Edward would need to be released. Warwick had started a rebellion but only a king could end it. Perhaps he fooled himself into believing that he had already achieved his goal. He had demonstrated to the king that he would not be written out of the script and he had disposed of several court favourites. Clarence was married to his daughter and support for the earl had been encouraging. For expediency's sake Edward would have to be released but it would still be possible to control him and ensure affairs were conducted under the supervision of Warwick. That may have been the theory. In September 1469 Edward was at liberty and appeared in York. He called his loyal nobles to his side, the earls of Suffolk, Arundel, Northumberland and Essex. Lord Hastings also arrived and with him a young man, now seventeen, named Richard, duke of Gloucester. Throughout the turmoil of the next eighteen months Richard remained steadfastly loyal to his brother, in stark contrast to the duke of Clarence.

Once affairs in the north had been sorted out Edward began to shore up his authority. He gave Richard – increasingly emerging as one of the most reliable and trustworthy of all the men at court – the Herbert estates in Wales. Richard never wavered in his loyalty to the king, a rare circumstance in the middle of the fifteenth century. We have a letter of Richard's, the earliest in existence, written at Castle Rising in Norfolk as he prepared to go north to help quell the rebellion in late June 1469. A rather anxious young man, suddenly thrust into the forefront of military responsibility and into the heart of danger, begs for money. Richard was expected to pay his own expenses, it would seem, and balance the books later from his own endowments. This was a difficult matter, as he explained:

> Right trusty and welbeloved We grete you wele. And forasmuch as the King's good Grace hathe appointed me to attende upon His Highnesse into the north parties of his lande, which wolbe to me gret cost and charge, whereunto I am soo sodenly called that I am not so wel purveide of money therfor as behoves me to be, and therefore pray you as my special trust is in you, to lend me an hundredth pounde of money unto Ester next commying, at whiche tyme I promise you shalbe truly therof content and paide again.

Richard wrote a postscript in his own hand:

> Sir J Say I pray you that ye fayle me not at this tyme in my grete need, as ye wule that
> I schewe yow my goode lordshype in that matter that ye labure to me for.[15]

Given the parchment to sign by his scribe he added a personal touch. His hand-
writing is as neat and competent as that of the secretary. Richard had clearly
been well schooled. Sir John Say was chancellor of the duchy of Lancaster and
it is interesting that he should already be seeking Richard's help in some way.
Good lordship was the great currency by which power flowed from the nobility
to their subordinates and service was rendered in return. Here we can see how
vital that service might be. John Say also lent money to Edward at this time and
was sufficiently valued by Edward to be asked to accompany him on a rather
hastily arranged trip abroad the following year. Such men as this were not only
lending money, no doubt at a handsome profit, but they also had to make difficult political decisions. Richard could offer something to Sir John in return for
his help; he could offer good lordship. There were others around at this juncture
who might also offer Sir John good lordship. The knight was forced to take a
risk. Civil war threw up these hard choices and as a consequence it corroded
the structure of lordship and service. After almost twenty years of attrition and
fracture Richard managed to restore something of its value in the areas under his
jurisdiction during the following decade of his brother's reign.

It was partly because Edward recognised the need for local people to respect
and share the interests of their lords that Edward restored Henry Percy to
the earldom of Northumberland. While this meant dispossessing John Neville,
the most useful and loyal of all his magnates, Edward was certain, and probably correct in his belief, that the north would never be secure unless a Percy
controlled it. Warwick, John's brother, may also have queered the patch. John
was, after all, a Neville and the Nevilles were not only rivals to the Percys but
were also becoming rivals to the king. Edward compensated John with the
marquisate of Montagu, which was a very noble distinction. He also offered
him the marriage of his own eldest child, Elizabeth of York, to John's son and
heir, George, and made this George the duke of Bedford. He also gave John
substantial estates in Devon which had, after Edgecote and a free-for-all in
Bridgewater, unexpectedly fallen into his possession. John Neville, formerly
earl of Northumberland and now Marquis of Montagu, was richly rewarded
for his priceless services. That was one way of looking at it. John Neville,
brother of the traitor Warwick, was deprived of his huge earldom which he
had so valiantly won and defended, and replaced with a disgraced Lancastrian.
That was another way of seeing things. But while Edward's logic was faultless,

his judgement here was disastrous. John was a courageous and astute commander, but he was not a saint. He perhaps shared a Neville disposition to baulk at retrograde career moves. Edward had created an enemy.

For the moment things remained relatively calm. It was clear that Warwick had support while he was remedying popular grievances but not while he was administering the realm. A way forward was urgently needed. The obvious solution to avoid a prolonged impasse was a public demonstration of an Edward-Warwick reconciliation. In the great chamber of Parliament at Westminster, at a grand council of all the peers, Warwick, Clarence and Edward swore to be friends. The Croyland chronicler perceptively observed:

> Still, however, there probably remained, on the one side, deeply seated in his mind, the injuries he had received and the contempt which had been shown to majesty, and on the other, a mind too conscious of a daring deed. [16]

The 'daring deed' had cost the queen her father and a brother. It had almost cost Edward his throne. If Warwick had thought that his interests in Wales would be served by killing the Herberts, he now had to contend with the fact that Edward was determined to give their lands and power to his own younger brother, Richard. There was to be no going back. It was only a matter of time before the deadly game of chess resumed again. In the meantime Edward seems to have woken up to the fact that his brother, Richard, had become a man. In these volatile days, fraught with intrigue, suspicion and manifest treason, Edward learnt that Richard could be trusted.

On 17 October 1469, Richard duke of Gloucester was made Constable of England. This was the post formerly held by the queen's father, Richard, Earl Rivers, murdered by Warwick. It was the highest military office in the land. We know virtually nothing of Richard's years at Middleham between 1465 and 1469, but the tutelage of Warwick had not tainted his fidelity. Perhaps, being younger than Clarence, he was able to escape the inducements and blandishments which so seduced his older brother. Perhaps Warwick, busy as he always was, paid little attention to the boy in his early teens exercising in the castle yard. He may have underestimated the lad. Edward may also have made this mistake, until he was shaken so violently out of his complacency and found that Richard could be very useful indeed. All we know about Richard's time under Warwick's wing is that he met two other young members of Warwick's household at Middleham who were to become his lifelong friends. The first was Francis, lord Lovell, a ward of Warwick, and the second was Anne Neville, Warwick's daughter. Francis was to become Richard's most trusted friend, and to die fighting his enemies, and Anne was to become his wife. It would seem that one character trait can already be dimly discerned as Richard reached his late teens: that of loyalty. Richard was loyal to those whom he trusted and was soon to show that he was loyal to those whom he served.

After the sham rapprochement at Westminster, Edward consolidated Richard's position in Wales. On 7 November 1469 Richard replaced Lord Hastings as justiciar of north Wales. Ten days later he was appointed chief steward of all the duchy of Lancaster lordships in south Wales, and on 30 November he was made chief steward, approver and surveyor of the principality of Wales and the earldom of March. Warwick had lands in Wales and had wanted to get rid of Herbert to extend his interests there. Richard was becoming something of a rival. In December Richard was given authority to subdue two castles in Wales that had fallen into rebel hands. These castles were Warwick's. There could be no doubt now that Richard was to be the instrument by which Warwick's ambitions in Wales were checked and the authority of the king was re-established.[17] On 7 February 1470 Richard displaced Warwick as chief steward and chamberlain of south Wales. A month later the earl was in open revolt again.

Edward was in a cleft stick. He had to endow the men he could trust with lands and offices as a matter of real urgency, but in so doing he was pushing the displaced and the discontented into opposition. Not only was Warwick's nose once again put out of joint, this time by the growing influence of Richard duke of Gloucester, but another powerful lord was also troubled by the grants made to the king's loyal brother. During 1469 Richard was given a major collection of duchy of Lancaster lands in both Lancashire and Cheshire. These included Clitheroe, Liverpool and Halton. These grants, with all the duchy offices that went with them, directly cut across the ambitions of the Stanleys, who intended to remain the dominant power in the north-west.[18]

Thomas, lord Stanley, was married to none other than Eleanor Neville, the sister of Warwick. In the next spasm of rebellion, Stanley, stood by Warwick and opposed the king. It was Richard's insertion into his sphere of influence that caused Stanley the most concern and he stood in open rivalry with the duke. Stanley's own interests were far more important to him than royal authority. Kings and the dynasties they represented came and went but the Stanleys always prospered. It is here, in the north-west, that Richard made his most deadly enemy and it was here, among the towns and villages of east Lancashire and over the hills into west Yorkshire, that he inspired his most loyal followers. There is no paradox in this observation; the enemies of Stanley became the friends of Richard. Richard was the only man with the power to match that of Stanley in the region and those who wanted to prevent the Stanleys from monopolising their resources soon saw Richard as their champion. Their lack of power was to cost Richard dearly. In opposing Stanley, Richard endowed himself with an Achilles heel. He discovered in the winter of 1469 and 1470 that Stanley was treacherous, self-seeking and ambitious, and he never forgot it. Richard did not like disloyal men. Stanley discovered that Richard was a threat, and he never forgot that.

The beginning of a long and, ultimately, tragic drama began in the woods and fields of the north-west. When Richard was appointed forester of Amounderness, Blackburn and Bowland in late 1469, he not only displaced Stanley, in those offices, but he also made the acquaintance of a certain James Harrington.[19] James had already locked horns with Stanley and had been forced to stand aside while Stanley swallowed up what Harrington believed to be his rightful inheritance. Stanley was his mortal foe. Nothing could have pleased James Harrington more than to see a strong rival to Stanley arrive in such a hotly contested region. James was steward of Amounderness Hundred and became deputy steward to Richard, duke of Gloucester, in Bowland.[20] James Harrington's brother, Robert, was bailiff of Amounderness and Blackburn but Thomas Stanley had put his own men in these offices and had refused to allow Robert to exercise his rights. James Harrington, for his part, was holding on to the family seat at Hornby which had been granted to Stanley. There was a virtual state of war between the two families for control of east Lancashire. Richard's presence could tip the balance against Stanley and protect the leading Yorkist gentry in the region. When the king's younger brother entered the region in late 1469, he was a young man earnestly trying to establish royal authority in very unsettled times. Stanley not only opposed him, he opposed his brother, the king, and joined Warwick's rebellion. For the rest of his reign Edward attempted to mediate fairly and dispassionately between the Stanleys and the Harringtons. When Richard became king himself, in 1483, he found this far more difficult to do. His early days in Stanley country had left a deep impression on him. He appears to have forged a bond with the trusty Harringtons, and a prejudice against the highly untrustworthy Stanleys, right from the start. James Harrington and Richard, duke of Gloucester, were to collaborate and cooperate for the rest of Edward's reign and their mutual dislike of Stanley was to cost them dear. The seeds being sown in 1469 were to bear bitter fruit at the battle of Bosworth in 1485.

Richard, only just seventeen, busied himself enforcing law and order in Wales, learning how to effect a commission of array, to supervise a muster, to account for supplies and wages, to reduce hostile fortresses and deploy siege weapons, to hunt down rebels and to hold judicial and military assizes. All this was invaluable training in the real world of high politics and service. He was assiduously performing his duties when disaster once again struck the house of York and threatened to topple it.

# FIVE

# SHOULDER
# TO SHOULDER

In the first two months of 1470 the smouldering embers of rebellion needed just a spark to set the country ablaze. Warwick and Clarence, though officially reconciled to the king, were more disgruntled than ever. They had achieved nothing in the previous year's rebellion except the manifest distrust of Edward, who had been left with the power to do them hurt if he so chose. The 'settlement' had seen Warwick's brother, John, demoted from the earldom of Northumberland in favour of the fourth Henry Percy. At the same time John's son, George, was made duke of Bedford and betrothed to Edward's oldest child, Elizabeth. What this in effect meant was that Warwick would never become a duke himself and Clarence would never become king. George Neville had been treated handsomely, but Warwick, Clarence and, as it turned out, John, could not care less about him. Edward had made very few concessions to them.

The trouble flared up again in February 1470 when the house of Sir Thomas Burgh of Gainsborough was attacked and destroyed by Sir Robert Welles in Lincolnshire. Thomas Burgh was Edward's master of horse; Robert Welles was one of Clarence's men. Welles posted notices in every church with a call to arms while Edward moved swiftly to intervene. A royal army mustered at Grantham on the Great North Road and moved towards the rebels. Welles meanwhile, was moving towards Leicester to join up with Warwick and Clarence. Before their forces combined, however, Edward forced the father of Welles, who had been taken hostage by the king, to write a letter to the son saying that if he did not submit his father would be put to death. This had the desired effect and the younger Welles immediately turned round and headed towards

Edward to rescue his father. On 12 March the two sides met near Stamford in Lincolnshire. Edward paraded Lord Welles between the opposing forces and executed him. He then opened up a barrage of cannon fire into the ranks of Welles' rebels who had begun to charge shouting 'A Warwick! A Clarence!' The cannon caused heavy casualties and as Edward's army began to advance the rebels broke ranks and fled. As they ran they discarded their livery jackets, provided by Warwick and Clarence. They either did this to make running easier or, more likely, to remove incriminating evidence. The battle has always been known as Lose-coat Field. The rebels having been routed by swift and decisive action on Edward's part, he moved west to hunt down Warwick and Clarence, whose involvement in the trouble had been so flagrant. Realising that they could not raise sufficient numbers on their own the two traitors fled south, took ship and washed up in Normandy on the shores of Louis XI.

Calais, where Warwick had intended to go, made its excuses and refused him entry. France it would have to be. Louis, known as 'the wily fox', made maximum capital out of this unexpected windfall. After several months of intense diplomatic manoeuvring he succeeded in achieving an extraordinary rapprochement between Warwick and Margaret of Anjou. Having managed to get the two of them to agree to meet at the town of Amboise, according to the Milanese ambassador:

> The same evening the king presented him [Warwick] to the queen. With great reverence Warwick went on his knees and asked her pardon for the injuries and wrongs done to her in the past. She graciously forgave him and he afterwards did homage and fealty there.[1]

The meeting must have been a wonderful occasion. The Coyland chronicler gives us a hint of the delightful pleasantries the two must have exchanged:

> They [Warwick and Clarence], were kindly received by king Louis, and being after some difficulty admitted into the favour of queen Margaret and her son prince Edward, made a promise that they would in future faithfully support their cause and that of king Henry.[2]

The 'difficulty' may have had something to do with the fact that they had been trying to destroy each other for at least fifteen years. All that time ago when the Wars of the Roses had first begun, at the first battle of St Albans in 1455, it had been Warwick's volley of arrows that had wounded Margaret's husband, Henry VI, and it had been his men who had killed her great friend, Edmund Beaufort, duke of Somerset. Had he not been instrumental in the capture of

Henry VI at the battle of Northampton? That had been an occasion on which four more of her tried and trusted lieutenants had been brutally done to death. He had done the same again at Towton the following year and had caused her to flee to Scotland with her incapacitated husband: a flight which had brought a decade of ignominious exile and bitter hopelessness.

Warwick had equally good reasons for adoring the ex-queen. At the battle of Wakefield in 1460 Warwick had lost his father and his brother to her Lancastrian henchmen. Many of his supporters and friends had died in the bloody aftermath of that grisly débâcle. As a consequence his subsequent career had been entirely predicated on eliminating her from English affairs. Nothing could be more evident to a neutral observer of these events than that Warwick and Margaret had their differences. The meeting and reconciliation effected by Louis must have been a thoroughly ghastly spectacle. It smacked of calculated policy, of expediency, of desperation. Neither had any other means by which their fortunes might be rescued. They would have to grit their teeth, hold their noses and make common cause against Edward. The lion and the bear would lie down together.

And so it was that in July 1470 Warwick agreed to restore Henry VI to the throne of England. The reconciliation was cemented by the betrothal of Warwick's daughter, Anne, to Margaret's only son, Prince Edward. This would finally allow Warwick to realise the dream of seeing one of his daughters on the throne. Clarence had been somewhat shunted sideways by all these novel arrangements, and in the denouement he appears as a reluctant collaborator. Never mind: Warwick would once again be the arbiter of English affairs with a pliant king and a deferential nobility, and no doubt Clarence could be fobbed off with the prospect of further gains in land and titles. Margaret, for her part, would only agree that the marriage of her beloved son to Warwick's daughter should take place after her husband had been restored to the throne. It was a price she was willing to pay in exchange for the inestimable triumph of Henry's return to glory. Only with this primary objective achieved would she make the concession. Although Warwick and Margaret undoubtedly loathed the sight of each other, their self-interest temporarily coincided. Warwick needed an alternative to Edward, and French backing: Margaret needed the kind of support he and Clarence could raise in England. The stage was set for the most remarkable comeback in English history.

Warwick's descent on England was carefully planned and timed. His brother-in-law, Henry, Lord Fitzhugh, who was married to Warwick's sister Alice, created a diversion in the north. While Edward was dealing with this, Warwick landed in Devon, in September 1470, accompanied by Jasper Tudor, earl of Pembroke, and John, earl of Oxford, who was another brother-in-law of Warwick, being married to his sister Margaret. The Burgundian fleet guarding the French coast had been scattered by a storm, granting the rebels an unopposed crossing. The Neville rebellion in Yorkshire had been easily put down by Edward but he seems to have delayed unnecessarily at Doncaster. Edward was an enigmatic mixture of vital energy and torpid lethargy. While he procrastinated in the north, Warwick was able to gather support at will. He had begun by issuing a proclamation describing Edward as 'late earl of March, usurper, oppressor and destroyer of our sovereign lord [Henry VI] and of the noble blood of this realm'. They had come to 'deliver our sovereign lord out of his great captivity'.[3] When one considers that Warwick was largely responsible for ensuring that Henry had been taken into captivity in the first place, one can only marvel at his shameless audacity.

Two events now caused the balance to swing in Warwick's favour. The first was the defection to his cause of Thomas Stanley. Having remained aloof the previous year Stanley now calculated he had more to gain by joining Warwick than in adhering to Edward. It was ever thus with Stanley: never predictable except in his unpredictability but always ready to take a calculated step up the ladder of ambition. Being married to Eleanor Neville, Warwick's sister, he had no doubt come to join the family party. The second event was something of a tragedy. John Neville, now marquis of Montagu, turned against the man he had so faithfully served for so long. While stripping John of the earldom of Northumberland, Edward had hoped he could keep him on board by lavish compensation. Edward needed a Percy restoration in the north and when it came to matters of state he could be quite ruthless and without sentimentality. John Neville did not have the luxury of the king's objectivity. He had defended the region from Scottish invasion, Percy treachery and even his own brother's insurgency. All the estates in Devon and the honours heaped on his son could not compensate for the humiliation of seeing his former enemies so elevated above him in his own heartlands.

Montagu's defection caught Edward completely by surprise. The king was actually waiting for him to arrive with the troops he needed to face Warwick and Clarence, who had already reached Coventry. It was only at the very last moment that a spy reported to Edward that Montagu had not come to the rescue but to betray him. Edward 'found himself compelled to consult his own safety, and that of his followers, by a precipitate flight'. Edward, with his brother Richard, his brother-in-law Anthony, earl Rivers, and his closest friend, William, lord Hastings, fled to King's Lynn in Norfolk and thence by ship to Holland. There they were welcomed by Charles of Burgundy's governor, Louis de Gruthuyse, an old acquaintance.[4] The king, or more precisely, ex-king, was so short of ready money that he rewarded the master of the ship that had conveyed him to safety with a furred gown, and his brother, Richard, had to borrow money from the bailiff of the town of Veere in Zeeland.[5]

There was once again, after almost a decade, merely a single king left in England. Henry VI was taken, bemused, pathetic, probably unable to understand the revolutionary events taking place around him, dressed in a blue gown and looking 'not so cleanly kept as should be such a prince', out of the Tower to be paraded before the citizens of London and publicly re-crowned. Years languishing in prison had clearly not helped his fragile condition. As he looked vacantly about him, his eyes would have passed over the earl of Warwick who was once again the Kingmaker, and once again attempting to hold on to the reins of power.[6] The Croyland chronicler, with his administrative background, rather enjoyed the novelty of the proceedings:

> Now all laws were once more enacted in the name of this king Henry, and all letters patent, writs, mandates, chirographs, and instruments whatsoever were published with a twofold mode of annotation in reference to this king's government – in this manner, 'In the year from the beginning of the reign of king Henry the Sixth, forty-eight, and in the first year of the recovery of his throne by the said king'.[7]

The Readeption of King Henry VI had begun.

Richard, duke of Gloucester, was back in the provinces of Burgundy. Once again he was a fugitive. Once again his future was obscure and his prospects uncertain. Once again he was heavily dependent on the hospitality and the security provided by the Burgundian people. Ten years had passed since the eight-year-old boy had been packed off in haste after the death of his father at Wakefield; Clarence had been with him then, and Edward had been fighting to win the throne of England. Now Clarence was in England, a traitor and an enemy, and Edward was with Richard, an exile and a supplicant. On the previous occasion Richard had been rescued by the triumph of Edward over his enemies. This time Richard would play a role in reversing Edward's fortunes and restoring him to the throne. While Clarence never seemed to know where he stood, or what value he should place on his fidelity and his oaths of fealty, there is no hint of Richard ever having wavered in his loyalty to Edward.

Their host in Holland, Louis de Gruthuyse, was a famous book collector and had amassed an outstanding collection of illuminated manuscripts. We know that Edward was very taken by this display and was later to commission books on history and chivalry from the workshops of Bruges. His friend, William, Lord Hastings, did likewise. Once again Richard was in the company of a man of taste and learning in a province of Burgundy. Once again he was dependent on his host in every respect and found him to be a model of knightly courtesy, a pillar of strength in the traumas of the house of York. On the other hand, the duke, Charles the Bold, was not as keen to accept the fugitives as his father had been a decade earlier. Charles had to be careful not to offend whatever government England ended up with. As it happened his difficult diplomatic problem was resolved when Louis XI of France suddenly declared war on him. This was all part of the bargain Warwick had secured when he and Margaret were negotiating with Louis for help in overthrowing Edward. All of a sudden Charles found himself free to abandon his pretence of friendship with the Lancastrian regime and able to cautiously acknowledge the exiles. In the event his backing for Edward's attempt to return to England was rather lacklustre, but it was better than nothing. At least Edward had permission to hire his own ships and men in Bruges and get together something of an invasion fleet. He was able to obtain the help of Duke Francis of Brittany and the Hanseatic League of north German towns which enabled him to fit out a fairly respectable fleet of thirty-six ships and about 1,200 men, some of whom were Flemish. His support came from those keen to prevent the king of France from expanding his influence and from those who took a gamble on winning future trading concessions from Edward if he ever got back his kingdom. Edward was in Holland for four months and appears to have been active and energetic, despite his desperate plight. It is the measure of the man that he could, under such extreme stress, act in a bold and confident manner. Although lethargy, complacency and inactivity sometimes dogged his presence, when decisive resolution was required, he could be strikingly effective.

During the entire four months of enforced sojourn in foreign parts, Richard, duke of Gloucester was at his brother's side. The awesome trepidation that accompanied the expedition to reclaim the kingdom and the dreadful razor's edge that separated power and security from failure and oblivion were shared by these two scions of the house of York. Richard, having turned eighteen, was about to help his brother regain the throne. He would find himself in the thick of battle, with death close at hand and naked swords covered in blood around him. He would risk his life and serve his lord. Throughout the difficult days ahead he would remain steadfastly loyal to his brother, the king. He would also discover the value of the loyalty of certain members of the northern gentry, and no doubt contrast their conduct in this darkest hour of need with that of Thomas, lord Stanley.

We are fortunate to have a detailed report of Edward's return to England known as the *Historie of the Arrival of Edward IV in England and the Finall Recoverye of His Kingdomes from Henry VI*. The anonymous author of the *Arrival* is heavily biased in favour of his patron, Edward IV, and the fact that Edward had a précis of the work sent to Burgundy shortly after the events it describes tells us that it is very much the 'authorised' version. Nevertheless it would be foolhardy to dismiss it entirely as propaganda. The author was present at much of the action and supplied some credible particulars. As he himself tells us, the account was:

> Compiled and put in this form ensuing by a servaunt of the Kyngs, that presently saw in effect a great parte of his exploytes, and the resydewe knewe by true relation of them that were present in every tyme.[9]

He described a rather hairy landing during which the fleet was hit by a storm and the 'wynds and tempests upon the sea' scattered the ships in different directions. Edward landed 'with his shippe aloone' at Ravenspur on the Humber. This was, by coincidence, where Henry Bolingbroke had landed before usurping the throne from Richard II. The chronicler mentioned this, informing us that Henry Bolingbroke had done this 'contrary and to the dissobeysance of his sovereigne lord, Kynge Richard the II'. The point of giving us this information is to explain that King Henry VI, whom Edward was intent on displacing, was lineally descended from Henry Bolingbroke and was therefore not a legitimate king at all. Either the irony of his remarks, which place Edward in the same case and in the same location as a 'Usurpowr', was lost on the author, or his subversive subtlety was cleverly disguised. Edward 'with a few with hym' spent what must have been a very difficult night 'lodged at a power village' two miles from his landing place. Unfortunately our chronicler does not describe the delicate moment when some hovel received a knock on the door that stormy night. It was not until the next day that 'the felowshipe came hole toward him'. Richard 'the Kynge's brothar' with three hundred men 'landyd at an other place iiii myle from thens'. Earl Rivers had landed fourteen miles away so Richard with his company would have been a welcome sight encouraging Edward to hope that he could successfully regroup. Hastings had been with the king throughout; part of the explanation for Edward's great trust in him must be the shared dangers and exertions of that very night.

The *Arrival* makes it clear how little support there was for Edward initially. Some towns, such as Hull, refused to admit him, and Yorkshire in general with its strong Neville sympathies was hostile territory. Edward was even reduced to pretending that he was loyal to King Henry VI and, like Bolingbroke seventy years before him, had come merely to claim his ducal inheritance. As he headed towards the city of York there were 'assembled great compaignies in divars places' and 'muche people of the contrie' gathered in order to resist him. The chronicler believed that one of the reasons why the hostile crowds allowed him to pass was that 'they durst not take upon them to make hym any manifest warre, knowyinge well the great curage and hardiness that he was of, with the parfete asswrance of the felowshipe that was with hym'. Personal courage and the perfect assurance of such a fellowship were wonderful assets to have at such a critical time. Perhaps Richard remembered that occasion fourteen years later at Bosworth Field when he too relied on that rare combination.

Edward only gained admittance to York itself by demonstrating intrepid courage. The recorder of the city, John Conyers, rode out to meet him and warned him that no good would come to him if he entered the city; his safety could not be guaranteed. Edward replied that he was determined to pursue what he had undertaken to the end, come what may. He was willing to accept 'what God and good fortune would gyve hym'. Nevertheless it must have been a highly charged occasion when he arrived at the gates of the city, again proclaiming that he had only come to reclaim the dukedom of York. How humiliating that must have been, but for the consoling thought that such dissembling would pay dividends soon enough. He was admitted on the condition that he was accompanied by only sixteen men, a fraction of his retinue, and found a crowd of 'worshipfull folks whicche were assembled a little within'. He walked into this highly dangerous situation shouting, according to one chronicler, 'A King Harry! A King and Prince Edward!' To reinforce the illusion that he supported Henry VI and his son, Prince Edward, he wore an ostrich feather: the emblem of the Prince of Wales. He had to placate the gathering with assurances of his good behaviour before they would allow him to stay and bring in the rest of his followers. After refreshing themselves they had to agree to be out of the city by noon the following day.[10] It should be remembered that this city was to become Richard's most fiercely loyal bastion: the one place in the world on which he could truly rely, and a city that mourned his death like no other. It is worth noting that their suspicion and trepidation in Edward's darkest hour, appeased only by his professions of loyalty to the Lancastrian king, contrast markedly with their love of Richard in the next decade. The change came about because Richard earned their respect and loyalty; it was not innately there.

These were times of unmitigated stress for Edward and those about him. Not only had they to take such enormous risks with potentially hostile mobs, but all the time enemy forces might descend upon them from any quarter. If they did so Edward had hardly enough men to put up a realistic defence. As he moved through Yorkshire the earl of Northumberland could have raised his levies and pounced. Thousands of Percy adherents could descend upon the relatively small force under Edward's command and extinguish the last glimmer of hope of a Yorkist restoration. Similarly the Neville forces of John, Marquis Montagu, were somewhere in the vicinity. They say that fortune favours the brave and Edward tested the adage to its fullest extent. Henry Percy did not move against him, perhaps grateful for his surprise restoration to the earldom of Northumberland. Montagu, the very man he had displaced and who had joined the rebellion for that reason, also failed to lift a finger against Edward. We can only guess at the strain suffered by poor old John as his loyalties were torn asunder. He had given so much to this former king of his, served him in his hour of need and been richly rewarded for it. Edward had taken the earldom from him but there was no reason to believe he had intended to harm his interests. Warwick was his brother, but revolt and treachery were not in John's nature; his heart was not in it and he let Edward pass.[11]

As Edward moved south, past Pontefract, Wakefield and Doncaster he received some reinforcements but 'not so many as he supposed'. It was when he reached Nottingham that his fortunes began to change. There, riding in to greet him, came Sir James Harrington and Sir William Parr with 600 men. These were the first substantial reinforcements to join Edward and they gave him the confidence to act more boldly and to convince others that he had the support and capability to win back his crown. It is no exaggeration to say that the arrival of these two northern knights and their retinues was a turning point in the fortunes of the Yorkists. William Parr was the brother of Margaret Parr who married Sir Richard Ratcliffe, one of Richard's most trusted servants. William Parr, made comptroller of the household by Edward for this brave and overt commitment, was to become Richard's lieutenant-warden of the west march and sheriff of Cumberland. James Harrington, as we know, had already made common cause with Richard against Thomas Stanley, and was to forge a bond with Richard that went far beyond the reciprocal commitment to shared interests so prevalent among the conventional arrangements of the time. Both Parr and Harrington were to fight with Richard in the forthcoming battles of Barnet and Tewkesbury, and to lose family and friends there. Richard never forgot that the help he had given Harrington at Hornby had been repaid by a conspicuous and wholehearted demonstration of loyalty at the very moment it was most needed.

What makes the behaviour of Harrington and Parr even more remarkable is that they both had strong Neville connections. These men, members of the gentry, chose to step beyond their ties with Warwick, their immediate lord, and to support the king. James Harrington's maternal grandmother was Philippa Neville and William Parr had even served Warwick when he had initially rebelled in 1469. In fact he first came to the attention of Edward when he acted as Warwick's messenger before the battle of Lose-coat Field. These men made a political choice. The fact that they could command a fairly substantial retinue of armed men should also alert us to the very real power that the upper reaches of the gentry could wield.

Edward continued to move south. His patrols reported enemy forces gathering to the east at Newark. Edward immediately turned towards them and approached the town. As he did so the duke of Exeter and the earl of Oxford promptly abandoned their forces and fled. Their confused army was left leaderless and in disarray. When Warwick had defeated Edward's army at Edgecote, Edward had not been there. Warwick had won his victory against William Herbert, earl of Pembroke. Edward himself had never lost a battle and perhaps this formidable reputation was sufficient to make Essex and Oxford realise that discretion was the better part of valour. Oxford was no slouch when it came to military command, as his subsequent performances at Bosworth and Stoke were to prove, but when he was confronted with a man with an aura of invincibility he chose not to chance his luck. As the chronicler put it, Oxford and Essex 'determyned shortly within themselfe that they might not abyde his comynge'. At Leicester 3,000 men loyal to William Hastings turned up and the tide had well and truly turned.

Warwick was by no means finished, however. On 27 March he took up quarters in the strongly defended town of Coventry with about 7,000 men. Edward's army was still not sufficient to attack such a strongly defended position against superior numbers and he billeted his forces in the town of Warwick, ironically enough. The earl of Warwick, meanwhile, could content himself in the knowledge that Montagu, Essex and Oxford were still in hostile array and aiming to rendezvous with him. He also had intelligence that Clarence was on the way with four thousand men. Edward's men failed to prevent Montagu, Essex and Oxford from joining Warwick and all now hinged on the arrival of Clarence. As he approached, Edward led his army out to meet him and three miles from the town of Warwick the two brothers faced each other. The author of the *Arrival* watched the dramatic scene as it unfolded. When the two armies were less than half a mile apart, Edward lined his men up in battle formation, banners flying and weapons at the ready. Then, unexpectedly and with perilous audacity, he left his army standing still, 'takyinge with hym his brothar of Glocestar, the Lord Rivers, Lord Hastings, and fewe othar, and went towards his brothar of Clarence'. Clarence responded by taking with him a few noble men and 'levinge his hoost in good order, departyd from them towards the Kynge'. With thousands watching, their lives dependent on the outcome, the brothers joined in fraternal embrace 'with as hartyly lovynge chere and countenanaunce as might be betwix two bretherne of so grete nobley and astate'. Then Richard and Clarence did likewise followed by the nobles with them. The onlookers were 'right glade and joyows, and thanked God highly of that joyows metynge, unitie, and accorde'.

Edward, again showing remarkable courage and presence of mind, entrusted himself to Clarence's safekeeping and went with him into his brother's army, still accompanied only by the few men he had chosen. He welcomed them cheerfully and promised them his good grace and received in return their cheers and gratitude. The two hosts then joined with much rejoicing and, no doubt, considerable relief before retiring to the town of Warwick for the night. Edward had a gift for man-management and a talent for pleasing crowds that few in positions of such authority had hitherto been granted. With Clarence back on board Edward could afford to take even greater risks. Warwick still had considerable forces at his disposal with the prospect of Margaret of Anjou arriving in England with strong support. Coventry could not be taken, nor the earl induced to emerge from it, and meanwhile Edward faced an invasion in the south. With time of the essence he once more took a risk and, leaving Warwick to fester in Coventry, he struck out for London.[12]

As Edward approached the seat of government, he wrote to the city magistrates commanding them to arrest Henry VI and prepare for his arrival. Warwick doubled the confusion and trepidation of the city fathers by writing to them also and commanding them to hold the city against Edward at all costs. London was buzzing with the news that Queen Margaret and Prince Edward were about to set sail from France. There were three Lancastrian lords holding the city but two of them, Edmund Beaufort, duke of Somerset, and John Courtenay, heir to the earl of Devon, had left to meet Margaret. This left George Neville, archbishop of York, who did his best to rally the people by organising a parade through the city with Henry VI as the centrepiece. It was a disaster. The *Great Chronicle of London* described the scene in painful detail:

> King Henry...being accompanied with the Archbishop of York which held him all the way by the hand and the Lord Zouche, an old and impotent man...bare the king's sword, and so with a small company of gentlemen going on foot before, and one being on horseback and bearing a pole or long shaft with two fox tails [an insulting symbol of defiance][13] fastened upon the said shaft's end, held with a small company of serving men following, the progress before shewed, the which was more liker a play than the showing of a prince to win men's hearts, for by this mean he lost many and won none or right few, and ever he was shewed in a blue gown of velvet as though he had no moo to change with.[14]

That blue gown was clearly a fashion faux pas. Whatever Henry's qualities were, kingly he was not. No greater demonstration of the contrast between the feeble and unmighty Henry VI, with all the pitiful suffering his pathetic senselessness had caused, and the flamboyant, decisive vigour of a regal warrior-king could have been provided than by the triumphant arrival, the very next day, of Edward IV. Preceded by 500 Flemish gunners he swept into the city and marched in an ostentatious spectacle directly to St Paul's for a service of thanksgiving. George Neville had secretly switched sides the previous evening and the aldermen and worthies of the city had met in common council to agree to admit the former king. The *Arrival* thought that the Londoners had sensibly reckoned that they did not have sufficient means to prevent Edward from entering without their having 'systeyned harmes and damagis irreparable'. Philippe de Commynes, a notoriously anti-Yorkist French chronicler, reporting to duke Charles of Burgundy, took a far more cynical view. He suggested that many of the city tradesmen were owed money by Edward and didn't want to lose it. Also, he ventured tartly, that 'the ladies of quality, and rich citizens' wives with whom he had formerly intrigued, forced their husbands and relations to declare themselves on his side'.[15] Edward had a reputation for being something of a ladies' man.

Two dramatic vignettes were then enacted, both tinged with pathos. First, Edward went to the 'Byshops paleis' where George Neville, archbishop of York, 'presentyd hym selfe to the Kyngs good grace, and, in his hand, the usurpowr, Kynge Henry'. One chronicler described Henry saying to Edward, 'My cousin of York, you are very welcome. I know that in your hands my life will not be in danger.' Part wishful thinking and part naivety: in a little less than six weeks Henry would be dead. Edward had learned the hard way that ex-kings had to be disposed of as a matter of priority. The apparent blamelessness of Henry, and an aura of harmlessness, had led Edward to believe that his survival was a matter of no consequence. He would not make the same mistake twice. The meeting of two monarchs, both crowned in Westminster Abbey on different occasions, was unique in English history. It must have been an uncomfortable and perhaps rather disturbing encounter for the casual onlooker. The bizarre proceedings ended rather abruptly as, in the words of the *Arrival*, Edward 'was seasyd of hym' and Henry was led away to the Tower to live out the few remaining days of his disastrous life.

The second event occurred at Westminster Abbey. While Edward was abroad in exile, Queen Elizabeth had given birth to a precious boy, the new heir to the throne. She had named him Edward in order to cause confusion among future generations of students studying the Wars of the Roses. Either that, or there was a desperate dearth of suitable names floating around. To be fair to Elizabeth, she had been forced to seek sanctuary in the Abbey during the difficult emergency created by Warwick's rebellion and the Readeption of Henry VI. Giving birth in such a holy place, in which the shrine of Edward the Confessor held sway, it must have made sense to placate the saint and hope for divine intervention in return for borrowing his name. It did mean that there were now three Edwards at large, two of whom were the sons of crowned kings. Henry VI's son, Edward,

Prince of Wales, was at that very moment sailing with his mother Margaret towards the other two Edwards, who were about to meet for the very first time. Edward IV had never seen his first born son but was careful to get his priorities right and had himself recrowned by Thomas Bouchier, the archbishop of Canterbury, before heading for the makeshift nursery. What transpired between Edward senior and Edward junior we cannot tell but the chronicler described Elizabeth presenting the baby to the king 'to his herts synguler comforte and gladnes'. No one present on that joyful occasion had sufficient prescience to be aware of the doleful melancholy pervading the scene. This was not to be the last time that Elizabeth was to seek sanctuary in the Abbey and it was not to be the last time that little Edward would find himself within its awesome confines. On this occasion he was liberated by his father, on the next, twelve years later, he would be taken into custody by his uncle Richard.

Edward and his reunited family did not have much time to celebrate. Warwick was on the move with a huge force of over 15,000 men and 'great puissaunce'. It was 13 April, Easter Saturday, and the Lancastrian scouts reached the town of Barnet, just ten miles north of London. Edward had only been in London two days but he was in a sufficient state of readiness to ride out immediately to meet his cousin. His advance guard encountered Warwick's scouts in the town and drove them back up the hill. Edward's army then moved through the town, up the steep slope to the plateau beyond and, as darkness fell, approached Warwick's army and fell silent. In the darkness Warwick was unsure how close Edward was and seems to have assumed that he had remained in the town for the night. He spent the night firing his guns at Edward unaware of the fact that he was overshooting and doing little damage. Edward had guns himself but refused to allow them to open fire, preferring to retain the advantage of surprise. Warwick, presuming his battery to have done some damage, began to advance at about 4.00 a.m. while it was still fairly dark. To make matters worse a thick mist reduced visibility. As it happened the two armies were not aligned facing each other so that as the battle began the earl of Oxford, on Warwick's right, pushed straight through Edward's left wing and streamed into Barnet. Some of Edward's men fled as their flank was turned and upon reaching London announced that Edward had lost. This was no doubt readily believed given that the odds were against him. The news was a little premature. The battle lines began to swivel round as Edward's right wing pushed back the duke of Exeter. Oxford, meanwhile, had managed to stop his men from looting Barnet and to regroup. What was left of his men, about 800 of them, came back up the hill to rejoin the battle. Unfortunately for them, with the mist still causing problems and the battle lines skewered, he attacked John Neville's men. John, the marquis of Montagu, now found himself attacked from behind and could not understand what was happening. Because Oxford's livery, a star with streams, was so similar to Edward's, the sun in splendour, it took some time before the Lancastrians realised that they were killing each other. One chronicler, John Warkworth, added the intriguing suggestion that John Neville had actually donned Edward's livery in a pre-arranged plan to betray his brother Warwick. This rumour probably accurately reflects both the confusion of the liveries and the difficulty everyone had in sorting out the loyalties of the unfortunate Montagu. His death in the thick of the fighting finally laid his internal conflicts to rest.

Oxford managed to escape and was to find salvation under Henry Tudor's banner. The duke of Exeter was badly wounded on the field of battle, though he did recover in the end. Warwick was not so fortunate. According to the unreliable Commynes, his brother Montagu had persuaded Warwick to dismount in order to inspire the troops with his commitment. Hitherto, it would seem, Warwick had gained a reputation for waiting to see which way the battle was going before deciding whether to spur his horse into the fray or to make good his escape. On this occasion his brother's advice cost him his life because he was too fat to make it back to the horse park and was cut down by Edward's men. Warkworth has more credible detail and believed that Warwick had been on horseback throughout but that he got trapped in Wrotham Wood as he attempted to escape. Either way his quest for power and control, fuelled by resentment and rancour, finally ended with a dagger thrust through the visor of his helmet.

If only contemporaries had been as interested in the exploits of the king's younger brother. Richard's conduct in his inaugural battle barely registered among the literary elite. Not a single contemporary chronicler bothered to mention his first battle experience. What little evidence we can piece together suggests that he was in the very thick of the fighting valiantly striving with his brother. Some historians have used what meagre scraps we do possess to give him a prominent role in the vanguard of Edward's army, and this may have been the case.[16] The first time this assertion was made was in a later source, *The Great Chronicle of London*. We do have some contemporary evidence: a newsletter written by a Hanseatic merchant living in London who reported that Richard had been slightly wounded.[17] What we do know is that when he came to command prayers to be said for those in his service who had died in the battle, the men he named were his personal retainers who would have been around his battle standard and at his side.[18] If these men were killed then we can be fairly certain that Richard had been in extreme danger. There is also an intriguing poem which eulogised Richard's role in the victory and seems to have been written to celebrate Edward's triumph:

The duke of Glocetter, that nobill prynce,
Yonge of age and victorius in batayle,
To the honoure of Hectour that he myghte comens,
Grace hym folowith, fortune, and good spede.
I suppose hes the same that clerkis of rede,
Fortune hathe hym chosyn, and forthe wyth hym wil goo,
Her husbonde to be, the wille of God is soo.[19]

Richard was still only eighteen years old at Barnet and had seen with his own eyes the reality of the struggle for supreme power: the narrow margin between death and glory, the trauma of existence crushed and of hopes wrecked, the noise and violence, the screams and wounds, the fear and pain, and, above all, the lost friends who had shared so much and would never be with him again. This nasty form of political arbitrament – barbaric, crude and violent, leaving the scars of unimaginable horror, had erupted several times in Richard's short life and would do so again. It formed the backdrop to the journey from his first breath at Fotheringhay to his last gasp at Bosworth. Brutal and sudden death cast a shadow over Richard's life and ultimately enveloped him.

One witness to the battle of Barnet was no stranger to such scenes of destruction. Henry VI had been brought along by Edward to be given a grand-stand view. The former king was now little more than an insurance policy to prevent Warwick from slipping in to London and setting up his puppet administration if Edward had been put to flight. Now that Warwick had gone and Edward's troubles were half over, Henry could be put back in the Tower. It all seems rather odd. Perhaps Edward did not deem it prudent to dispose of this superfluous royal baggage while the old king's son was still around. At least Prince Edward, who landed in Dorset with his mother Margaret the same evening of the battle, could not claim the throne while his father was alive. Margaret, however, was clearly placing her hopes on the boy Edward in any case. King Edward had little time to enjoy his success as news of her growing forces reached his ears.

Margaret had obviously been shocked by news of Warwick's defeat but had been considerably comforted by the level of support flooding in to her from all parts of the south-west. Edmund Beaufort, duke of Somerset, who had met her at Weymouth, was an experienced commander, and the death of Warwick at least had the advantage of making the politics of the whole enterprise somewhat simpler. Margaret was very cautious and as her army moved eastward she sent decoy detachments towards London to try to throw Edward's spies off her trail. She was keen to move north from the county of Somerset instead of directly east towards London. She knew that Jasper Tudor was busy raising troops for her in Wales and there might be further gains in Cheshire and Lancashire. Her son, the Prince of Wales, might inspire the loyalty of Lancastrians in that area. There was also the matter of the Stanleys. They are curiously anonymous at this time. Thomas, lord Stanley, had supported Margaret and got in the way of the duke of York at various times in the past. He had shifted his allegiances with the prevailing political wind but might provide her with support. The fact that Margaret contemplated heading towards his area of influence at least suggests that she did not expect any opposition from him. In any case Margaret far preferred the north to London.

Edward, having spent five days restoring his army at Windsor, slowly moved up the Thames valley. As April 1471 drew to a close the two rival armies readied themselves for battle. Margaret had been welcomed at Bristol and her forces had emerged refreshed and replenished. Although she had a slight advantage over Edward in numerical terms she was still keen to feint towards London and strike north. Edward was having none of it and suddenly, with great speed, marched to Malmesbury and cut off the northern route. Margaret, for her part, fooled Edward into believing that she was about to give battle at Sodbury; he prepared to meet her army only to discover that she had slipped past him by means of a night march along the banks of the River Severn towards Gloucester. Edward hastily sent a rider to Richard Beauchamp, governor of Gloucester town and castle, to tell him to hold the town against her and thereby prevent her crossing the river. This singular service the governor succeeded in performing, and was knighted shortly afterwards for his efforts. Margaret had to attempt to cross further upstream. By the time her army had reached Tewkesbury it was the evening of 3 May and her men were exhausted. Even if there had been sufficient light to effect a crossing Edward's army was too close to enable it to be accomplished safely. Edward had force marched his own men to within a few miles of the Lancastrians, determined to prevent her escaping north. He had marched thirty miles in a day and taken his men to the limits of physical endurance but his tactical skill had given him the chance he needed. If Margaret had escaped who knows what trouble she would have caused across the land and who could guess how long the next phase of the Wars of the Roses would last? Edward had given himself the opportunity to finally rid himself of the Lancastrian threat.

Both armies rested fitfully during the night, but as soon as dawn broke Edward advanced to Tewkesbury and prepared to fight. He arranged his army into three battalions or 'wards', the vanward, or vanguard, on the right, the mainward, which now took the centre, and the rearward which now moved up to take the left. This was to be Richard, duke of Gloucester's command. (The chronicler believed Richard commanded the 'vaward' but his description places him on the left.) Edward took the centre and on his right he placed Clarence, but with Hastings in command. The apportioning of responsibility tells us what everybody already knew: Richard was utterly trustworthy and highly competent, despite his youth and relative inexperience, while Clarence needed to be chaperoned and monitored. Edward, whose personal courage and brilliant swordsmanship had thrilled the chronicler at Barnet and set an inspiring example to his army, now unfurled his banners and advanced:

> [The King] dyd blowe up the trumpets; sommytted his caws and qwarell to Almyghty God, to owr most blessyd lady his mothar Vyrgyn Mary, the glroious martyr, Seint George, and all the saynts; and avaunced, directly upon his enemyes.[20]

Edward opened up with a barrage from the guns he had brought from Windsor. These, with archers in support, inflicted heavy casualties on the Lancastrians. In their vanguard, Edmund, duke of Somerset was so frustrated by the devastating ordinance deployed against him and the fact that his men were hampered by hedges and ditches, that he launched a full assault right at the centre of the Yorkist army. The *Arrival* was not sure whether this was prompted by the storm of missiles 'which they wowld not durst abyde' or an act of 'great harte and corage'. Either way, his charge smashed into the left of Edward's own battle, glanced off the right of Richard's, and caused dreadful confusion. Somerset found himself directly confronting Edward. The chronicler described Edward resisting 'full manly' and pushing Somerset's forces back up a small hill 'with great violence'. For the first time we have an accurate account of Richard's behaviour in battle. Richard moved to his right to join his brother and help in repulsing the Lancastrian thrust: 'The Kynge ... set forth even upon them and ... put them upe towards the hyll, and so also, the Kyng's vaward, being in the rule of the Duke of Gloucestar'. Richard had not only acquitted himself with great distinction, he had made a major difference to the outcome.

Just as the fighting reached its climax, two hundred mounted spearmen, who had been posted by Edward in woods on his left flank, charged into the fray. Having been given the rather desultory task of preventing an ambush they were keen for some real action and, seeing Edmund Beaufort's men in front of them, knew that they could get some. The Lancastrian line gave way under the pressure of the combined efforts of Richard and Edward and with the additional impetus of the spearmen. This was the first time Richard had been able to see how effective horsemen might be in battles of this kind and the experience may have had a lasting influence on him. Lord Wenlock, right in the centre of the Lancastrian vanguard, was killed. John Courtenay, earl of Devon, and John Beaufort, marquis of Dorset and brother of Edmund, fell in the ensuing rout. Prince Edward had been with Lord Wenlock and tried to make good his escape but 'was taken, fleinge to the towne wards and slayne in the fielde'. The last direct descendent of Henry V was thus unceremoniously despatched. As they fled, many of the Lancastrians could find no escape. Ahead of them was the River Avon, where many drowned, but the majority of the casualties were hacked down before they got there in what is still called the 'Bloody Meadow'. Some fled to the sanctuary of the nearby abbey but this proved to be a deadly mistake. A clever lawyer in Edward's company explained to him that the abbey did not possess the necessary franchise to enable it to give protection 'for any offendars agaynst theyr prince havynge recowrse thethar'. Edward did not wait to enquire more fully into the ancient rights of sanctuary but ordered the fugitives to be dragged out and executed as traitors. The *Arrival* is keen to emphasise how kindly and reverently Edward allowed the bodies of the massacred to be buried decently and the author chooses not to dwell on the appalling violation of the abbey's sacred precincts. The abbey was considered to have been so badly polluted that day by the spilling of blood that it was reconsecrated a few weeks later by the bishop of Worcester.

John Warkworth's *Chronicle* adds some details concerning this unsavoury episode. He described how Edward had burst into the abbey with his bloody sword drawn but that a priest, who happened to be celebrating mass while twelve thousand men were killing each other outside, bravely stood in front of the king and held up the 'host', the consecrated bread, the body of Christ, and declared that, in the name of the sacrament, Edward should pardon those cowering behind the altar. Edward agreed; the Lancastrians, including Edmund Beaufort, surrendered themselves. John Warkworth's account thus shows Edward not only violating the rights of sanctuary, but also traducing the sacrament and breaking his word. It is this sort of testimony, written by a supposedly learned scholar, the master of Peterhouse, Cambridge, that makes use of the original sources such a tricky business. He appended his chronicle to another one at some point after 1473. As he lived until 1500 he may have altered his text after Henry Tudor came to power in 1485. The fact is, his praise for Edward is tempered by strong Lancastrian sentiments and, whenever he can, he strikes out at Richard. Reading his text one would not have guessed that Richard was present at the battle at all. It is also strange that he should have so carefully listed the names of all those who thought they had been pardoned by Edward but were executed two days later. Who would be interested in such a list, one wonders? It is not only Edward and Richard whose reputations were subtly undermined by Warkworth; he blames the death of Prince Edward on Clarence. The prince was slain 'whiche cryede for socure to his brother-in-law the duke of Clarence'.[21] The fact that Clarence had married Warwick's daughter, Isabel, and that Prince Edward had just married the other daughter, Anne, to cement Warwick and Margaret's new friendship, did indeed make Clarence the brother-in-law of Edward. The only purpose for presenting this unlikely battlefield encounter is to suggest that Clarence not only killed the young man begging for help, but also broke some sort of family bond as well.

With this sort of reporting we have to tread warily, alert to the possibility of some serious doctoring of the text, but also keeping an open mind about the details it offers. Warkworth proceeded to implicate Richard in two dark deeds performed shortly after the battle.

The first involved the suppression of a rebellion by the Bastard of Fauconberg. The man who gloried in this appellation was Thomas Fauconberg, the illegitimate son of William Neville, Warwick's uncle. He was therefore a cousin of Warwick. He raised a considerable force from Calais and from Kent and marched on London. Joined by all kinds of peasants and merchants, farmers and sailors, carrying anything from good swords to pitchforks, he attacked the city and, despite well organised resistance, did a fair amount of damage in Bishopsgate and Aldgate and also on Southwark Bridge. The Croyland chronicler witnessed the damage, reporting that 'the vestiges of their misdeeds are even yet to be seen upon the said bridge, as they burned all the houses which lay between the draw-bridge, and the outer gate, that looks towards the High Street of Southwark, and which had been built at vast expense'. The 'Bastard' was held off by Anthony, earl Rivers, until King Edward arrived. News had begun to reach the rebels, most of whom probably just wanted to get their hands on a bit of London plunder, that King Edward had just won two outstanding victories and killed Warwick and Prince Edward. They also heard that the duke of Somerset had been executed and the Lancastrian cause was in ruins. As Edward's victorious army approached, the Londoners, led by Rivers, drove the rebels out. The Croyland chronicle clearly relished the spectacle: 'then might you have seen all the remnants of this band of robbers hastening with all speed to their ships and other hiding places.' The rebels out of London, they still posed a threat: Fauconberg had a fleet of about forty ships, and Edward chose a pragmatic approach, offering Fauconberg a pardon in return for submission. On 27 May the rebel leader duly accepted the offer and surrendered his fleet to Richard, duke of Gloucester. In September, despite the pardon, he was executed. Warkworth is quick to pin the blame on Richard and at the same time highlight the immorality of the proceedings: 'for anone after, by the Duke of Gloucetre in Yorkeschyre, the seide Bastarde was behedede, notwithstondynge he hade a chartere of pardone'. Shortly after this statement Warkworth described the 'Bastard' very much alive and being taken around Kent by Edward, presumably to encourage any remaining rebels to surrender. Fauconberg was indeed put to death later in the year, possibly because of further indiscretions, but there is no evidence that the man who originally arrested him was anywhere near. Fauconberg was executed in London and his head displayed on London Bridge looking towards Kent.

Richard was constable of England, which explains why many of these judicial proceedings fell to him, particularly if they involved high treason. After the battle of Tewkesbury, Richard presided over the execution of the captured rebels, including that of Edmund Beaufort. Later Tudor historians made much of this as it provided such an early example of the brutal savagery of Richard. The truth is that the proceedings in the marketplace at Tewkesbury were conducted in a proper and judicial manner. Richard was accompanied by the duke of Norfolk, marshal of England, in a properly constituted commission. Most of the rebels were indeed beheaded, no doubt providing some entertainment for the townsfolk, but some, such as Sir John Fortescue, adviser to Margaret, and Henry VI's lord chief justice, were pardoned. The difference between the sentences was simple: those who had previously received pardons from Edward, but had reneged on them, were executed, while those who had not, now received them.

Edmund Beaufort, duke of Somerset, was the son of the Edmund Beaufort who had died fighting valiantly for the Lancastrians in the first battle of St Albans. His brother, Henry, had been killed at Hexham in the same cause. There was not the remotest possibility that men like this would sit down and drink a glass of wine and share a joke with a Yorkist. They got precisely what they expected, and would have reciprocated given half a chance.

With Edmund Beaufort's death the rather troublesome descendants of John of Gaunt's mistress, Katherine Swynford, were left thin on the ground. Her daughter Joan had married Ralph Neville and spawned Warwick's family. Only Warwick's daughter Anne was to live in to the next reign and even she did not survive long. All that remained of the proud Beaufort clan was a cousin of Edmund named Margaret. She had had a son, just fifteen years old in 1471, who was to surprise most people and become King Henry VII in due course. There are lessons to be learnt here, apart from the fact that Henry Tudor's great-grandfather was illegitimate: royal blood had such a magical power that even a drop of it might get you somewhere. From such a slender thread was a dynasty spun. Having seized power in 1485 the first of that dynasty set about amending the record. Tudor propagandists not only vilified Richard for executing the indomitable Edmund, they also blamed Richard for the death of Prince Edward. At least Warkworth, while trying to implicate Clarence, confirmed that the prince had died on the field of battle. The *Arrival*, writing at King Edward's official behest, puts the blame for all the deaths squarely and unashamedly where it belonged:

> Here is it to be remembered, that, from the time of Tewkesbury fielde, where Edward, called Prince, was slayne, thanne, and sonne aftar wer taken and slayne at the Kynges will, all the noblemen that came from beyond the see with the sayde Edward, called Prince, and othar also theyr parte-takers, as many as were eny might or puissance.

Far more serious is Warkworth's accusation that Richard killed Henry VI in the Tower. Edward arrived in London in triumph on 21 May 1471. All rebellion had been crushed. His policy of restoring Henry Percy to the earldom of Northumberland finally reaped dividends and all was quiet there. There were a few pockets of isolated resistance, such as Jasper Tudor in Pembroke, but these were soon to dissipate. Edward marched in to his favourite city basking in his restored regality and martial renown. At the head of the parade, which contained most of the peers of the realm including five dukes and six earls, was Richard, duke of Gloucester with the king just behind him. At the back of the parade was Margaret of Anjou, a captive at last. She had been arrested by none other than Sir William Stanley the day after the battle of Tewkesbury, seeking the protection of a 'poor religious house'. With her was the newly widowed Anne, daughter of Warwick and future wife to Richard. The two ladies must have made a sorry spectacle. At least their arrest provides a clue as to what the very covert Stanleys were up to during all the excitement. If you can't be present at the battle, and the Stanleys always had remarkably full diaries on the days in question, then the least you can do is hover around to see who wins, step in and bask in reflected glory. For this signal service William was well rewarded, and his brother, Thomas, likewise. They joined the procession through the streets of London and no doubt celebrated like everybody else that night.

Everybody, that is, except the luckless Henry VI. On the very same evening Henry was finally put to death. Few commentators today question the necessity for this action and most agree it should have been done a decade earlier.[22] The *Arrival* covers up the involvement of its patron and tells us that Henry, on hearing the news that all hope had been lost, his wife captured, his son killed, 'he toke it so great dispite, ire, indignation, that, of pure displeasure, and melancoly, he dyed'. Few possess the requisite naïveté to swallow that one. Plenty, however, have accepted Warkworth's dark hint:

> And the same nyghte that Kygne Edwarde came to London, Kynge Herry, beynge inwarde in presone in the Toure of Londone, was putt to dethe...beynge thenne at the Toure the Duke of Gloucetre...

Warkworth was probably repeating a rumour he had heard. Philippe de Commynes certainly heard it:

> if what was told me was true, after the battle was over, the Duke of Gloucester slew this poor King Henry with his own hand, or caused him to be carried to some private place, and stood by himself, while he was killed.

None of the chroniclers liked the fact that Henry had been killed. It would have made no difference to their views to have pointed out to them that his survival had already cost thousands of lives. It would not have made an iota of difference to remind them that dishonour and disgrace abroad had brought violence and disorder at home and that both had led to poverty, trauma and misery for countless individuals and their communities. What mattered to them was that Henry was a king. To kill a king was to strike at the very heart of the cosmic weal upon which the health and prosperity of the whole body politic depended. God was a mysterious presence who might be invoked in prayer and appeased through worship. His saints mediated his power and his priests communicated his grace. Since biblical times when the children of Israel had called upon God to give them a king, the lord's anointed was sacred. He might be bad, like Saul, or sin, like David, but he had been anointed by the prophet according to the will of the Lord. Only God could authorise his removal. To lay a hand on a consecrated king was to commit sacrilege.

The Croyland chronicler expresses the dichotomy perfectly. Edward was a 'renowned conqueror and mighty monarch whose praises resounded far and wide throughout the land'. The very next sentence he reports Henry's death:

> I would pass over in silence the fact that at this period King Henry was found dead in the Tower of London; may God spare and grant time for repentance to the person, whoever he was, who thus dared lay sacrilegious hands upon the Lord's anointed! Hence it is that he who perpetrated this has justly earned the title of tyrant while he who thus suffered had gained that of a glorious Martyr.

The body was then displayed in St Paul's and, according to Warkworth, also at Blackfriars. Warkworth added the morbid detail that the dead king bled on the pavement in both places. A solemn funeral barge then conveyed the body to Chertsey Abbey, ten miles upriver. The Croyland chronicler had more to say about Henry:

> How great his deserts were, by reason of his innocence of life, his love of God and of the Church, his patience in adversity, and his other remarkable virtues, is abundantly

testified by the miracles which God wrought in favour of those who have, with devout hearts, implored his intercession.

While remembering that these chroniclers were ordained clergymen we should also remember that the Croyland scribe had seen royal service at Edward's court and must have been aware of the political realities. You can't have two kings. Perhaps the resolution to the problem of eulogising Edward without imputing the sin of regicide to him lay in the simple artifice of blaming Richard. If Richard killed Henry then not only was Edward innocent of the crime but Richard's character could be besmirched with the sin of regicide.

This would also explain why the Croyland chronicle hinted that Richard had been responsible for the death of Prince Edward: 'there were slain on the queen's side, either in the field or after the battle, by the avenging hands of certain persons, prince Edward, the only son of king Henry'. These smears and the poisonous tone infecting them could only have come from a prejudice or an agenda. The agenda of the later writers is clear enough. Henry Tudor needed more than a battle and a thin trace of royal blood to shore up his shaky credentials; defame Richard and Henry becomes a saviour. This does not account for the poor reputation Richard seems to have attracted during Edward's reign, as illustrated, for example, by the hostility of Commynes. We may never know the answer to this question. It might be that Richard was unfortunate in the commentators with whom he was blessed and that they do not represent the general view. It may also be that when trying to retain a veneer of civility while brutal savagery is being committed, the chroniclers found a useful foil in Richard.

Richard had certainly shown in the previous two years that he could do his brother's business efficiently and without sentimentality. The king needed men such as this. He had been in the thick of battle in which violent men had tried to kill him. He had seen all the hopes of his house dashed and then valiantly restored. The legacy of his father, who had died fighting for strong rule and the restoration of honour, now rested on his brother and Richard had shown that he cared about it very much. Whatever they said about Richard no one ever accused him of cowardice or incompetence. His loyalty to his brother, shining more brightly against the treachery of Clarence and Warwick, was unquestioned.

There now began what has become known as 'the second reign of Edward IV'. It began in a flurry of frantic activity in the confines of Westminster Abbey in April 1471. Edward had himself hurriedly re-crowned before seeing his wife and their new-born son, and then marched out to face Warwick. It heralded the advent of twelve years of peace and prosperity which few would have been bold enough to predict at the time. The author of the *Arrival*, signing off his account, his commission fulfilled, could only hope 'that peace and tranquilitie shall growe and multiplye...from day to day, to the honour and lovynge of Almiyghty God'. His invocation brought its reward: more than a decade was to pass before that tranquillity was shattered again.

Richard at eighteen was a man. He had come of age and was about to establish himself as the king's lieutenant in the north. This would involve building up the support of the leading gentry families and strengthening their ties with the court and with royal administration. One family, the Stanleys, would not be very happy about this and their quarrel with the Harringtons was to become the crux of the power struggle about to ensue. Richard was about to become dangerously embroiled. At the battle of Tewkesbury, knighted for valour on the field, had been Robert Harrington. The Harringtons knew that this service to Richard's family would always be remembered and would bring them 'good lordship' and powerful protection. The problem was Stanley.

# SIX

# FEUD

At the height of Warwick's rebellion Thomas Lord Stanley had tried to take the castle of Hornby by force and had been prevented from doing so by James Harrington and his guest, Richard, duke of Gloucester. If Richard had travelled from Middleham, where he had been living under Warwick's tutelage, he would have found that the most direct route to Hornby would have been to strike east and follow the valley of the River Ure. Galloping hard, the journey would have taken him three or four hours, provided he could get fresh horses on the way. The valley of the Ure is called Wensleydale, after the village of Wensley near Middleham, and is famous for its cheese. Today the trip takes less than an hour by car, but only the careworn worker delivering goods or meeting clients would aim to rush along the route. The leisurely stranger with time to admire the views might need all day. The journey would have taken Richard through a breath-taking scene of swirling, strangely carved hills covered in dark green pasture and purple heather. When his horses halted for drink, beyond the chatter of his attendants, he might have heard the sounds of bleating sheep, startled larks and the low roar of cascading water. Moving up the valley the views became dra-matic, the hills arduous, the river swift, and everywhere was stone: the timeless stone of the Yorkshire Dales in a patchwork riot of higgledy-piggledy dry-stone walls dividing every field, providing every bridge and sheltering every barn, every shed and every home from the long, dark winters.

Past Aysgarth Falls to the town of Hawes, between Great Shunner Fell and Wether Fell, up past Hardraw Force to Garsdale Head, Richard would have made his way to the very western edge of the Dales and the craggy defiance of the village of Sedburgh, wrapped up in weathered walls. From here he would have turned south and followed the valley of the River Lune to Kirby Lonsdale. This was Lancashire, and the journey to Hornby was almost done. As he followed the valley he would have been conscious of the strength and breadth of the River Lune on his right as it flowed towards the Lancastrian coast just a dozen miles away. As he approached the village of Hornby he would have passed the striking remains of a Norman motte and bailey castle called Castle Stede: an impressive man-made hill dominating the valley below. The castle he was about to visit was strategically placed to command the same route. The remnant of the Norman earthwork was a powerful reminder of the dauntless confidence and practical skill of those ruthless conquerors. Richard was descended from that stock. A direct descendent of Henry II, the first Plantagenet king, Richard Plantagenet would have known that his great Angevin forebear Henry, ruler of Britain, Ireland, Normandy, Anjou, Aquitaine, Maine and Poitou, was himself the great-grandson of William the Conqueror. At Richard's adopted home, Middleham castle, he could look out directly on another huge mound of earth left by the Normans and dominating the surroundings. Middleham, impressive, impregnable and built to last for ever, stood in a Norman shadow. The Normans had introduced the art of castle-building and used it to enforce their will wherever they went. They chose their sites with unfailing precision. The medieval descendants of those structures, so familiar to Richard and so essential to the exercise of lordship, administration, justice and control, formed the very fabric from which the politics and social structure of the medieval world were made. Few could see in Richard's day that between the prototypes left by the Normans and the complex, mighty structures of more recent days, the entire history of castles as military strongholds was contained. Castles had had their day. For over four hundred years they had shaped the world about them, both physically in their visual impact, and subliminally in their demonstration of authority, but all that was about to end. As Richard passed the Norman motte, descended into Hornby village and began the climb up to Hornby castle, a wry smile may have crossed the face of the ghost of William the Conqueror. While he had stood at the beginning of an era, Richard would fall at the end. With the advent of artillery and the abolition of private armies, the Tudor era would see these formidable garrisons begin a transformation into stately homes.

Hornby sat on a hill overlooking the confluence of the River Lune and the River Wenning. It was built to control the route from Lancashire northwards, through Penrith to Carlisle and on to Scotland. From its keep, over four hundred feet above sea level, James Harrington and Richard would have seen the River Lune winding its way to Lancaster, a dozen miles downstream, and beyond, to the sea at Morcambe Bay. Built on an outcrop of rock bounded by the two rivers, it presented an impregnable obstacle to any who dared challenge it. A third river, the Hindrush, provided extra security at the base of the hill and the woods behind completed the quintessential defences. No wonder Stanley wanted it. A regional magnate intent on carving a pre-eminence for himself between the sea and the western Pennines could not tolerate such a powerful challenge to his dominion. Hornby might be a useful outpost for a Yorkshire knight, a valuable addition to the properties of a northern lord, but its proximity to the Dales was only a minor part of its attraction. It was near to the lakes of Cumbria and the important western march, it was close to the administrative capital of Lancashire with the sea beyond, but above all it was on Stanley's very doorstep. If Hornby was to be held by anyone apart from Stanley himself then that person would need to be a very close associate who was indelibly identified with his interests.

The obstacle faced by the Stanleys, and the Harringtons who were to be their challengers, was that in the county palatine of Lancashire, a man holding Hornby, who also possessed rights in the duchy, would be too strong to shift. Duchy of Lancaster officials, and there were many of them, from bailiffs to receivers, foresters to stewards, auditors to sergeants, escheators, attorneys, chamberlains and clerks, all answered to the duchy council alone. They held their posts and exercised their functions by virtue of the royal prerogative. They had authority and tenure that no man could challenge because it came from the king. This was his land. The real problem faced by Stanley was a structural one: he could never become the magnate of the region he so desired to be, like his aristocratic equivalents in the earldoms of Northumberland or Somerset, the dukedoms of Norfolk or Buckingham, or any of the regions of England outside the duchy of Lancaster. Those lords were the highest authority in their regions because they represented the king. In the county palatine of Lancashire it was the officials of the duchy of Lancaster that represented the king for the simple reason that the king himself was the duke of Lancaster. When Henry Bolingbroke, the duke of Lancaster, had seized the throne in 1399 he had kept the duchy as his own personal possession, perhaps as an insurance policy in case he lost the throne himself. It was the base from which he had launched his bid for the throne and he could not bear to part with its resources and financial security. It had passed through hereditary succession to Henry V and so to Henry VI. They were Lancastrian kings because their father and grandfather had been the duke of Lancaster, and so were they. Edward, of course, was a Yorkist, and not the duke of Lancaster.

Rather than surrender the duchy to the heirs of Henry VI, Edward kept it as a crown possession and his first Parliament in November 1461 ordained the Lancastrian lands to be 'corporate and be called the Duchie of Lancastre'. Edward declared that he held it to himself and his heirs by right of inheriting the crown. Having overcome the tricky legal problem of transferring ownership of the duchy of Lancaster to a Yorkist, Edward cleverly kept it separate from all the rest of his dominions so that he could directly reap the financial benefits of its very efficient administrative system. Although he was king, he was also, in a sense, the new duke of Lancaster. Like all his magnates who rendered revenue and service to him by virtue of their territorial hegemonies, Edward could behave like a duke in the duchy territories and take the money directly for himself without an intermediary. To do this, all the historic privileges, jurisdictions, liberties, and franchises that would normally belong to the lord of the region, had to be retained by the king. In a county palatine the lord exercised the 'lawes roiall' through his officials: the chancellor and chief officers. By the authority of letters patent under the Great Seal of England there was ordained another seal called the seal of the duchy of Lancaster, with a chancellor to keep it and officers and councillors to rule the particular officials, ministers, tenants and inhabitants under its authority.[1]

Stanley was hedged in by duchy officials. Men exercising these functions were only answerable to their immediate superiors who, in turn, were only answerable to the duchy council. Stanley needed to be on that council if his authority in the north-west was not to be seriously undermined. Edward needed a powerful figure in the area to get things done locally and so he allowed Stanley to retain his recently acquired office of receiver in Lancashire and Cheshire. This was not sufficient to guarantee a place on the council, though it was very influential and the administrative officers, the receiver general and the clerk of the council would be expected to take his views into account. The man who dominated the council was the chief steward. This had been Warwick until his fall and for a brief period after the battle of Tewkesbury, Thomas Lord Stanley had replaced him. That brief spell in elysium was cut short on 19 June 1471 when Richard, duke of Gloucester, was given the job. The Harringtons, doggedly clinging on to Hornby against the repeated efforts of Stanley to get them out, suddenly found themselves with a familiar and very powerful friend. It was inevitable that Gloucester, seeking to establish his own regional power base, should see the Harringtons, his personal retainers, as kindred spirits in the fight to challenge Stanley's vexing ambitions. The Stanley-Harrington feud would engulf him in the end, but joining in seemed to make good sense at the time.

To fully understand why the Stanleys and their neighbours, the Harringtons, fell out so dramatically we have to go back seventy years to the beginning of the fifteenth century. In the reign of Henry V we find the grandfathers of the two protagonists both serving the Lancastrian king and co-operating with each other very happily. They were important members of the upper gentry, of equal rank and with very close family ties. Sir William Harrington served Henry V while he was still prince of Wales and, when he became king, Harrington became one of his knights and his banner-bearer. At the great English victory at Agincourt in 1415, it was Sir William Harrington who stood by the king's side and held the royal banner aloft. His grandson, James, may well have done the same for Richard III at Bosworth seventy years later. Sir William was made a knight of the Garter in 1417 in recognition of his outstanding military service. The Order of the Garter was already the senior order of chivalry and the award was an honour of such distinction that his descendants were unlikely to forget it. He went on to serve in the king's subsequent campaigns in France and was seriously wounded at the siege of Rouen in 1419. He recovered and lived another twenty years with the satisfaction of having had a good war. He married Margaret, the daughter and heiress of Sir Robert Neville of Hornby in Lancashire; this was how the Harringtons acquired Hornby.[2]

Sir John Stanley meanwhile was also serving Henry V and led a company of Cheshire men at Agincourt. Although the details of his service are hazy, he was certainly present with the king in France in 1418.[3] He had inherited a strong tradition of royal service from his father, also called John, who had died in 1414. The first Sir John had been richly rewarded by Henry IV for not intervening when he was busy usurping the throne and overthrowing Richard II. The great Stanley tradition of remaining aloof at moments of crisis and then backing the winning side seems to have begun here. Certainly the first Sir John was richly rewarded by Henry IV and went on to serve him with distinction. He had acquired Lathom in Lancashire, which was to become the fulcrum of Stanley power in the years ahead, by marrying Isobel Lathom, and spent the rest of his life adding to its already extensive manors and appurtenances. Like William Harrington he served in the household of the prince of Wales, and managed to become the steward of the household. He lent Henry IV money and was rewarded with lands and preferment. This was the way to go about climbing up the social scale. He was promoted from the prince's household to become steward of the king's household. For helping to suppress the rebellion of Henry Percy and Glendower, he received estates in Cheshire and north Wales. He was granted the Isle of Man in 1405, confiscated from Henry Percy, and the grant was made perpetual the following year. With the island came the title king of Man. The Stanleys were careful not to use this title in England for fear of offending their royal benefactors, but their sense of predominance over the other gentry families in the north-west was no doubt inflated by the acquisition. John Stanley I was also made lieutenant in Ireland for a time which gave him immense freedom of action and the opportunity to build up a fiercely loyal band of local retainers who could serve him in Ireland and profit with him. Needless to say the Irish hated Stanley.[4]

Sir William Harrington was appointed to the important duchy of Lancaster post of steward of Amounderness Hundred. The hundreds, of which there were six in Lancashire, were ancient administrative districts formerly consisting of a hundred households. The hundreds of Lancashire in the fifteenth century covered large areas of about 150,000 acres and contained thousands of households. Amounderness hundred had the River Lune as its northern boundary and therefore included Hornby. To the north was the hundred of Lonsdale and to the immediate south the hundred of Blackburn. Sweeping across Blackburn and into Amounderness was the forest of Bowland. The stewards of the hundreds and the foresters had influential judicial and financial responsibilities that gave them power in these regions. They answered only to the chief steward or the master forester. It is not difficult to imagine the frustration of Thomas Stanley when Richard of Gloucester was appointed master forester of Bowland in his stead, with James Harrington as his deputy (1471), and also chief steward in Lancashire, again in Stanley's place. But this is to look ahead. The grandfathers of Thomas Lord Stanley and James Harrington could not have predicted that their grandsons would have clashed with such bitterness. They co-operated throughout the early years of the reign of Henry VI. In 1425 we find them adjudicating a lawsuit together concerning lands in Yorkshire and Lancashire. In the 1430s they were asked by the government to negotiate a settlement between the two most powerful men in the kingdom: the dukes of Gloucester and Bedford, brothers of Henry V. William Harrington and John Stanley II served on many commissions together in Lancashire and left no trace of any discord or difference between them.

The striking thing about this period in the history of the relationship between the two is their equality in rank and in social status. This was confirmed by the marriage of John Stanley II to the sister of William Harrington. When Isabel Harrington married John Stanley the two families were both members of the upper gentry with influential connections at court and substantial properties in the north. As the clouds darkened over the sunny friendship and co-operation which had characterised the connections and discourse between their grand-fathers, it is sometimes easy to forget that Thomas Stanley's grandmother was a Harrington and that Thomas was a cousin of James Harrington.

John Stanley died in 1437 and William Harrington in 1440. They were both succeeded by their eldest sons, both called Thomas. Co-operation between the families continued but they began to take different directions. Thomas Stanley had been returned as MP for Lancashire in 1433, with his uncle William

Harrington. In 1443, 1446 and 1449 he was returned as MP again, this time with his first cousin Thomas Harrington. A hint of future trouble can just be discerned in the duchy appointments that Henry VI's government began to give Thomas Stanley. In 1439 he was appointed steward of the duchy of Lancaster north of the Trent, and in 1443 he became receiver general of the whole duchy.

The 1439 appointment is strange because the office of steward had traditionally been hereditary. William Harrington was ailing and surrendered the office, but both his own son, Thomas, and Thomas Stanley were about thirty years of age. Thomas Stanley was preferred over Thomas Harrington for what had been a Harrington post. It would seem that Stanley was busy strengthening his local connections while Harrington was looking further afield. Stanley was appointed constable for Chester in 1437, for instance, and lieutenant-justice for Cheshire, Flint and north Wales while his Harrington cousin followed his father into royal service in France. Thomas Harrington married the daughter of Lord Dacre, acted as deputy to the earl of Salisbury as steward of Amounderness, and, increasingly identified with Neville interests, he seemed keen to have a distinguished military career, as his father had done, and perhaps bridge that invisible gap between his inherited gentry status and the glittering and expansive world of the aristocracy. In the 1440s it would have baffled Thomas Harrington to be told that his cousin would get there first and, even more remarkable, that the Harringtons never would.

With the war going badly in France and, with the English triumphs of the great Henry V being gradually reversed under his inept successor, Henry VI, the Lancastrian government was seriously short of money. Rather than the martial heroes of the older generation, such as William Harrington, the royal coffers needed hard-nosed money-makers who could rake in the profits of local lordship. Stanley was not only receiver general of the duchy of Lancaster, he was also controller of the royal household. This put him in a very fortunate position and he was able to use the un-appropriated revenues of the duchy and allocate them to the household. He could also make substantial profits himself and invest them in leases and other forms of landholding in the northwest. The Lancastrian regime found him useful for harnessing the resources of the palatinates of Chester and Lancaster, and the principality of Wales. They also found his ability to raise loyal tenants an invaluable boon when military strength was required to suppress rebellion and disorder at home. In the aftermath of Jack Cade's rebellion in 1450, Stanley led troops from the north-west to ravage Kent.[5] The duke of York was to make an uncomfortable discovery of Stanley's military strength in Lancashire and Cheshire when Stanley impeded the duke's progress through the counties on his return from Ireland.

Stanley had opted to make himself useful to the court and to profit from it, but there were risks involved in this game. When the duke of Suffolk was overthrown in 1450-51, Stanley suffered a reverse. Suffolk was the ideal sort of man to work for. He exercised the king's authority and tried to make the day-to-day running of the court function 'as best it could without a real king, but he had to pay for support and reward men like Stanley who provided it. At the same time the realm at large and the war abroad were neglected, but that was not Stanley's concern. Not, that is, until Suffolk fell. In October 1450 Stanley had to surrender the justiciarship of north Wales and, the following year, the lordship of Mold. Parliament then demanded his removal from the royal household and he was replaced as controller by none other than his cousin Richard Harrington. Richard was the son of William Harrington's brother, and so was a cousin of Thomas Harrington as well. For the first time, and somewhat indirectly, Stanley found himself put out by a Harrington. He was able to recover soon enough; he had a stable power base and a strong and disciplined following. Not only did the power he had already accumulated make it impossible now for any government to ignore him, but he also proved adept at manipulating political crises and turning them to his advantage.

While it was possible for Stanley to remain aloof and distance himself quickly from factions, the Harringtons were, conversely, moving further into the Neville orbit and through it towards the duke of York, the husband of Cecily Neville. York himself had good reason to mistrust Thomas Stanley after what had happened in 1450. The duke had been returning from Ireland and, after landing at Beaumaris, had found 'gangs' at Holt and Chester attempting to intercept him as he marched to his estates on the Welsh border. The duke was, understandably, infuriated by this incident and blamed it on the most powerful man in the locality. In a petition to the king he specifically mentioned Sir Thomas Stanley who had 'lain in wait for to hearken upon me'. Stanley was stripped of his offices but probably knew that this was just a forlorn attempt by the court to placate the duke and, given time, they would come knocking on his door again.

With the duke of York at the centre of power it was the turn of the Harringtons to prosper. Stanley, as he expected, was needed as much by the duke of York as he had been by Suffolk and Somerset. So it was that Thomas Stanley and Thomas Harrington found themselves working together again. During the king's mental illness and York's first 'protectorate', they were required to attend upon the duke to help him disperse insurgents of the Percy family who had raised rebellion in Yorkshire and Lancashire. They were instructed to discourage any movement 'in the contree where as ye be'. Stanley could command greater forces than the Harringtons, however, and at the first battle of St Albans in 1455 he used them to good effect. The duke of York had been summarily dismissed from his protectorate by a somewhat restored Henry VI. At the same time the earl of Salisbury, Richard Neville senior, was also dismissed as chancellor. Summoned to attend a great council at Leicester the duke of York and his brother-in-law, Salisbury, suspected the worst and armed themselves. Richard Neville junior, Warwick, joined them and the Wars of the Roses began. The Yorkist victory at St Albans was a close-run thing. There were only about two or three thousand men on either side. Stanley was on his way to support the Lancastrians but unfortunately got delayed in heavy traffic. If he had turned up it is likely that his numbers alone would have swung the affair in favour of Somerset and the court party. By 'waiting on events', a technique he would now specialise in and refine into a high art, he capitalised on the outcome. York recognised that Stanley could easily have prevented a Yorkist victory. Shortly afterwards Stanley was at the heart of the government again as a member of the king's council and chamberlain of the household.

In November of the same year Stanley's fortunes reached heights which placed him forever above and beyond the reach of his gentry rivals. He became a peer of the realm and, in January 1456, was summoned to Parliament as Lord Stanley. In the struggle for power between Margaret of Anjou and Richard, duke of York, Stanley had made himself indispensable to both sides. York had been exercising his second protectorate at this time but he was away in Devon when Stanley was elevated and it is more than likely that it was Margaret who had ensured he received his peerage. She entrusted the counsel and care of her precious son, Edward, to Stanley, and installed him as a knight of the Garter in May 1457. One might pause to consider the decline of the dignity of this noble order of chivalry in the years since William Harrington had won his garter in France with Henry V. Here was Stanley basking in an honour many brave and faithful servants of the state had failed to achieve. And for what? Margaret needed him and considered him to be a trusted Lancastrian. He certainly deserved some award or other for managing to improve both his Lancastrian and his Yorkist credentials at the same time.[6]

As a peer of the realm Stanley had advantages over men like the Harringtons that, unless they too were ennobled, could never be overcome. His presence at court, in Parliament and on commissions gave him access to considerable patronage and influence. Above all, he could join the aristocratic marriage market and consolidate the rank of his successors. Before he died in February 1459 he had managed to secure for his eldest son, also called Thomas, the hand in marriage of Eleanor Neville, daughter of Richard Neville, the earl of Salisbury, and sister of Richard Neville, the earl of Warwick. When his father died, Thomas, the second lord Stanley, was well placed to advance the Stanley cause, providing he proved as adroit as his father in negotiating the stormy waters of the growing conflict between the houses of York and Lancaster. The younger Thomas first appeared in the records in 1454 as one of the squires of Henry VI. He would have been familiar with the royal household and the nuances of court protocol which were to prove invaluable in the years ahead. After the death of his father he was suddenly confronted with his first serious test.

The accord between Margaret and the duke of York broke down in the summer of 1459 and Margaret and the Lancastrian lords brought immense pressure to bear on Stanley. The earl of Salisbury was mobilising his forces in Yorkshire and heading south-west to join the duke of York at Ludlow. Margaret appealed on behalf of the prince of Wales for the loyalty of the men of the palatinate of Chester and ordered Stanley to intercept the duke of York. The earl of Salisbury was also in touch with Stanley, his son-in-law, and expected him to throw his forces in against the Lancastrians. Here was precisely the tricky sort of situation which the first lord Stanley had used so brilliantly to his own advantage. He would have been immensely proud of the marvellous way the second lord Stanley upheld the family tradition as the rival armies clashed at Blore Heath in September 1459. Though only a few miles away with 2,000 men, Stanley held off, sending letters of support to Salisbury before and after the battle and sending his excuses to Margaret. His brother, William, committed himself to the winning side and threw in his men as Salisbury gained the advantage. Both behaved in exactly the same way as they were to behave at Bosworth over a quarter of a century later. The lords and commons who met at Coventry in November to attaint the Yorkists were furious with Stanley's behaviour and strongly petitioned the queen to strip him of all his possessions. She could not bring herself to do this and protected him from being added to the list of twenty-six. The earl of Salisbury believed that Stanley had assisted him and ensured that he had achieved his objective. Stanley had managed to remain popular with both the Yorkist leaders and with Margaret of Anjou.

On the night before the battle of Blore Heath a cameo was played out in Salisbury's camp which gives us an insight into the characters of the Stanley and Harrington families. Salisbury received a letter from Thomas Stanley expressing support. The earl, having read it, sent it to his lieutenant. This trusted officer was none other than Thomas Harrington. Thomas showed it to the rest of the company with the words 'Sirs, be merry, for yet we have more friends.' Thomas Harrington, brave, committed and trusted, was at the heart of the action, while Thomas Stanley, powerful, untrustworthy and uncommitted, hedged his bets and kept everyone guessing. For their respective endeavours at Blore Heath, Stanley escaped the censure of the queen and prospered under the Yorkists, while Thomas and his second son James were captured in the confusion afterwards and imprisoned at Chester. It was only after the Yorkist victory at the battle of Northampton in July of the following year that the Harringtons were released along with two other prisoners who had been captured with them: John and Thomas Neville, sons of the earl of Salisbury and brothers of Warwick. Five months later Thomas Harrington's wholehearted commitment to the duke of York and his Neville kinsmen was to cost him his life. That was the danger that came with fidelity and the heavy price that might have to be paid by those who followed its call during a civil war. It would be impossible to imagine Stanley ever having to pay so much.

We know what Thomas Harrington said when he read the letter Stanley sent to Salisbury at Blore Heath, because it was reported in the Commons' indictment of Stanley in the Coventry Parliament. Harrington's cheerful words (in the original they have a hint of the north about them: Sirres, be mery, for yet we have moo frendis) show that Harrington had no reason to distrust Stanley. Parliament took quite the opposite view. Its petition detailing the manifest treachery of Stanley was rejected by Margaret but accepted by the Court of History. Whoever framed the petition was very clear what Stanley's behaviour revealed about him:

To the King our Sovereign Lord show the Commons in this present Parliament assembled: That whereas it pleased your Highness to send to the Lord Stanley...charging him that upon his faith and allegiance he should come to your Highness in all haste, with such fellowship as he might make, the said Lord Stanley, notwithstanding the said commandment, came not to you....Also whereas your said Highness gave in commandment to your first begotten son, Edward, Prince of Wales, to assemble your people and his tenants, to resist the malice of your rebels, and thereupon the same noble Prince sent to the said Lord Stanley to come to him in all haste possible, with such fellowship as he might make – the said Lord Stanley, putting the said matter in delay, faintly excused himself, saying he was not ready. Howbeit, of his own confession, he had before a commandment from your Highness to be ready to come to the same with his said fellowship, upon a day's warning; which delay and absence was a great cause of the loss and distress of your said people at Blore Heath.[7]

The outraged Commons also reported that the letter Stanley had sent, which Thomas Harrington had showed to his men, had congratulated Salisbury, 'thanking God of the good speed of the said Earl, rejoicing him greatly of the same, trusting to God that he should be with the said Earl in other places to stand him in as good stead as he should have done if he had been with them there'. Students of Stanley military tactics will recognise the phrase 'if he had been there'. He had not been, of course, and despite the Commons begging for his impeachment, he profited in the usual way.

In the following summer, July 1460, the Lancastrians were beaten at the battle of Northampton and the king, Henry VI, captured. Warwick was in charge of the government in London because the duke of York had fled to Ireland after the rout at Ludlow. Warwick obviously enjoyed the experience of running affairs. While he was waiting for the duke of York to arrive he could do pretty much as he liked. The king was too enfeebled to protest, even had he wanted to do so. Warwick was to specialise in pliant kings, and become rather upset when they proved to be less than pliant. The Harringtons were not present at the battle of Northampton and there is no evidence that the Stanleys were either. Thomas Harrington and his second son James were otherwise occupied, imprisoned at Chester castle from where they were not released until November 1460. The prior of Durham wrote to Thomas shortly afterwards, 'thankyng God that ye are past the trouble that ye were in'. Defenders of Thomas Stanley have not been able to provide an equally impressive alibi. He didn't participate in the Yorkist victory at Northampton but in the aftermath, with Margaret and her son hiding in Wales and the duke of York once again in charge, he made himself useful to the winning side and was soon engaged on Yorkist business. The duke of York arrived from Ireland and one of the first things he did was to issue instructions to Stanley to release those imprisoned in Chester castle who had been captured after Blore Heath. Stanley, now a regular member of the duke of York's council meetings in London, complied. There must have been a strong whiff of irony in the breeze as Stanley freed James Harrington from prison. These two men were about to engage in a bitter, and ultimately deadly feud. If either of them could have foreseen the events that were about to unfold they may have attempted to settle their personal differences in the precincts of Chester castle. The sight would not have been a pleasant one.

The duke of York immediately began to use Thomas Harrington, and his second son James, on important commissions in the north. On 12 November 1460 they were instructed to gather all the loyal men of Westmorland, Cumberland and the adjacent counties, to prevent and resist all unlawful gatherings. Thomas Harrington had become a loyal and trusted servant of the duke of York with growing responsibilities for security. As the duke left London for the last time, to confront Margaret in the north, Harrington was high on a chronicler's list of those accompanying the duke: 'The duke of York, the earl of Salisbury, the earl of Rutland, and Sir Thomas Harrington, with many more knights and squires and the great people with them ... departed out of London toward York'.[8] With a Yorkist triumph that would see the advent of the reign of a Yorkist king only three months away, Thomas Harrington and his offspring were perfectly placed to reap the benefits of their valuable contribution to

Edward IV's pulpit in Fotheringhay church

Fotheringhay church

Fotheringhay church from the remains of the castle

Hornby castle

Hornby castle from the River Wenning

Hornby castle keep, rebuilt by Edward Stanley

Hornby castle keep, rebuilt by Edward Stanley

Middleham castle in Wensleydale

KING RICHARD III
YOUNGEST SON OF RICHARD
DUKE OF YORK AND CICELY
NEVILL WAS BORN IN THIS
CASTLE OCTOBER 2ND 1452

RICHARD III SOCIETY
HON. SECRETARY MISS E NOKES,
4 OAKLEY STREET S.W.3 NN.
TEL: 071-351-3391.

*Above:* Plaque recording the birth of Richard at Fotheringhay

*Left:* The east window at Fotheringhay church, showing the royal arms and Richard's white boar badge

The gates and churchyard at Fotheringhay

The remains of the great hall at Middleham castle

The remains of the motte at Fotheringhay castle, with the church in the background

The royal arms with the white boar of Richard to the right, on the pulpit at Fotheringhay

View down the Lune Valley from the keep at Hornby

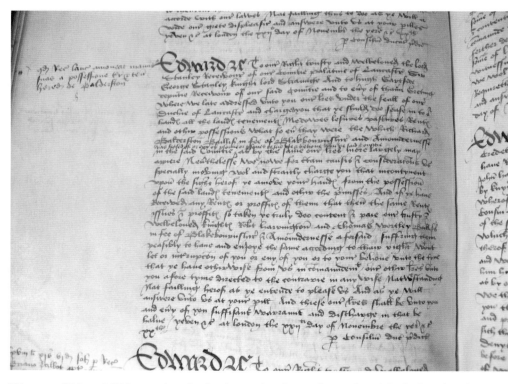

Warrant of Edward IV instructing the Stanleys to hand over the profits of the bailiwicks of Blackburn and Amounderness to Robert Harrington

the Yorkist cause. Their elevation to the peerage would have been a formality after the battle of Wakefield and they might have begun to emulate the rise of Stanley, who, incidentally, seems to have been conveniently delayed in London. As it turned out, all the hopes and realistic aspirations of the Harringtons, so nearly fulfilled, were dashed to pieces.

Defeat in the battle of Wakefield on 30 December 1460 only temporarily hampered the progress of the Yorkists. The duke of York and his son Edmund, earl of Rutland, were killed, along with Richard Neville, earl of Salisbury, and there can be little doubt that this was a tremendous blow to the house of York, but Edward, York's eldest son, would avenge them all and be crowned king in March 1461. The same could not be said of the fortunes of the Harringtons. Fighting with the duke of York, Thomas Harrington's oldest son, John, was killed and Thomas himself, badly wounded, died the next day. The reason why these deaths were so debilitating to the Harrington cause was because Thomas Stanley was so determined to profit from them. Thomas Harrington's surviving sons, James and Robert would do their best to stop him, and succeed for a while, but, in the end, their struggle proved futile. The opportunity for the Stanleys to monopolise power in the north-west was one they were quick to exploit.

Despite the family tragedy at Wakefield it would still be possible for the Harringtons to recover their losses provided that they could hold on to the family seat at Hornby and the inheritance of their father, Thomas. James Harrington immediately took possession of Hornby, and with it the two daughters of his brother John, Anne and Elizabeth. These two girls, described as 'infants' in one source, were to be crucial in the feud that was about to begin. They were the heiresses of Thomas and John Harrington. Because John had died without sons, these girls would jointly inherit the family estates and pass them on to the ownership of whomsoever they married. Stanley was determined to get possession of them in order to marry them to his own family and so see the castle at Hornby with its commanding views and strategic importance fall under his control. James Harrington was equally determined to prevent him from doing so. James, in a later indictment, was accused of imprisoning his nieces and unlawfully occupying Hornby. He argued, fairly plausibly, that because John had died on 30 December during the battle of Wakefield while his father survived until 31 December, for that one day James had been the oldest surviving son of his father and therefore his heir. When his father died of his wounds the next day, he, James, should have lawfully inherited the Harrington lands, so he argued. The daughters of John were not, therefore, the heirs of Thomas.

James might have been able to get away with this argument if the king had supported him as fully as Richard, duke of York, would have done. Edward, however, unlike his father, was king. Other considerations would have to come into play. The Harrington inheritance was safe for only as long as it took for Edward to realise, as others had done before him, that he needed Stanley. In their efforts to resist the grasping hands of Thomas Stanley, the Harringtons were to come into conflict with a power in Lancashire too well entrenched for them to resist without royal help, but it was a power that Edward needed for his own purposes.

While James was taking over Hornby and securing the custody of his nieces, Robert Harrington was also doing his bit. Shortly after his father's death at Wakefield, he married Isabel Balderston. Like the Harrington girls, two Balderston sisters, Isabel and Joan, had recently lost their father, William Balderston, who had died without male heirs. The Balderston girls would, therefore, jointly inherit their father's legacy and pass it on to their husbands. Robert Harrington married Isabel and John Pilkington married Joan. The Balderston inheritance was well worth having. It consisted of the hereditary bailiwicks of Blackburn and Amounderness. A bailiwick was simply the jurisdiction of a bailiff, and so by their marriages, Robert Harrington and John Pilkington had garnered the right to appoint the bailiffs in two of the six hundreds in Lancashire, a vast area covering a third of the county, and all the rights that went with the offices. Bailiships came with the financially lucrative rights to collect rents, fees, fines and confiscations, but also with the power associated with patronage, appointments, arbitration and dictating the terms of leases. Thomas lord Stanley was the receiver to whom all the dues should have been ultimately destined. If the receiver was at loggerheads with the bailiffs there could be considerable trouble. Robert Harrington had not only intruded significantly onto Stanley's patch, he had done so at the same time as strengthening his ties with another powerful Lancashire family. Robert Harrington's second cousins, Margaret and William Harrington, had both married brother and sister Pilkingtons in a double wedding. John Pilkington and his brother Charles were, like the Harrington brothers, to become close associates of Richard, duke of Gloucester. Before that they would do well under Edward after supporting his progress to the throne. Four months after his victory at Towton, John Pilkington was appointed 'esquire of the body' for life with substantial revenues to support him. At the same time he received the rights over certain custom in the port of London, profits from farms and issues in London and Middlesex, the leases of four shops and a hospice in London, and the revenues from certain subsidies. His brother Thomas was granted substantial estates in Ireland. In 1462 John Pilkington continued to receive marks of royal favour with the grant of certain manors in Yorkshire and further privileges. It was this John who was to be appointed to assist the young duke of Gloucester when he received his first political responsibilities in Wales during Warwick's rebellion. The Pilkingtons and the Harringtons now formed a formidable combination against the Stanleys. If the Harringtons had suffered a serious setback at Wakefield they were clearly not going to slink off into a corner and sulk about it. James and Robert were doing their very best to shore up the family legacy and to consolidate their position in the north-east of Lancashire.

There were now two contentious issues causing tension between the Stanleys and the Harringtons. On the one hand, James Harrington had seized his father's property at Hornby which Stanley coveted, and on the other, Robert Harrington had gained for himself control of significant authority in Blackburn and Amounderness, much to the consternation of Stanley. While Stanley could not as yet get his hands on the Harrington seat at Hornby and the two female heiresses, he certainly had the strength and power to prevent Robert from interfering with his own rights as receiver. In the duchy of Lancaster records in the National Archives we can trace the power struggle taking place in Lancashire in the warrants and letters issued by the king under the duchy seal. Edward IV needed the help of both the leading Yorkist gentry families who had participated in his family's struggle for power, and also the leading magnate in the region who could raise a substantial body of men. The bitter dispute between the Harringtons and the Stanleys was not one he wanted and was one he found very difficult to deal with. He couldn't really afford to offend either party, and it is evident from the records that the feud was not only baffling and unwelcome to him but also slipping out of his control. On 2 July 1462 Edward issued a warrant to Giles Elston, a man otherwise unknown, but in all probability a crony of Stanley:

Edward R to Giles Elston, gretyng. For asmoche as it is understonde to oure Counsell of oure Duchie of Lancastre upon the sight of certain sufficient and credible evidence shewed unto oure said Counsell as touching the offices of Bailywyk of Amoundernesse and Blackbourne within oure Countie palatyn of Lancastre, that the heres of William Balderston Esquire and theyre auncestors in the tymes of oure noble progenitours by many yere passed, have had and occupied as there olde enheritaunce, the Bailishippe of Amoundernesse and Blackbourne aforsaide, and have continually accoumted for the saide offices by all the tyme aforsaide, Wherfor the premises considered we woll and straitly charge you that all suche somes of money appertenyng unto us whiche ye have received, levied or in any waye taken of the saide offices ye do deliver, or do to be delivered unto the saide heres or to thair deputies. And also that ye surcesse in occupiying the saide Bailyshipps or any parcel of theyme, any commandment, letter patente or thing by us afore this tyme to you made or graunted notwithstanding, as ye will eschewe oure grete displeasure.[9]

This warrant had been preceded by letters patent sent to Giles in February 1462 ordering him to hand over the offices of bailiff to their rightful owners but also revealing that violence had been used to prevent Robert Harrington from getting them. The king states that the bailiffs appointed on behalf of the Balderston heiresses, 'were by you put oute ... and that you wrongly by grete force and might took the money of the saide offices'.

The 'bailyship', the office of bailiff and the rights and authority pertaining to it, were obviously profitable to the holder, and also to the king. This was not simply a case of an illegal seizure by Stanley of someone else's rights, but also a reduction in the profitability of the offices to the crown. The unlawful seizure had been brought to the duchy council's attention by Robert Harrington, but the lack of revenue coming in to the coffers of the duchy had made them act. The pressure Edward was bringing to bear on Stanley related as much to royal rights, and more specifically to his financial rights, as it did to the rights and wrongs of the case. Edward was busy attempting to exploit all his duchy rights for financial gain at a time when the royal coffers were badly in need of funds. He did not set out to offend Stanley but he did want money. Robert Harrington was no doubt willing to pay the necessary price to gain control of the bailiwicks but had little success; it is clear from the records that the orders issued in the name of the king were blatantly ignored. It was eighteen months later, in February 1464, that the king issued a warrant addressed to the man who really mattered, Thomas lord Stanley, ordering him and the sheriff to take possession of the two bailiwicks and then to release them to Joan and Isabel and their two husbands. With rebellion rife in the north in 1464, Edward could not afford to get on the wrong side of Stanley and the saga continued. Stanley may have been assisted by members of the duchy council: Warwick, for instance, was chief steward until his fall and brother-in-law of Stanley, and the three chancellors during Edward's reign, Say, Fowler and Thwaites, all worked closely with Stanley in his role as receiver. Stanley managed to evade the royal commands and retain the rights and all the profits accruing from them in Blackburn and Amounderness.

As late as November 1480, almost twenty years after Robert had married Isabel, Stanley was still preventing him from enjoying his rights. A warrant was issued at that time repeating the earlier demands. John Pilkington had died and Joan had remarried: her new husband, Thomas Wortley, joined Robert Harrington in the struggle to get their wives' inheritance. Again the king ordered Stanley to 'seize' what belonged to Harrington, in order to give it back to him; the convenient fiction that it wasn't Stanley robbing Harrington was maintained for the purposes of protocol:

> Edward R. To oure trusty and welbeloved lord Stanley, Receiver of oure countie palatine of Lancastre, Sir George Sharpe and Hugh Garside deputie receivers, to seize into oure hands all the landes tenements etc and other possessions of Richard Balderston

bailiff in fee of Blackbournshire and Amoundernesse. And if you have received eny rentes or profits of them, the same rentes, offices and profits so taken ye fairly doo content and paie oure trusty and welbeloved knight Robert Harrington and Thomas Wortley Bailiffs in fee ... suffering them peaceably to have and enjoy the same according to their right withoute let or interrupption of you or eny of you or to your behove unto the tyme that ye have otherwyse from us in commandment... not failing herof as ye entende to please us and as ye must answerre unto us at youre peril.[10]

Another warrant a few months later gives us an insight into the power of the bailiffs, and also the financial incentive for the king to sort the dispute out:

Edward R. To oure trusty and welbeloved Robert Harrington and Thomas Wortley knights and baillifs in fee of Blackbourneshire and Amoundernesse in the Countie of Lancastre Greetyng. Concerning the grete somes of money sette in arrears from the said bailiwicks ... And therefore entending to save youre right in their behalf and to avoid the perills that to us might growe by sufferaunce of the non paiment of oure said tenure Wol and straitly charge you that ye or your deputie baillifs there require every of your said tenants within your said bailiwicks to make payment in oure right according to the custom and value of their tenures. And such as refuse that to doo within a resonable tyme to them limited, ye do put such of their lands and tenements in seasure in oure name as they hold from us within your said bailiwicks, and them to kepe in oure hands till of oure duties we be fully satisfied and contented. To be assisted by mayors, sheriffs, bailiffs, constables and all other officers of oure said duchie.[11]

If the 'bailiffs in fee' could be assisted by such a cast of supporting characters and had the authority to seize lands and tenements, and profit from them in lieu of payment, it is no wonder that Robert Harrington and Thomas Stanley vied for possession. At this late stage Richard duke of Gloucester was attempting to help Robert, and in retaliation the duchy council complained to the king that the duke and his associates were wasting the assets of the duchy, but once again national politics intervened.[12] The king was preparing for war with Scotland and needed all the protagonists of the feud, the Stanleys the Harringtons and perhaps we should now include the duke of Gloucester, to arm, raise troops and render service against a common enemy.[13] Edward could always put sentimentality aside and the needs of state first. Perhaps he had not invested as much personal energy as Richard had in attempting to support their natural allies and resist Stanley. When Richard seized the throne in 1483 the Balderston inheritance dispute still lingered on, but an ominous warning signal must have been sent to Stanley when Richard moved the chancellor of the duchy, Thomas Thwaites, into another post outside the duchy and replaced him with his own man, Thomas Metcalfe.

Stanley's dispute with Robert Harrington may have demonstrated the simmering tension created across the region by his feud with the Harrington brothers, but it was a mere sideshow compared to his determined fight to wrest Hornby castle from James' grip. James Harrington, having occupied the castle as quickly as he could, and taken possession of the two little Harrington heiresses, was adamant that nothing would induce him to surrender the Harrington patrimony into the grasping and untrustworthy hands of Thomas lord Stanley. The whole country was still in a state of some disorder following Edward's victory at the battle of Towton. A long period of misrule under Henry VI had come to an end but the legacy of uncertainty, violence and abuse of power by dominant local lords was still rife in many areas. Edward's authority at ground level depended on the men who ruled each region. His efforts to intervene in the Harrington-Stanley feud show how lawless and violent some areas could become when the most powerful men in those localities were at war with each other. On 31 May 1463 a warrant was issued under the seal of the duchy of Lancaster and addressed to the justices of the county:

> For asmoche as oure humble servant James Haryngton, knight, and many others divers persones to the nombre of iii ti [30] and more whose names been contained in a schedule Whiche we send yow herin closed, were wronfuly indited at oure town of Preston in Amoundernesse in oure countie aforsaide...as we been informed, we therefore wol and straitly charge yow that of all maner processe herafter to be made or awarded against theym or any of theym by reson of the saide inditement, ye surcesse and put in respite.[14]

This was followed on 10 July by a far more comprehensive order to the justices to stop all proceedings against any person whose indictment was made in the previous reign. It would seem that malicious prosecutions were being brought in Lancashire and some, purporting to have been initiated in the previous reign, were designed to trap Edward's loyal supporters in the county. On 16 July Edward issued a warrant specifically naming the culprits:

> Edward R. To oure justices of assise and coroner of oure countie palatyn of Lancastre gretyng. For asmoche as Thomas lord Stanley and Richard Carlill oure attorney and justice of the peace of oure said countie satte at oure town of Preston in Amoundernesse in the saide countie [February last], And than and there they made an inpanell and returned afore theym in the name of Sir John Assheton knight, late sheriff of oure saide countie, 24 personnes, menyell [menial] men and servants of the said lord, of the whiche panel and sitting the said sheriff knewe not, nor precept or commaundment had from the said lord nor from us to retorne...maliciously

withoute cause and against oure lawes, endited oure true lege man James Haryngton knight and the said sheriff and many othere personnes to the nombre iiii ti or more of ryatours confederatys and othere offences...we therefore wol and charge yow that ye surcesse of making any processe, writte or warrant against the said James, the saide sheriff or any other personne or personnes at the saide day and place endited afore the said lord....[15]

In order to bring false charges against James Harrington and attempt to arrest him and put him away, Stanley had been forced to resort to gangsterism. James had powerful friends: the sheriff, Assheton, was an associate of the Harringtons, as was another sheriff, Sir Nicholas Byron. The two other sheriffs on the list at this time were John Pilkington and his cousin Thomas. In order to proceed against James Harrington in the county court Stanley would have needed the compliance of at least one of Harrington's friends or relatives just to convene the court. Not being able to proceed lawfully, Stanley trespassed on the king's rights by acting without the knowledge of the royal officials, and for good measure, indicting the sheriff himself. James and his brother were still in the king's favour and he managed to rescue them from harm, but he did not proceed against Stanley. No action was taken against him for subverting the king's laws and abusing his prerogatives. Stanley and his henchmen were throwing their weight around in Lancashire, almost with impunity, and much of it was directed against the Harringtons.

The dispute over Hornby castle was a complex one. Before his death at the battle of Wakefield, Sir Thomas Harrington had issued a will and conveyed his property to trustees. These granted the custody and marriage of the elder daughter Anne to Geoffrey Middleton, esquire. In March 1463 the trustees, who included the Archbishop of York and Sir John Huddleston, granted James Harrington possession of Thomas's estates at Brierley in Yorkshire. While James was happy to inherit his father's estates in Yorkshire it was evident to him that by the same right he should inherit all his father's property, and this included his nieces. Geoffrey Middleton paid good money for the wardship and marriage of Anne, rendering 100 marks for 'one of the daughters and heirs of John Harrington, knight, deceased, a minor and in the king's custody'. He never got Anne. Considering that she must have been about two years old in 1461, and her sister only one, perhaps she was better off staying at Hornby. It may have become a little noisy from time to time but James had fortified it considerably. We should certainly treat with the utmost suspicion the plaintive appeals addressed to the king in the name of Anne and her sister. They protested that their uncle Sir James 'took the said complainants and them kept as prisoners contrary to their wills, in divers places by long space, intending the utter destruction and disinheritance of the said complainants'. Both Stanley and Harrington were needed by the king and he was reluctant to get involved. He needed Stanley to present him with large sums of money from the receipts of the duchy of Lancaster. These had to be collected by Stanley and any shortfalls paid by Stanley himself. This guaranteed the king essential funds, and no doubt profits for Stanley, but no one else had the same authority or strength in the region and Stanley had to be content.

Harrington was also useful. In 1465, after the battle of Hexham, Henry VI was left to wander around as a fugitive. The capture of the deposed monarch was of the greatest importance to Edward IV and he was delighted when his rival was discovered and captured at Waddington Hall in Yorkshire. There was something of a tussle involved, with Henry's partisans putting up resistance and Henry temporarily escaping into some woods. The detection of the ex-king, and the operation to arrest him and bring him into custody, was led by James Harrington. Edward IV showed his gratitude by granting James the castle, manor and lordship of Thurland 'for his good service in the capture of Henry VI'. James was also given all the properties belonging to Richard Tunstell, a rebel, including 'all land, rents and services in the town of Tunstell, ditto the towns or hamlets of Wharton, Overborowe, Netherborowe, Oldwenyngton, Gale and Ergham, co. Lancaster, and Bentham, Burton and Lonnesdale, co. Yorks, and the town of Holme in Kendall, co. Westmorland'. All this was confirmed by an Act of Parliament in July 1465 and further grants were recorded in the Patent Rolls throughout 1465 and 1466.[16]

The balance finally shifted in Stanley's favour when both Thomas and his brother William were needed to resist the threat of a Welsh rebellion. William Stanley was instructed to issue proclamations throughout the county of Cheshire, where he was the sheriff, to prepare all able-bodied men to resist the rebels believed to be gathering in the south of the county. Shortly afterwards Thomas Stanley was able to achieve his goal and secure a grant of the Harrington heiresses. In October 1466 custody of Anne and Elizabeth, with the lands and castle of Hornby, were officially transferred to the wardship of Stanley. In the final analysis, the threat of insurrection, and Stanley's ability to deal with it, outweighed the loyalty, service and usefulness of the Harringtons, at least in the eyes of this particular king. The next king would take an altogether different view, but the calamitous consequences of it perhaps endorsed Edward's judgement.

The judgement in favour of Stanley was by no means the end of the matter. James Harrington refused to surrender Hornby and kept his nieces with him. James was defiant and, it would seem, prepared to go to any lengths to prevent Stanley from getting his father's lands. If the Harrington loyalty and good service were to be rewarded in this despicable fashion then what was it worth? Perhaps the king could tell him. Exactly how far was Edward prepared to go to endorse the overweening ambition of Thomas Stanley, a man who had hardly lifted a finger when it really mattered? Thomas Harrington had died with the king's father, and their sons had been killed together: what kind of gratitude was this? Was this the reward a king made for faithful allegiance and the ultimate sacrifice? Stanley could go to hell and the king had better change his mind. The king knew the strength of James' views and was understandably sympathetic. He ordered two inquiries, to be undertaken under the arbitration of the earl of Warwick. Warwick was acceptable to both parties and both sides gave substantial sureties. There were to be two inquiries because Edward was determined to get the legal facts of the case and wanted the will of Thomas Harrington investigated, and also the status and eligibility of John and his heirs. Warwick at first found the situation just as difficult as the king did. He also did not want to offend either party, and the legal complexities were quite beyond him. He handed the case over to his deputy, Henry Sotehill. He was able to show in Chancery that the granddaughters of Thomas Harrington were indeed his heirs. They were aged eight and nine at the time of the inquest and Sotehill concluded that they were being held by Sir James Harrington and Sir John Huddleston, with their manors and their lands, unlawfully, without legal title or right. Chancery issued a writ, summoning the parties to Westminster to hear the award, in December 1468. In March 1469 the summons was repeated. James Harrington and his friend John Huddleston, had not appeared, no doubt because the judgement against them also stated that they had been in transgression of the law for eight years. When they did eventually appear, whatever sureties they had managed to obtain for their own safety were ignored and they found themselves temporarily imprisoned in the chancellor's prison in Fleet.[17]

How they secured their release is not recorded but the spring of 1469 was a period of increasing tension at court leading to the outright defiance and rebellion of Warwick in the summer. In the turmoil and confusion of the period from the battle of Edgecote in July 1469 to the battle of Tewkesbury in May 1471, the Hornby inheritance was not on the top of Edward's agenda. Stanley's commitment to Warwick during the rebellion, and the appearance of the king's brother, Richard, in north Wales, Cheshire and Lancashire, allowed James Harrington to continue to occupy Hornby and to resist any attempt to take it from him. When Stanley tried to blast his way in using cannon he was prevented from doing so by James's new friend, Richard duke of Gloucester, who stayed at Hornby during the thick of the trouble. Gloucester's intervention on behalf of James Harrington came at a time when Stanley was still a putative supporter of Edward and the king was considerably alarmed to find that his brother had confronted Stanley in such a remarkable way. He had enough disorder and rebellious rioting on his hands without two of his magnates having a spat; the consequences for law and order could be disastrous. King Edward sent instructions to his officials:

> To the sheriff of York. Order to cause proclamations to be made. The king our sovereign lord, straightly commandeth that no man of whatsoever degree under colour of any wrong done unto him for any matter of variance late fallen between his brother, the duke of Gloucester, and the lord Stanley, distress, rob or despoil any of his subjects: but that he that shall find himself wronged, shall sue his remedy by the course of the king's law or by none otherwise, upon pain of death.[18]

This order was dated 25 March 1470, the day before a warrant issued by Richard showed that he was at Hornby. By October of the same year the Stanley v Harrington fixture in which Richard had made a guest appearance, had plummeted down the scale of royal concerns. Harrington's problems in retaining ownership of Hornby were as nothing compared to Edward's difficulties in holding on to his kingdom. The problems Edward had encountered at York gathered momentum and span out of control. Edward found himself without a kingdom and enjoying the hospitality of the Hollanders. When he was joined by his brother Richard it was clear that James Harrington was going to have to fend for himself. The Readeption of Henry VI on 6 October 1470 made things far worse because Stanley had openly joined the new regime. Here was a golden opportunity for the master of opportunism. Remarkably, and with tremendous tenacity, James held on to Hornby. Stanley probably felt he had bigger fish to fry for the moment and he does not appear to have taken much advantage of the temporary collapse in James' support. We have already seen how Edward's return was greeted by James Harrington's speedy and welcome contribution of assistance at Nottingham, and the importance of that support, but it now becomes clear why James' unshakeable loyalty to the Yorkist regime never wavered. By Edward's side at Nottingham was Richard, duke of Gloucester, and he had become James Harrington's 'good lord'.

Once restored, and with most of his enemies slaughtered at Barnet or Tewkesbury, Edward must have been irritated to hear that the Hornby dispute was still unresolved. Warwick had been killed and so, in the absence of his arbitrator, Edward decided to settle the matter himself, once and for all. Stanley, needless to say, had been restored to favour and had managed, particularly in his arrest of Queen Margaret, to appear helpful. Before the first year of Edward's second reign was out Stanley had managed to become steward of the royal household, a post of enormous trust and responsibility. He had followed his father's footsteps into the inner circle of the royal household. Edward, in other words, continued to back Stanley despite his manifest treachery the year before. Stanley's wife, Eleanor Neville, had conveniently died by the time Edward began his comeback reign and this at least cleared Stanley of the Neville taint. He promptly married Margaret Beaufort, the mother of Henry Tudor. Ironically this was not seen as a threat by Edward, but more a strengthening of Stanley's Welsh connections which would enable him to deliver reliable forces across the north-west. Edward was looking to the future and there would be a need for such powerful regional lords to support his projected wars with France and Scotland. Hornby castle was neither here nor there. No one recorded the duke of Gloucester's reaction to the news that Thomas lord Stanley had married the mother of the only surviving Lancastrian claimant to the throne. Perhaps he wasn't too surprised.

In April 1472 both Thomas lord Stanley and his adversary James Harrington were bound for the sum of 3,000 marks while the king made a decision over Hornby. The decision would include the disposition of the castle and the 'manors, lands, rents, reversions and advowsons of abbeys, priories, churches and chapels' of the late Thomas Harrington and his son John. It would also include the wardship of the two heiresses, still described as 'infants', though Anne must have been about thirteen and Elizabeth twelve.[19] The king meant business and heard the evidence in person. After having done so and without further ado he awarded the lot to Stanley. It might seem remarkable and unsatisfactory to us that such an unreliable toady should profit so notably and at the expense of a family who were about to lose their most important property because of their unflinching loyalty to Edward's family. Our difficulty is that we don't understand fifteenth century *realpolitik* in the way that Edward did. Even his brother, Richard, had difficulty understanding some aspects of it, though perhaps not all.

A year passed before Edward heard, to his utter astonishment, that his award had been completely ignored by the Harringtons and that they had turned Hornby castle into a warzone ready to repel the entire might of any magnate foolish enough to attempt to set foot in it. It is a wonder that this matter came to the notice of a busy king, though the rumour that the steward of the household may have mentioned it over supper one evening must surely be discounted. History cannot tolerate malicious gossip. If Edward had chanced to casually ask Stanley, as the solicitous royal servant had been attending to his personal needs, how he was enjoying the view from Hornby, then perhaps it is possible that the king may have assumed from Stanley's downcast expression and the momentary loss of his ready smile, that all was not as it should be ten miles or so up the River Lune from Lancaster. Edward ordered writs to be sent to the sheriff of York and to the sheriffs of Westmorland and Cumberland. He could not afford to be defied in this way by anybody:

[To the sheriffs, order to cause proclamations to be made in the matter of the castle of Hornby] Whereas all the castles, manors, lordships, lands, rents, and services with knights' fees and advowsons to churches, which were of John Harrington, knight, son and heir of Thomas Harrington, knight, within the county palatine of Lancaster, came to the hands of our lord the king after the death of the said John and Thomas, and in his hands be yet by reason of the minor age of Anne and Elizabeth, daughters of John and heirs of Thomas Harrington; as by divers inquisitions taken within the county palatine and into his chancery returned plainly appeareth; and howbeit that our lord king being so possessed of the said castles etc. and the issues, profits and revenue of the same coming and growing, he by his laws ought to receive; nevertheless James Harrington and Robert Harrington, knights, and also Christopher Persume, priest, gathering to them a great number of evil disposed persons with force of arms arrayed in form of war, having no dread of his laws nor to offend his majesty's realm, now entered into the said castle of Hornby and have stuffed and enforced it with men, victuals and habiliments of war, as the king is credibly informed to his great displeasure, in contempt of his laws, to the worst example to all his well disposed lieges; which his highness will not of his royal duty suffer to remain unpunished. Wherefore our said lord commands that the said James, Robert and Christopher and all other persons within the castle of Hornby, incontinent after this proclamation, without delay utterly depart out of the same, and that they nor any other person thenceforth without a special command of the king, enter into the said castle, upon the faith and allegiance that they owe us, and upon pain of forfeit of all that they may, and their bodies to be at the king's will, and that none of the king's subjects upon the said pain from the time of this proclamation, aid, succour or receive any of the said James etc. in the castle, in keeping it against this proclamation: and further that the said James etc. upon their faith and allegiance appear within fifteen days upon pain of forfeiture, before our lord and his council, wherever he be then, to answer to the things as shall be objected to then and to receive as shall be ordained according to law.[20]

To make absolutely sure that this proclamation was obeyed, Edward sent his brother Richard to enforce it. This was a masterstroke and finally saw the Harringtons surrender their beloved Hornby. Richard had no choice but to obey his brother, and he was the only man the Harringtons could really trust. Richard took his time, and it was not until 1475 that Stanley finally got his way at Hornby, but get his way he did. He also took possession of the heiresses and promptly married them to his relatives in order to gain legal title to Hornby. Anne Harrington was married to Stanley's younger son, Edward, and Elizabeth Harrington to his nephew, John. Edward Stanley and his cousin John were now the joint heirs of Thomas Harrington.

The Harringtons had committed *lèse-majesté* and would have to pay a price. Richard was able to protect them from the full force of the king's wrath and under his lordship they recovered and began to prosper again. In 1479 James Harrington was granted a licence 'to build walls and towers with stone, lime and sand around and within his manors of Farleton, co. Lancaster, and Brierley, co. Yorks, and to crenellate the same and to enclose and impark all his lands, meadows, pastures and woods in Farleton and Brierley'.[21] We also find that James Harrington served on Commissions of the Peace in the West Riding of Yorkshire with Richard, from 1477 onwards. Their friendship and mutual respect grew after James lost Hornby to Stanley. James and Richard had both lost a father and a brother at the battle of Wakefield and that shared loss could not be forgotten, overlooked or swept aside by Richard. He was only eight when that loss had occurred but the year after James Harrington handed Hornby over to Stanley, Richard was to publicly remember his father in a most ostentatious and solemn ceremony. If your family served and died for Richard's father, then your place in Richard's heart was assured.

# SEVEN

# IN MEMORIAM

In July 1476, Thomas Whiting, the Chester Herald, recorded that the bodies of Richard duke of York and Edmund earl of Rutland were displayed in the house of the Mendicant Friars at Pontefract. They had been hastily interred here after their violent deaths at the battle of Wakefield, sixteen years before. Richard duke of York had had to wait three months to be reunited with his head, which had been cut off and barbarously displayed on Micklegate Bar in York. Now, what remained of the duke and his second son, Edmund, lay in state at Pontefract in preparation for the proper funeral they had been denied for so many years. The duke's body was 'garbed in an ermine-furred mantle and cap of maintenance, covered with a cloth of gold'. The hearse blazed with candles and was guarded by an angel made of silver and bearing a crown of gold 'as a reminder that by right the duke had been king'. At a requiem mass held in the friar's church, the duke's youngest son, Richard, duke of Gloucester, acted as chief mourner. He had come on behalf of King Edward to oversee the removal and transfer of the bodies to their final resting place in the family vaults at Fotheringhay.

After mass, the 'chariot' carrying the body of the duke was drawn by six horses covered to the ground with black trappings charged with the arms of France and England. Ahead of these rode a solitary knight bearing the duke's banner with his heraldic arms fully displayed. Immediately behind the hearse, dressed in mourning, rode Richard, duke of Gloucester, Constable of England. He headed a mighty procession of nobles, officers of arms, knights, burgesses and common people. He was not only Constable but also Admiral and Great Chamberlain. The twenty-three-year old Richard, brother of the king, was the most senior ranking lord in the hauntingly sombre crowds which slowly and silently followed the bier. Edward had directed his brother to supervise this stately ceremonial that served to honour the noble progenitor of the royal family and, through the power of ritual and symbolism, to embellish the credentials of the anointed king. Richard followed his father's body for seven days in a poignant solemnisation of his respect and admiration. At every stage, Doncaster, Blithe, Toxford, Newark and Grantham, the hearses and the procession rested for the night in an elaborate and highly organised programme involving every religious house, church, bishop, abbot, monk and nun on the route.

The noble cortege arrived at Fotheringhay on Monday 29 July 1476 to be greeted by several high-ranking prelates, ex-servants of the duke and members of Fotheringhay College. They processed towards the church, the route lined by thousands of spectators, until they approached the long churchyard. The road led directly to the gates of the church, which stands on a crossroad, and the welcoming party could see the magnificent spectacle edging towards them from afar. At the entrance to the churchyard was the king, waiting patiently with Clarence, Dorset, Rivers and Hastings. All other dukes, earls and barons were present, dressed in mourning. As the hearse entered through the massive wrought iron gates, the king 'made obeisance to the body right humbly and put his hand on the body and kissed it, crying all the time'. The procession then entered the church, where the queen and her two daughters, all in black, were seated and waiting with their ladies and gentlewomen in attendance. Two splendid coffins, decorated in beaten gold with the arms of France and England, and covered in black sarcenet (a rich velvet of silk known as 'cloth of majesty') were laid out in readiness, one for the duke in the choir and one for the earl of Rutland in the Lady Chapel. Masses were sung and then the king's chamberlain laid seven pieces of gold in the shape of a cross on the duke's body. On the following day, after a candlelit vigil, three masses were sung before the main service of burial took place and a sermon was preached by the bishop of London. Following this, offerings were made by Richard duke of Gloucester, and by other unnamed lords.

After the funeral people were admitted to receive alms and over 5,000 came to receive them. A dinner was then held in the castle nearby attended by an incredible 20,000 people, some in the castle itself and the rest in the pavilions and tents erected in the castle precincts. The meal cost the Exchequer £3,000. Throughout the herald's account the duke of Gloucester plays a prominent role.[1] As Constable he would have been responsible for organising the spectacle and attending to the considerable arrangements and complex management required for such large numbers, such an extensive journey and all the security and protocol needed for the attendance of so many high-ranking persons. There was more to his presence, however, than the simple discharge of his duties might warrant. This unforgettable display was a very public demonstration of all that Richard stood for. The man whose bones now rested at Fotheringhay was not only Richard's father, he was the last man who embodied the ancient spirit of an earlier age. He had been a man of valour, a man of nobility, a man of principle and a man of virtue. Richard followed his hearse for a week in 1476, but in many ways he followed him all his life.

Almost exactly a year later, in July 1477, Richard made an indenture with Queens' College Cambridge to admit four priests to preach the word of God to the fellows for an annual salary. Among their duties it was stipulated that they should say prayers for a number of Richard's living relatives and for the souls of his departed loved ones. Among these were his brother the king, Elizabeth the queen (and also the foundress of the college), 'the prince and all the kynges childer', somewhat ironic in the light of the fate of two of these 'childer', and for the 'good astate' of Cecily his mother. After this there appears a name which resonates in filial gratitude: 'for the soule of the right high and mighty prince of blessed memorie Richarde duke of Yorke fader to oure sovereyne lorde the kynge and to the sayde duke of Gloucetre'. Similarly, when in the following year Richard founded a college at Middleham for a dean, six priests, four clerks, six choristers and a sacristan, their primary function was 'to do divyne service there daily' and to pray. These prayers were an essential element in the religious conduct and conventional piety of the day.

Medieval cosmology saw the universe as emanating from a creator and being perpetually sustained by His presence. The divine world, with God as king, Christ as his prince on earth, the angels, seraphim and cherubim his ministers administering his thrones, dominions and powers, and his saints reporting and interceding on a regional basis, directly corresponded to and reflected the medieval social and administrative structure. God ran the world in the same way a monarch ran his kingdom. A vital element in the scheme was the continual correspondence between God and his creatures which was communicated by prayer. In exactly the same way that a king could not possibly govern his realm, and thereby ensure the health of the commonweal, without his ministers and counsellors communicating with him, passing petitions to him and returning his judgements back to the people, so the Creator relied on an effective system of correspondence between the divine and the secular worlds. This function was performed by men and women who lived lives apart from the commonalty in order to pass on messages from below and to hear and interpret his instructions from above. These special ones, living according to their vocation and their vows, had their own hierarchy which, like its earthly counterpart, was ordained by God. In the same way that a crowned king had divine sanction to rule his people, who were bound to him by sacred oaths according to rank, so the Pope governed the religious community with his cardinals, metropolitans, bishops and priests. Prayer in the medieval world was as important to each community, and for many individuals, as email and mobile phone technology are for many today. The important thing was that it worked. Prayers sung by trained choristers were particularly effective.

Part of the scheme was the belief that after death, each soul, on its onward journey after leaving its temporary earthly home, could be assisted by the prayers of the living. Every cathedral, church and chapel was a sacred space in which the sound of the names of these departed souls, the smell of the incense, the light from the candles and the thoughts and prayers of their loved ones, reached up to the heavens and that mysterious place where souls gathered awaiting judgement. These prayers were for their benefit alone and helped them find rest. Such prayers, or 'obits' were chanted, usually on a daily basis, in particularly propitious places called 'chantries'. Often these would be within the vicinity of the body of the departed one but this was not essential. Providing that the participants were virtuous, well-trained and meticulous in carrying out their task, the prayers would reach beyond this world and be heard in eternity. There was some doubt about how long a soul would need to spend in the departure lounge of purgatory before receiving its boarding pass and climbing aboard the next flight. There would be the customary delays and the confusing signs and announcements before further interminable and inexplicable hindrances until the final call was heard. Woe betide the unready.

Chantries were seen as vital to the spiritual health of the world and the comfort of the departed. Establishing them was an act of piety, of sacrifice and of charity. Maintaining them and renewing them was as necessary as tending a field or repairing a roof. Life without them was unthinkable and life with them was made more bearable. Their beauty, quietness, harmony and unfailing ritual provided a stability, a peace and a consolation that everyone could experience and enjoy. No one in Richard's day would have believed that just sixty years after the foundation of the college and chantry at Middleham it would be torn down in a whirlwind of destruction, bigotry and greed. Henry VIII destroyed the chantries of England because the Reformation had taken religion beyond such childish superstition and into an age of rational belief. More particularly Henry VIII brought the music and colours, the shapes and movements, the joy and solace of sacrifice, to a deathly silence amid a pile of rubble because he wanted to marry Anne Boleyn, the woman he executed on trumped-up charges three years later for having a girl instead of a boy. It was here in Yorkshire that the forlorn protest known as the Pilgrimage of Grace, clinging on to a vanishing era and desperately trying to stop the bewildering vandalism around it, was so savagely repressed.

In the statutes drawn up at Middleham, Richard stipulated that prayers should be offered:

> ...for the soules of my soverayn lord the King, the Quene, and of me, my wiff, and myn issue after our decesses, and specially for the soules of my Lord and fader Richard Duc of York, of my brethren and susters, and oyer my progenitours and successors, and all Christen soules, in part of satisfaction of suche things as at the dredfull day of dome I shal answere for.[2]

The statutes for the foundations at Queens' College Cambridge and Middleham are rich sources in which to explore the heart and character of Richard. Through them we can begin to understand what he believed in and what mattered to him. There can be no doubt that his father was pivotal in shaping Richard's political views. As constable of England Richard had instructed the heralds to pay tribute to his father's military successes. He wanted it remembered that his father had driven away Charles VII at Pontoise and almost captured the French king in the summer of 1441. He was tremendously proud of this achievement and was aware of how keenly his father felt the humiliating disappointment of the abject defeats of the English in France after he had been dismissed. The only manuscript work known to have been commissioned by the duke of York was Claudian's 'Life of Stilicho' which told the heroic history of one of Rome's last great commanders struggling to defend her frontiers from the encroaching barbarians and constantly undermined by a hostile court party at home. Stilicho's efforts to revive the fortunes of his great country were wrecked by the malicious plotting of his rivals. The duke of York commissioned the work at the end of 1446 when he too had been recalled home and stripped of his command through the pernicious intrigue of his enemies at court.[3] Richard inherited his love of chivalry and martial virtue from his father and not only revered his memory but also longed to finish his father's work in France and return to the glorious days of triumph when English valour was renowned and feared.

Richard's love of chivalry is reflected in his patronage of the heralds and their role as officers of arms. When he was king he granted them a charter of incorporation and gave them the London house of Coldharbour as their headquarters. He was in contact with John Kendale, an officer of the order of the Knights of St John at Rhodes and appointed him to present his obedience to Pope Innocent VIII. The Knights of St John were the extraordinary military-medical-monks who formed the oldest order of chivalry in the world and ran the hospital for pilgrims in Jerusalem as well as defending the Latin kingdom in the east from the Turks. They had been founded during the eleventh century after the First

Crusade and had become a powerful and revered military force by the time that the greatest crusading hero of them all, Richard the Lionheart, launched the Third Crusade. His heart was believed to be buried at All Hallows in Barking and his namesake, Richard III, gave the church his patronage. Almost three hundred years after Richard I's death, his name was revered, his deeds embedded in the collective consciousness, his heroic virtues immortalised in popular ballads. The crusading ideal was very much alive too.

Since the Lionheart's day no self-respecting king could fail to understand that his reputation at home and abroad would always be measured against the bench-mark of Christian chivalry established by Richard I. Edward I had been on crusade when he had become king of England in 1272. Since that formidable warrior's reign the kings of England had had little time, opportunity or inclination to leave their kingdoms and march through hostile mountains and deserts in order to be betrayed by their Byzantine hosts and annihilated by their Muslim adversaries. One or two nurtured the ambition of reviving the crusading tradition with its lure of glory, salvation and miraculous power, but winds in the Channel and a lack of sun cream had prevented them from translating their laudable hopes into reality. One can scarcely imagine Edward II or Henry III leading a great expedition across 1,500 miles of hostile terrain and into Asia Minor to try their luck in Palestine. They would have had problems negotiating their way out of Calais. There were one or two kings that may have had a more realistic chance of wearing the mantle of Richard I; Edward III, for instance, but they were either fighting the French in the Hundred Years War or fighting their own rivals in England. Even Richard I had had to dash home with the job unfinished, his country on the brink of bankruptcy and his French possessions being pilfered by King Philip of France. The one king who had the belief, the charisma and the leadership qualities to launch a military venture of such magnitude was Henry V. His invasion of France, leading to the victory at Agincourt in 1415, may have just been the first stage in his real plan to retake the Holy Land for Christendom. As it happened he died before his intentions were realised though his foundation of a religious house called Syon, the biblical name for Jerusalem, to the west of London, may bear an echo of his dream.

Henry V was an exemplar to Richard as much as Richard the Lionheart was. He had not only revived the memory of English greatness and re-established the mystique of monarchy in his audacious conquests, but he had adopted Richard's father. There was a personal bond between the duke of York and his patron which reinforced the adulation of the great king and the reverence paid to his memory. It may be too far-fetched to imagine Richard duke of Gloucester, as a small boy aged six or seven, listening to his father's reminiscences of the life he lived as a small boy in the household of the incomparable Henry V, but

Richard's father would have been eleven when Henry V died and certainly old enough for the king to have made an impression. When Nicolas von Poppelau, a Silesian knight who visited Richard when he was king, in 1484, described the king of Hungary's great victory over the Turks in the previous year, Richard was moved to exclaim, 'I wish that my kingdom lay upon the confines of Turkey. With my own people alone and without the help of other princes I should like to drive away not only the Turks, but all my foes.' Poppelau was an odd and gossipy diplomat on some sort of nebulous fact-finding mission for Frederick III of Bohemia but his account of his stay with Richard at Pontefract gives us a fascinating insight into the personal life of his host. Von Poppelau was a lover of heroic tales of chivalry and could perform feats of strength himself. He seems to have liked Richard and took his remark about defeating the Turks as a genuine reflection of his noble character. As with most aspects of the life of Richard, historians have wildly differing views about the significance of von Poppelau's testimony, from believing it showed Richard's 'active thirst for warfare' and his 'egocentric echo of Henry V's great dream' to a cuddlier version of Richard as 'a bold romantic'.[4] There can be no doubt, though, that Richard would certainly have liked to rid himself of all his foes by strength of arms. Much of his father's life had been spent in trying to hold on to Henry V's conquests in France. Richard's own life was to show that he inherited his father's diplomatic and military aims. The record of his written and spoken word suggests that he also inherited his father's love of loyalty and of justice and perhaps other, less tangible notions, nurtured in cherishing his father's memory.

Among those whom Richard required the priests at Queens' College to include in their prayers were a group of soldiers who had fought with him and died at the battles of Barnet and Tewkesbury. Prayers were to be said for his family and his ancestors and a few friends who were benefactors of the college, including John Pilkington and John Huddleston, but also for the souls of Thomas Parr, John Milewater, Christopher Worsely, Thomas Huddleston and John Harper 'and all other gentilmen and yomen servants and lovers of the saide duke of Gloucetre, the wiche were slayn in his service'. Six years after Tewkesbury, Richard remembered those loyal servants who had died fighting with him and included them in his prayers. These men meant a great deal to him and their service and sacrifice would never be forgotten. The co-benefactors, John Pilkington and John Huddleston, are also interesting. Sir John Pilkington was an esquire of the body to Edward IV, a sheriff of Lancashire and a justice of the peace in Yorkshire. He was not only a member of the interwoven gentry network that became closely associated with Richard during the 1470s and early 1480s in Lancashire and Yorkshire, but he was also one of those who had suffered in the Yorkist cause. In June 1470 he had been left high and dry by Edward's flight abroad, captured and imprisoned at Pontefract. A contemporary source, unsure about his fate, reflected the danger he was forced to endure by recording that he was 'lyke to die hastily withowte [unless] they be dead'.[5] He was freed on Edward's return, fought for him at Barnet and was knighted at Tewkesbury. He had been one of those who had accompanied Richard on his first commission to enquire into rebellion in Wales in 1469. With his castle at Bury in Lancashire, deep in Stanley territory, his impeccable service in the Yorkist cause, his mentoring of the young Richard in the difficult period of rebellion in 1469 and his valiant efforts on the battlefield on Richard's side, it is hardly surprising that he was a friend of the duke of Gloucester.[6]

There was one other connection between John Pilkington and Richard that brought him within a very close-knit band of trusted associates: he was the brother-in-law of Robert Harrington. John Pilkington's wife was Joan Balderston whose sister Isabel was married to Robert Harrington. John, in other words, shared the Balderston inheritance of the bailiwicks of Blackburn and Amounderness that was causing so much friction in Lancashire. John Pilkington was not only a friend of Richard he was an enemy of Stanley. John was to die in 1479 but his younger brother Charles was to become a knight of the body under Richard and be knighted by him in Scotland. His cousin Thomas, married to James Harrington's cousin, Margaret Harrington, was to fight for Richard at Bosworth. A taste of the relationship between John Pilkington and Richard duke of Gloucester may be glimpsed in a bequest Sir John made to Richard in 1478 of a great emerald, set in gold, which had attracted the duke and for which he had offered 100 marks, a princely sum. Sir John gave it to him as a gift.[7]

The other benefactor mentioned in the indenture was John Huddleston. Here was another stalwart Yorkist member of a gentry clan who not only made considerable sacrifices for Richard and his family but also crossed swords with Stanley. John had been an associate of Thomas Harrington and had been made a trustee of his will before the battle of Wakefield. This was the John Huddleston mentioned with James Harrington in the indictments over Hornby. John had landed up in Fleet prison with James Harrington and had done his best to ensure that Hornby passed to James after his father's death at Wakefield. When Henry Sotehill found against James Harrington in the inquiry into the ownership of Hornby, he had clearly ignored the man who probably knew better than anybody what Thomas Harrington would have wanted to happen to his property. John Huddleston acted as Richard's attorney in the grant to Queens' College and was to go on to fight with him at Bosworth. He had many sons and they, too, became loyal servants to Richard. The eldest, Richard Huddleston, became a knight of the body in Richard's household, captain of Beaumaris and captain and sheriff of Anglesey. John Huddleston junior became an esquire of the body in Richard's household where his kinsman James Huddleston also served. His younger brother Henry was also there when not attending to his important commands in Anglesey and Caernarvonshire. This family exercised authority in north Wales which was coveted by Stanley. Loyalty to Richard duke of Gloucester and difficulties with Thomas Stanley seemed to go hand in hand.

In the list of five men who had died fighting by Richard's side, Thomas Huddleston, another son of the attorney John, appears. John also had connections with another of those named, Thomas Parr, who was killed at Barnet. Thomas Parr's brother William was to become Richard's lieutenant-warden of the west march and John Huddleston his under-sheriff. This William Parr of Kendal had another brother, John, who fought with him at Tewkesbury and was knighted. William Parr had been with James Harrington when they appeared at Nottingham to greet the returning Edward, with 600 men, and so help him win back his throne.[8] The other men who died in the battles of 1471 and were enrolled in the Queens' College charter, were members of Edward's household who had been with Richard on that first commission in Wales. There is something touching about Richard's commitment to the memory of these men. In a way he was repaying a debt he owed them. This was good lordship in action. To those who gave him service Richard would reciprocate with his lordship; those who died in his service would not be forgotten. Richard attracted loyalty and gratitude in the north because he repaid service and took care of his retainers. There was more to this, however, than advertising his gifts and renders in order to strengthen and attract loyal ties. Richard cared about these people; he valued them and looked after them in life and in death. These were the relatives of the men who were to ride with him at Bosworth Field. A close-knit group united by family, geography and mutual interests, their loyalty to Richard was to be outflanked by the self-interest of Stanley.

The prayers recited for these men in perpetuity had to be offered by priests and choristers of exemplary character and holiness of life and also addressed to certain saints. The provisions Richard made in these matters tells us a little more about him. At Queens' the saints to be venerated were Saints Anthony, Ninian and George. At Middleham the saints whose days were to be principle feast days were exactly the same, with the addition of Saint Cuthbert. All these saints were popular in the late middle ages but they have particular relevance to the north and also to the house of York. They are as much personal and local as they are conventional. Saint Anthony was a fifth-century hermit of Roman Egypt. He popularised asceticism, established the first rule for the solitary life and was considered to be the patriarch of monks. His life was characterised by extreme austerity, having spent twenty-four years in complete solitude in the Egyptian desert. The connection with the house of York seems to stem from the fact that it was said that the only company he kept in the desert was a wild boar. The story went that when the demons attempted to overthrow Anthony's virtue they commanded all the beasts to threaten him, but the wild boar refused. The boar was a symbol, therefore, of the rejection of evil and the acceptance of good. The association of the boar with the city of York, the Roman town of Eboravicum, made Saint Anthony the ideal choice for Richard.[9] Saint Ninian was another saint with strong northern associations. He had been the 'Apostle of the Picts' according to Bede, and made his base at Whithorn in the western march. Richard was warden of this region and Saint Ninian was the patron saint. His *Life* had been written by Abbot Ailred of Rievaulx in the twelfth century and his cult was very popular in the north.[10]

Saint Cuthbert was another very popular northern saint, as indeed he still is. Associated particularly with Durham and the eastern march, he was the patron saint of Middleham College and when Richard's own son was installed as prince of Wales, Saint Cuthbert's banner was displayed with that of Saint George. Cuthbert was not only revered for his simplicity of life and his asceticism, so typical of the Celtic Church, but also for the protection it was believed that his coffin and his incorrupt body provided against the Vikings. The miracle of the body which would not decay and the long journey of the coffin from Lindisfarne to its final resting place in Durham was a legend which lived in the hearts of every child of the north. Prayers to Cuthbert always worked and his benign influence and protection were felt across the region. The struggle of the monks who fled from Lindisfarne and protected his body from the marauding Norsemen was vivid in the collective consciousness of the north. He was a symbol of northern identity, national defiance against invasion and the triumph of Christianity over paganism. Richard's choice of Cuthbert was a demonstration of his identification with the north and his adoption of its values and beliefs.

Middleham was also dedicated to Saints Alkelda and Mary. Saint Mary is addressed as 'His Blissid moder our Lady Seint Marie, socour and refuge of all sinners repentant'. All saints played a role in interceding between man and God, but Mary was the most important when it came to the hope of remission of sins. This dedication does not demonstrate that Richard was conscious of being any more of a sinner than the next man. Living on earth involved sin and it was best to take no chances. Saint Alkelda was a very local saint, already the patron of the church at Middleham, of which the college was an extension, and also of Giggleswick in Yorkshire. She was said to have been a holy virgin, strangled to death by Viking women and buried in the church at Middleham. Richard's saints all struggled against evil, both within themselves in their spiritual quests to overcome the temptations of the devil, and in the external world in the form of the heathen, the heretical and the enemies of the people. The presence of Saint George on the lists should be no surprise. He was the patron saint of England and of soldiers. The personification of chivalry, associated with crusading, his cult was fostered and developed by the house of York. Saint George was a favourite saint of Richard for obvious reasons. He was not only holy and virtuous but he was also a valiant soldier: the perfect combination. Again, his story illustrated the fight within and the fight without. Saint George slew a dragon, not only to rescue the archetypal damsel in distress, but also to conquer evil.

There is nothing startlingly original or unusual in the choice of these saints and many other benefactors of the period chose in a similar vein. Nor can we be sure that they reveal as much about the inner man as we would like, but there is a prayer within the dedication to Middleham which seems to have come from Richard's heart:

> Know ye that where it haith pleased Almighty God, Creatour and Redemer of all mankind, of His most bounteuouse and manyfold graces to enhabile, enhaunce and exalte me His most simple creature, nakedly borne into this wretched world, destitute of possessions, goods and enheretaments, to the grete astate, honor and dignite that He hath called me now unto, to be named, knowed, reputed and called Richard Duc of Gloucestre, and of His infynyte goodnesse not oonly to endewe me with grete possessions and of giftys of His divine grace, but also to preserve, kep and deliver me of many grete jeopardy, parells and hurts, for the which and other the manyfold benyfits of His bounteuouse grace and goodnesse to me, without any my desert or cause in sundry behalves shewed and geven, I, daily and ourly according to my deuty remembering the premisses, and in recognicion that all such goodness cometh of Hyme, an finally determyned, into the loving and thankyng of His Deite... [11]

Although hyperbole may be detected in the notion that Richard was born destitute of possessions and inheritance, his prospects as the youngest son of a duke whose enemies at court far outnumbered his friends, were certainly not guaranteed. There is no doubt that he had been delivered from many great dangers and hurts and there can be no argument about the manifold benefits he now enjoyed. He was still a young man whose memories of tragedy, exile and those sharp blades that separated life from death, were recent and fresh, but he was also the most trusted brother of the king with enormous power across the north, the greatest landholder in the kingdom apart from the king, and living a life adorned by the trappings of majesty and regalian privilege. He did well to remember that.

Some of the detail of the stipulations for Middleham, shows that Richard enjoyed and understood music. He not only required the dean and the priests to have 'literal cunning, good disposition and in worldly policy may be founden able' but were also to be sufficiently learned, not only in understanding and literature but also in singing. Their musical qualifications are specified precisely: the priests must be able to sing 'playne song, priked song, faburden, and descant of two mynymes at the lest'. One of these priests had to be 'a player upon the organs, and daily to play as oft it shalbe requisite and appoynted'. When von Poppelau visited Richard's court in 1484, he was much struck by the quality of the music played during the royal mass.[12]

These musical and literate priests, studious servants of God, graduates from Cambridge, were not likely to be the genteel, scholarly choristers their modern counterparts might be, however. Another stricture in the statutes lists the scale of punishments they might expect for any violent knife-crime they committed on or off the premises. The matter of fact tone and the relative leniency of the sentences suggest that these offences were not entirely unknown:

> Also, I statute, make, and ordeyne that if eny prest, clerk, or oder minister of the same College use at eny tyme in ire eny inhonest or slaunderous words ayenst his fellow, his superior or inferior, of the same College, he shal pay of his wagys at evere tyme two pennez. If he draw violently a knyff, he shal pay of his saide wage at evere tyme so doing four penys, and if he draw blode he shal pay of his saide wage as moch as the deane, with one of the saide six prests, shal reasonable deme hyme to pay to be convectid in, to ye reparacion of the saide College.

Middleham on a Saturday night in 1478 was obviously far less pleasant than it is today. This record alerts us to the danger of making the anachronistic assumption that the security accepted and enjoyed in 'civilised' communities in the past conforms to the same ideal to which we vainly aspire today.

In 1478 Richard could be well satisfied with his achievements. He had attained his pre-eminence among the upper nobility through his own efforts as much as by good fortune and birth. He was in his prime, married and secure. There must have been few clouds on the horizon. He was not to know that his troublesome brother Clarence was about to embark on the road to destruction, nor that his own way of life in the peace and security of the Yorkshire countryside, with occasional forays against the Scots, would become one of confusion and danger within five years. At least the problem of Clarence did not come as any great surprise. Richard had carved his swathe of northern lands and hegemony at the expense of other ambitious lords, and one of those was his brother Clarence.

Clarence had been a major beneficiary of Edward's generosity in forgiving those who had plotted his ruin. In 1471 Clarence had been restored to his estates, except the lands given back to Henry Percy in Northumberland, and even for these Clarence received ample recompense in the form of the Courtenay lands in Devon and Cornwall. Perhaps there was something wrong with the Courtenay lands in the south-west; John Neville, Marquis of Montagu, had also rebelled when he was given these instead of the Percy lands in the north. These men clearly did not appreciate the rugged beauty of the moors, the crystal clear waters of the Atlantic crashing on to little smugglers' coves, or the strange dialect and cider of the inhabitants. There again, their disdain for this part of the world may have had something to do with the phenomenal time it took to get there. Such men had no desire to get away from it all; quite the opposite.

Clarence had few grounds for complaint. He had joined Warwick's rebellion, defied the king and helped to drive him into exile. He had the remarkably good fortune to then profit from Warwick's fall. He was granted the Beauchamp-Despenser lands Warwick had enjoyed in right of his wife. He was also promised all the estates of Warwick and his wife that had not already been granted to Richard. This was the nub of the problem. It was one thing to come back from the error of betrayal and ignominy; it was quite another to have to suffer a younger brother profiting from your mistake. Clarence was furious at the marks of favour now being shown to the duke of Gloucester. He was so jealous that his persistent wrangling forced Edward to revoke the grant to Richard of the office of chamberlain of England. We do not have any record of Richard's reaction to this demotion, caused by the whingeing of a treasonable and self-seeking reprobate. Clarence was made chamberlain in Richard's place on 20 May 1472. If bad feeling between the two did not exist after this episode, it must have done following Clarence's attempts to prevent Richard from marrying Anne Neville. Anne was the daughter of Warwick, an early companion of Richard during his teen years at Middleham and the sister of Isabel, who was married to Clarence. She was an obvious choice for Richard. Whether they liked each other mattered not. As Charles Ross brilliantly put it, 'Medieval marriages of the upper-class variety had much more to do with lawyers than with love, liking or lust.'[13]

Anne was the daughter of Richard's cousin, but there was nothing unseemly in that, despite one historian, with a curious devotion to the 'evil Richard' myth, recently describing their relationship as 'incestuous, sinful, prohibited, deeply shocking and probably incapable of being dispensed.'[14] The fact that Anne's sister was married to Richard's brother created a degree of affinity that was routinely dispensed with. Describing them as 'siblings-in-law', a term presumably invented for the sole purpose of suggesting that Richard was closer to Anne than he actually was, is mere obfuscation. Marrying a brother-in-law was fine, is fine, and had a long and distinguished line of medieval precedents, as the Harringtons and Pilkingtons would have testified. Consanguinity, blood relations, were a different matter, but Richard's kinship with Anne was also commonplace, acceptable and in no way shocking to contemporaries. They were cousins once removed. Only a pathological distortion of the facts could create a sin out of this perfectly normal marriage. To give a measure of the case, none of Richard and Anne's various connections would fit into any of the twenty-five degrees of 'kindred and affinity' that would require dispensation in the Church of England today. But for those determined to render Richard in an exclusively negative light, portraying his marriage as sinful makes sense.

The difficulty for Clarence was that Anne's portion of Warwick's inheritance would now go to Richard rather than himself. Clarence's efforts to prevent this from happening provide the background to the very public quarrel that then broke out between the king's brothers. The Croyland chronicler was on hand to describe for us what happened. Anne, he reminds us, had been married to Edward, the son of Henry VI, killed at Tewkesbury. We might remember this hastily arranged union as part of Warwick's attempt to construct an alliance with his old Lancastrian enemy, Margaret of Anjou. Anne and Edward were only briefly acquainted before he set sail for England and an early grave. Richard, the chronicler tells us 'sought the said Anne in marriage. This proposal, however, did not suit the views of his brother, the duke of Clarence, who had previously married the eldest daughter of the same earl'. The chronicler then described Clarence's real objections to the marriage and his rather farcical attempt to hide the eligible young lady:

> He caused the damsel to be concealed, in order that it might not be known by his brother where she was; as he was afraid of a division of the earl's property, which he wished to come to himself alone in right of his wife, and not to be obliged to share it with any other person. Still however, the craftiness of the duke of Gloucester so far prevailed that he discovered the young lady in the city of London disguised in the habit of a cookmaid; upon which he had her removed to the sanctuary of St Martin's.[15]

We note in passing the epithet 'craftiness' creeping into descriptions of Richard's behaviour at an early stage. Spotting one's bride-to-be dressed as a kitchen maid no doubt required considerable craftiness and probably shocked contemporaries into the bargain. Having craftily spied his sinful quarry, Richard had her removed into the local brothel known as the sanctuary of St Martin's. The chronicler provides the sequel:

In consequence of this, such a violent discussion arose between the brothers, and so many arguments were, with the greatest acuteness, put forth on either side, in the king's presence, who sat in judgement in the council chamber, that all present, and the lawyers even, were quite surprised that these princes should find arguments in such abundance by means of which to support their respective causes. In fact, these brothers, the king and the two dukes, were possessed of such surpassing talents that, if they had been able to live without dissensions, such a threefold cord could never have been broken without the utmost difficulty.

The Croyland chronicler was probably a witness to this heated debate and, as he himself tells us he was a Doctor of Canon Law, his admiration for the 'acuteness' of the protagonists is high praise indeed. The chronicler goes on to describe Edward's efforts to settle the 'discord between princes of such high rank'. His solution involved allowing Gloucester to marry Anne and receiving the lands she was entitled to as agreed 'through the mediation of arbitrators', and guaranteeing the rest of her mother's inheritance to Clarence. The whole affair was clearly difficult and unwelcome for the king. We can almost see the shudder of the chronicler as he moves on in his narrative, 'However, I readily pass over a matter so incurable as this, without attempting to find a cause for it, and so leave these strong-willed men to the impulse of their own wills.'

The matter of the Warwick inheritance was settled by the king in Parliament in 1474 with Warwick's lands in Wales and the north going to Richard and those in the Midlands going to Clarence. This did not satisfy Clarence and nor, from what we can tell, did it satisfy Richard. Richard, it would be fair to assume, did not get on with his brother. Clarence was untrustworthy: he had betrayed the king in 1469, he was implicated in a rebellion led by John de Vere, the earl of Oxford, in 1473, and he was eventually disloyal once too often and executed in 1478 for treason. Some commentators have suggested that Richard blamed the Woodvilles for Clarence's fall and point out that Richard came to court less frequently after Clarence's execution than he had before. What the dispute over Richard's marriage to Anne, and the division of the Warwick inheritance shows, is that Richard had little reason to love Clarence before 1478 and probably considered his fate as self-inflicted. Richard, still only twenty years old when he married Anne, was not a man prepared to be pushed around when it came to establishing himself as a lord in the north.

Anne may have been only sixteen when they married, but the very next year, 1473, saw the birth of their only child, named Edward. In the following year Richard put pressure on the earl of Northumberland over rights of lordship. The earl had complained to the king in 1473 that Richard had recruited John Wedrington, under-sheriff of Northumberland, as one of his retainers.

This man was one of the earl's men and he felt that Richard had trespassed on his rights in the matter. The king and council agreed and instructed Richard to retain none of the earl's men in the future. A year later, on 28 July 1474, the earl signed an indenture with Richard that not only reversed the earlier decision but that went much further than anybody would have expected. The earl promised, in a solemn treaty, to be 'the faithful servant' of Richard who, in turn, promised to be Henry Percy's 'good and faithful lord'. In practice Richard and Percy achieved a *modus vivendi* which allowed each a proper sphere of influence, but nevertheless Richard was making it quite clear who the boss was. The treaty began with a telling description of the two parties:

> The indenture made the 28th day of July the 14th year of the reign of our sovereign lord King Edward IV between the right high and mighty prince Richard Duke of Gloucester on the one part and the right worshipful lord Henry Earl of Northumberland on the other part...[16]

The difference between the two northern magnates was that Richard was a 'right high and mighty prince' while Henry Percy was merely a 'right worshipful lord'. This was a difference Richard was keen to have acknowledged and to enforce. Richard may have been young but he was a royal prince and therefore in an altogether different league to Percy. There was never the slightest chance that Stanley would acknowledge the superiority of Richard in his own sphere of influence in this way.

Richard was carving a large but close-knit niche for himself in the north of England where he was the royal representative and no other authority superseded his. He had a wife and an heir, a strong group of associates from among the most significant regional families and a base at Middleham which, with its proximity to the city of York, gave him an influence and an authority second to none between the Don and the Tweed. He had earned much of this by his bravery in action and by his loyalty to his brother, the king. He was as ambitious as any young prince would be and as conscious of his heritage, particularly as the son of Richard duke of York. He was also keen to participate in the unfinished business for which his father had lived and died: a revival of English military triumph in France.

# EIGHT

# THE HOPE OF GLORY

In 1475, when Richard was twenty-two years-old, the prospect of military triumph on the Continent seemed to have become a tangible reality. Edward IV invaded France with 'the finest, largest and best appointed force that has ever left England' according to an Italian visitor.[1] Philippe de Commynes, now back in France as one of Louis XI's councillors, agreed: the army was 'the most numerous, the best disciplined, the best mounted, and the best armed that ever any king of that nation invaded France with'.[2] Martial glory beckoned. All the wrongs suffered by his father, whose efforts to reverse the tide in France had been so grievously thwarted by his enemies at home, could now be remedied. The prospect of vindication and exculpation hovered in the air and with it the lure of glory, of lasting fame and of undying renown. The trajectory of Richard's life until this moment seemed to point towards the ancient enemy. Two of the greatest English kings, Edward III and Henry V, had both won fabulous victories in France and secured lasting memorials in the annals of chivalry. To be a part of the revival of those great days was an aspiration which resonated with Richard. His great-uncle had served Henry V in France, at Agincourt itself, and his father had done his best to serve Henry VI there. How fitting for Richard to serve his brother, Edward IV, in a return of English might to the fields of France.

After his restoration in 1471 Edward had been left with bitter resentment towards the France of Louis XI, and particularly against Louis himself whom he believed to be 'the principal ground, root, and provoker of the King's let and trouble'. Louis' persistent and material support for the enemies of Edward in general and the Lancastrians in particular, was a challenge and an affront to Edward's honour. The king of England's security was still being undermined by 'subtle and crafty means', despite the death of Henry VI and his son. Both Burgundy and Brittany were keen to engage English support against Louis, though Edward was disinclined to give any encouragement to Duke Charles the Bold of Burgundy after the decidedly cool reception of Edward and his fellow fugitives in October 1470. Brittany was a different matter and a French invasion there in 1472 was repulsed with the help of English archers under Anthony Earl Rivers and his brother, Sir Edward Woodville. Edward IV was on very good terms with Duke Francis of Brittany and their joint operations in the Channel against Louis had been to the advantage of both Brittany and England. Edward knew that if he was really serious about launching an invasion against France, and there was no apparent reason to suppose that he wasn't, then he would need the security of alliances with Brittany, Burgundy and Scotland. He broke the ice with Charles the Bold and his advances were reciprocated with the arrival in England of his old friend Louis de Gruthuyse. The governor of Holland was warmly received by Edward and entertained in lavish style. De Gruthuyse had given Edward hospitality at a time of grave crisis and he was rewarded in England by the grant of the earldom of Winchester. Charles the Bold, still driving a hard bargain, agreed to an alliance with Edward and the project began to materialise.

Parliament was persuaded to raise a massive tax, though not without considerable difficulty. The tax amounted to an income tax of ten percent on all lords and a lump sum from the commons. The difficulties Edward had in raising the money once it had been granted stemmed from the two previous occasions he had been granted taxation for war and had used the money for other purposes. This time Parliament appointed special commissioners to hold the money at St Paul's and to release it when the expedition was ready to set sail. It still took two years for some areas to produce the money due from them. No one likes paying tax but it would seem also that there was only lukewarm enthusiasm for war with France. A whole generation had passed since the glory days when reputations, wealth and opportunities had been made in waging war against the traditional enemy. The current generation of eligible soldiers expected only disaster and ruinous expense to come from fighting in France. Twenty years of civil war had not persuaded them that money spent on killing people was necessarily money well spent. Edward pushed on undaunted, squeezing the rich by raising cash through the despised system of 'benevolences'. Treasury officials would recommend the value of the generous gift a subject was required to make to the king in his hour of need. It was possible to refuse to pay the sum but the price of turning down such an opportunity to contribute to the national war effort, in terms of career-damage and loss of future prospects, invariably tipped the balance in favour of stumping up the necessary.

Louis, realising that Edward might actually be serious in his plans to invade, began a diplomatic assault of his own and managed to persuade both Francis of Brittany and Charles of Burgundy to renew their truces with him. Charles was a very unreliable ally. He had ambitions in the east which involved marrying his daughter to the heir of the Emperor Frederick III and thus elevating his dukedom to a kingdom. He wanted to recover French lands to the south of Holland which separated his duchy in two halves and he was busy preparing a war with the Swiss, attacking the Rhineland town of Neuss and threatening the Archbishop of Cologne. None of this had any advantage for England and gave Charles far too many distractions and excuses to be an enthusiastic participant in a war with France. After two years of shilly-shallying, renewing truces with France and negotiating with Frederick III's son, the Archduke Maximilian, Charles at last came round to the idea of a formal alliance with England and a war with his nemesis, Louis. His decision was perhaps made simpler by the defeat of his army by the Swiss. By the treaty of London signed on 25 July 1474 Charles agreed to acknowledge Edward as king of France providing Burgundy got a whole shopping list of territories from the dismemberment of France. The deal was done and Edward could finally report to Parliament that he was ready to go. Scotland had been brought on side by offering James III a marriage between his newly born son and Edward's third daughter Cecily. The scene was set for the biggest invasion of France from England ever before attempted.

Not everyone in England was as committed to the enterprise as Edward appeared to be. Louis, as wily as ever, had sent messages to England pointing out that Burgundy was not the force it once was and that an accommodation between Louis and Edward might be very much in Edward's interests. Edward responded by sending Garter Herald to Louis to tell him that the king of England would be prepared to listen to his overtures but only after he had landed in France. At that stage he would be happy to receive envoys and to allow Louis to make approaches to two men who were high in his confidence and would act as negotiators. These two royal diplomats were John, Lord Howard, and the steward of the household, Thomas lord Stanley.[3] Their work behind the scenes, and the failure of the duke of Burgundy to provide any real assistance, led to an early and controversial end to the expedition. One man who was unlikely to forget the experience afforded by this tremendous escapade was Richard duke of Gloucester. He arrived to join the royal army with perhaps the largest contingent of fighting men: ten knights, 100 lancers and 1,000 archers, with high hopes of an illustrious adventure to emulate the feats of his ancestors. The army that duly disembarked at Calais numbered over 11,000 fighting men and a host of supporting contingents bringing supplies and logistical apparatus. This was more than Henry V himself had been able to muster. The peers of the realm were arrayed for war, including five dukes, three earls and twenty-three barons. Surely this great force would accomplish the cherished dream of a revival of English fortunes in France with all the wealth and prestige that would attend upon it.

Soon after arriving in Calais the deflation of English hopes began. Having waited ten days for the duke of Burgundy to arrive, the English were astonished to see him march in to the garrison accompanied only by his bodyguard. The duke explained that he had left his army in the east ready to destroy the duke of Lorraine and that, rather than spurn such a marvellous opportunity, he preferred the English to join him there, conquer Champagne and crown Edward as king of France in Rheims. Edward had little choice but to acquiesce in the scheme. He knew that he could not conquer France without a powerful ally but he must also have been aware of the growing realisation among the English nobility that the once-proud armies of Burgundy, famed for their discipline and training, were a thing of the past and could no longer be relied upon. Edward marched his army eastwards, much to the surprise of Louis who had expected an attack on Normandy. As Edward reached the fortress of St Quentin, which his supposed ally the count of St Pol commanded, the garrison opened fire with cannon supported by skirmishers. Reaching the towns under the rule of Charles of Burgundy, he found their gates closed and the duke safely behind their walls refusing to allow the English to enter. Louis, meanwhile, had been shadowing the English army and had been busy destroying all the crops in his own fields. As it became clear that both Charles' promises and his dukedom were bankrupt and that he was a spent force in European politics, so it also became apparent that the English army would not be able to find sufficient supplies to sustain itself through the winter. As Louis' army, outnumbering the English, tentatively approached, the time had come for ignominious diplomacy. Edward had just the right men for the job. He released a French prisoner, a valet in Louis' service named Jacques de Gracay, and gave him two crowns with instructions to inform the French king that these gifts were from the Lords Howard and Stanley. The valet was to recommend these two noblemen to the king. Louis was swift to take the hint and sent another valet from his household offering Edward peace on favourable terms.

There can be no doubt that the terms were indeed remarkably favourable. Louis was to make an immediate payment of 75,000 crowns, about £15,000, and an annual payment of 50,000 crowns, or £10,000, for as long as both kings lived. The dauphin, heir to the French throne, was to marry one of Edward's daughters and instead of expecting a dowry to come with the bride he was instead to provide her with a jointure, an annual income, of £60,000. On top of all this and a seven year truce there were commercial agreements and provisions for mutual assistance in time of need. Louis was certainly in earnest and began raising the money straight away. A good deal of gold was splashed around the English negotiators who found that their more serious misgivings and reticence about traducing English honour mysteriously vanished. Louis not only understood the English lords, he knew how to soften up their soldiers too and when the armies met at Amiens on the Somme he supplied the English with an abundance of food and wine, issuing instructions to the innkeepers to give free drink to any soldier who cared to ask for it. Louis had obviously been studying English national characteristics with some care and had discovered that if they are plied with quantities of alcohol while in a foreign city their martial vigour expended itself in destroying property, picking fights with each other and rolling over in the gutters in a drunken stupor. Philippe de Commynes was back in harness as a chief negotiator for Louis and has left us with a vivid account of the whole proceedings. Nine or ten taverns entertained the English:

> ...liberally furnished with all that they wanted, where they had whatever they had a mind to call for, without paying for it, according to the King of France's orders, who bore all the expense of that entertainment, which lasted three or four days.

This was a cruel method of warfare with the English soldiers incapable of standing on their own two feet and likely to suffer from blinding headaches for some time. Commynes grew a little concerned after a while and informed the French king that the presence of 9,000 armed drunks in Amiens was likely to cause a public nuisance. It was agreed that the English commanders would get their men out of what was left of the town but this they failed to manage. Commynes took a walk round the town at nine o'clock in the morning on the fourth day and found that the English were so much the worse for wear that they posed no threat. Edward nevertheless began to forcibly eject his men and posted a guard at the city gates to prevent them from getting back in.

It was now decided that the two kings should meet in person to conclude the business. At Picquigny, three miles down the river, elaborate arrangements were put in place to enable the two monarchs to converse in safety. A bridge was flung up over the river with a screen across the middle and a strong wooden lattice in the centre of it allowing communication to take place. Amiable though the participants had become, no one was prepared to risk another Montereau. John duke of Burgundy had been assassinated there at just such a meeting in 1419. When John the Fearless had arrived on his similarly constructed bridge all those years ago, he had been struck down at the feet of the dauphin, the future

Charles VII of France, while in the act of kneeling in polite welcome. No one was too sure what had happened or why. France and Burgundy were allies at the time and the crime seemed senseless. Both countries needed the help of each other against the English. The most likely explanation was that the duke's hand had moved to his sword to push it out of the way. Most people find that when they kneel in deference before the heir to the throne of France, the sword can play havoc with their efforts to perform the manoeuvre in a decorous fashion. Adjusting it at the wrong moment, however, can be fatal. Some zealous brute by the dauphin's side slaughtered the duke in cold blood. On that occasion two fenced enclosures had been deployed on the bridge and only the leaders' most trusted confidants had been permitted to enter. The security advisers of John the Fearless had got it badly wrong. At high-profile meetings of this sort when the temptation to make a name for yourself in defence of your master may prove to be overwhelming, it is best to make a comprehensive risk assessment. In many ways the consequences of Montereau were still being felt in France and Burgundy. Picquigny would not be making the same headlines.

Commynes witnessed the unfolding drama. The area designated for the meeting had been covered by boards to keep off rain and so the spaces on either side of the barrier resembled lions' cages. The holes between the bars of the lattice were not wide enough to thrust an arm through and security on either side of the bridge was tight. The king of France approached with 800 men-at-arms. The king of England brought the whole of his army up to his side of the river in battle order. Commynes was worried about the disparity in numbers but trusted the English because 'they do not manage their treaties and capitulations with as much cunning and policy as the French do'. He nevertheless warned that, though they proceeded with 'greater straightforwardness in their affairs, yet a man must be cautious, and have a care not to affront them, for it is dangerous meddling with them'. Twelve men from either side were selected to accompany the monarchs with four observers from each side in the ranks of their rivals on the other side of the bridge. The king of France came to the barrier first, accompanied by a select group that happened to include Commynes. Our reporter was dressed in identical fashion to the king and explained this strange circumstance by informing his readers that, 'It was the king's royal pleasure, according to an old and common custom that he had, that I should be dressed like him on that day.' It seems scarcely credible that Commynes was too naïve to realise that this singular honour afforded to him might also be a means by which to thwart an assassination. There were probably few of his fellow courtiers going green with envy and there must have been some suppressed sniggering when Commynes was granted the favour. The king of England then arrived and Commynes carefully noted what he saw:

The King of England advanced along the causeway (which I mentioned before) very nobly attended, with the air and presence of a king: there were in his train his brother the Duke of Clarence, the earl of Northumberland, his chamberlain the Lord Hastings, his chancellor, and other peers of the realm; among whom there were not above three or four dressed in cloth of gold like himself. King Edward wore a black velvet cap on his head decorated with a large fleur de lys made of precious stones. He was a prince of noble and majestic presence but beginning to get a little fat and I remember that when I last saw him, when Warwick had forced him to flee from England, he had seemed better-looking. Indeed I remember thinking then that I had never beheld such a handsome person before.[4]

Regal life had clearly begun to take its toll on Edward's appearance in the five years since Commynes had last seen him. Wearing the fleur de lys, the national symbol of France, was presumably not intended as a gesture of goodwill. However, as Edward approached the barrier, whatever defiance he had planned to show he seems to have thought better of it and, pulling off his cap, bowed low to the ground in front of Louis. Commynes did not concede any reciprocal gesture on the part of the king of France but acknowledged that he 'received him with abundance of reverence and respect'. The two kings 'embraced through the holes of the grate' and spoke to each other in friendly terms. Commynes was impressed with Edward's knowledge of French but less impressed by the chancellor, Thomas Rotherham bishop of Rochester, whose felt it necessary to harangue the gathering. Copies of the treaty were furnished and both kings somehow managed to put one hand on the parchment and another on 'the holy true cross' before swearing religiously to observe the contents. Louis did, as a matter of fact, take these obligations seriously and continued to pay Edward, apart from in 1480, until 1482 when Edward's own breaches of the treaty released him from his bond.

Commynes continued to observe the historic occasion at Picquigny with a keen interest and described the king of France ordering his subordinates to withdraw so that he could speak alone with Edward. The English nobles took the hint and followed suit. After a while Commynes found himself called back again by King Louis who asked Edward if he recognised the man. Much to Commynes delight and admiration, Edward not only remembered him but could recall all the places they had previously met and recounted their conversations in Calais when Commynes had been in the service of the duke of Burgundy. This led the conversation on to the topic of the allies of the English king. Edward reassured Louis that he would not make much effort to bring the duke of Burgundy round to the idea of a truce with France. If he disagreed he could go his own way. As for the duke of Brittany, that was a different matter.

Edward told Louis that he desired him not to attempt anything against Duke Francis because 'he had never found so true and faithful a friend'. We are very fortunate to have this first-hand account of such a rare and intimate exchange between two kings, standing almost alone on a bridge over a river while their armies, retinues, courtiers and lackeys could only watch and wait at a distance. Edward's remark about Duke Francis tells us a good deal about the English king, as do many of Commynes' astute observations. Edward was thirty-three years old but had aged quite quickly and signs of corpulence, for which he was soon to be known, had begun to appear. He was intelligent and good-looking with a charisma evident in his bearing. He was also faithful to his friends. Perhaps this was a family trait.

The main business concluded, Louis began to joke with Edward and told his fellow-king that he should come to Paris and be royally entertained with wine, women and song. He need not fear straying off the path of virtue because Louis would give him the cardinal of Bourbon as his confessor, 'since he would very willingly absolve him from sin if he should have committed any, because he knew the cardinal was a jolly good fellow'. Louis and Edward parted on excellent terms. Both had secured terms that enabled their countries to avoid war and both were satisfied with the outcome. Edward had not had the co-operation he expected from Burgundy and had no intention of fighting a war on his own. Louis had succeeded in rescuing his country from a joint attack by both his major competitors and could enjoy the prospects of a beneficial alliance with a major trading partner. He paid Edward a ransom of £10,000 for Margaret of Anjou who was duly released from English custody and spent the rest of her life – she died in 1482 – living in quietude on a small pension in France. The English were not sorry to see her return to her native soil.

One man, at least, did not share the satisfaction of Edward's court. Commynes reported that 'the Duke of Gloucester, the King of England's brother, and some other persons of quality, were not present at this interview, as being adverse to the treaty'. This explains why the king's most trusted lieutenant was not mentioned in any of the formalities and subsequent celebrations. He had refused to attend. Historians agree that in the short and the long term the Treaty of Picquigny was a good deal from the English point of view. Certainly there was some dissension among the ranks and some unrest at home at what was initially perceived to be a waste of taxpayers' money, but Louis lavished the English nobility with bribes and Edward remitted a substantial portion of the tax he had been granted by Parliament. The Croyland chronicler wrote about complaints at home being savagely dealt with by Edward. The chronicler expressed the view that the king's swift action to stifle unrest had been necessary because no one among the king's advisers was safe who 'induced by the friendship of the French king or by his presents, had persuaded the king to make peace'.[5] The chronicler's verdict was, nevertheless, a favourable one: 'Accordingly, our lord the king returned to England, having thus concluded an honourable treaty of peace'. Commynes noted that Richard was reconciled to the French king at Amiens, where Louis ensured that the duke was 'splendidly entertained and nobly presented both with plate and fine horses'. We do not know what Richard's private thoughts were on this occasion, nor subsequently; he remained a loyal servant of the king for the rest of the reign. The episode merely tells us what we already know: that Richard did not like making peace with France, and that he put his loyalty to his brother, the king, ahead of his own ambitions. His absence from the negotiations does, however, suggest that all was not well with Richard. He must have felt very strongly about something. Perhaps he was astounded by the appalling affront to English arms, the shameful triumph of money-grubbing policy over the hope of military success, the damage to his nation's prestige at home and abroad, the victory of dissembling diplomacy over martial vigour, the stomach-churning use of blackmail and bribery rather than the trial of national strength for which he had so longed. Perhaps the contrast between the hopes and courage of his brave retinue as it arrived in France, willing to chance everything for the glory of England, and the grins and taunts they now endured, made his heart sink.

Just a few weeks earlier the proud and glittering array of English warriors had paused for two nights at the historic site of the battle of Agincourt. Richard and his men had stood in awe as they beheld that sacred field. Here Henry V had won a victory that would be remembered for ever. Those who had fought with him on that great day, men like Thomas Erpingham and Walter Hungerford, were the immortals known to all in Richard's youth. Richard himself bore the title of the duke of Gloucester who had been injured on that day and whose life had been saved by the great King Henry in the heat of battle. Richard's father bore the title of the duke of York who had been killed that day in the service of King Harry. By Richard's side, surveying the field of glory with him, were the descendants of those who had fought on St Crispin's day sixty years before, including the redoubtable James Harrington. How Richard and his companions-in-arms must have prayed for the chance to emulate their ancestors, and how close they had come to doing so. This magnificent English army must surely have done wonders and helped to bury the grim memories of the countless humiliations troubling the spirits of those heroes from another age. Here was the golden opportunity to right the wrongs of recent times and salve the wounds of civil war in noble quests and honourable triumphs. We can be confident in taking the liberty of assuming that when Commynes reported that the duke of Gloucester was 'adverse' he was, in truth, devastated.

Richard had not set out for France to suffer disgrace and capitulation. There is some evidence that the rank and file shared his views. Louis de Bretelles, a Gascon serving in the retinue of Anthony Earl Rivers, told Commynes that Edward had won nine victories and suffered only one defeat, the present one; and that the shame of returning to England after this defeat outweighed all the honour he had gained from the other nine. This soldier was exaggerating a little: Edward had only won four battles. But they were all ferocious pitched battles, at Mortimer's Cross, Towton, Barnet and Tewkesbury. How fitting it would have been to turn those great victories fought against his own people into a victory on foreign soil that might unite them all. The king of France did his best to avoid crowing about his skilful machinations but a slip of the royal tongue quickly gave rise to a popular French song mocking the English for being conquered by venison pasties and fine wine. The English nobles left in France as surety suffered humiliating jibes from some of the lesser nobility in Paris.[6] In time Edward was able to overcome any residual resentment in England at the return of such a large army without a blow being struck, but Richard's hopes had been higher than most and the evidence shows that he would have preferred a proper war.

The débâcle in France in 1475 provides a backdrop to the grand reburial of the duke of York and his son at Fotheringhay in 1476. The timing of the ceremony has always been a puzzle but the events of the previous year may have influenced Edward. In his own mind he had settled matters with France for the foreseeable future, and on English terms. The work of his father, to gain an honourable peace, had been completed and his body could be laid to rest. The prominence granted to his brother in the solemnities was perhaps an acknowledgement that Richard had felt dismayed by events in France. The ritual and the subsequent festivities demonstrated Edward's commitment to the family heritage and his continued trust in Richard. From Richard's point of view there must have been an added poignancy to the proceedings following his experience in France. His father was being buried in the collegiate church founded by his great-uncle, Edward, duke of York, who had died at the battle of Agincourt. Richard, the second duke of York, was to be laid to rest next to Edward, the first duke of York, as if they were lineally descended. Whatever thoughts Richard harboured over the Treaty of Picquigny, his visit to Agincourt and the bringing of his father to Fotheringhay can only have strengthened his notion of a destiny yet to be fulfilled. Fotheringhay was not only the place where the hopes of the Yorkists were buried, but also where they had been reborn.

To commemorate the special role played by the church at Fotheringhay in the history of his family, Edward commissioned a splendid pulpit which still dominates the nave. As the priest preached to the congregation he would have found himself surrounded by the heraldic emblems of the king. At his back he would have been conscious of a splendid coat of arms belonging to the king himself. The three lions of England were quartered with the fleur de lys of France, symbolising, rather ironically given the circumstances, the English claim to both crowns. The arms are supported by a black unicorn on the right and a white lion on the left. Atop the shield rests the golden crown of the king of England. To his left the priest would have seen, carved in wood and brightly painted, a white boar: the badge of the king's brother Richard. On his right he would have seen another beast carved and decorated in the same manner. This was, and still is, a black bear representing the elder brother Clarence. The iconography is a manifest demonstration of the establishment of the house of York. Here, in the presence of their noble ancestors, were the heraldic devices of the king of England, supported on either side by his two brothers. The three surviving sons of the duke of York were united under the royal canopy. Shortly after the erection of this beautiful monument to medieval royal piety and pride it became a permanent reminder of the mutability of human affairs. Clarence fell out with Edward and their quarrel so angered the king that he had his brother put to death. So much for the dream of family solidarity.

George duke of Clarence, unlike Richard, does not seem to have been able to settle for second place. A life lived under his brother's sovereignty was a life lived in the shade, always eclipsed and never free to sparkle. Clarence could not be satisfied with the life of dedicated service that Richard had chosen. Being the elder brother, royal ambitions were bound to be nearer the surface and conflict was also more likely. In 1469 he had rebelled against Edward under the understanding that his cause would advance. He had suffered a reversal of his hopes, not so much when Edward won his kingdom back, as when Warwick opted to restore Henry VI. This turn around had helped Clarence realign his allegiance in favour of his brother. The problems resurfaced in 1476 when Isabel, his wife, died after giving birth to their second son, Richard. Clarence had always been an unstable character but the loss of Isabel hurt him badly. To compound his difficulties Edward opposed his remarriage to Mary of Burgundy, the heiress of Charles. This is exactly the sort of thing Edward had been doing before Clarence's first marriage. Edward did not trust Clarence, with excellent reason, and he could not afford to allow him to make a powerful diplomatic marriage that could lead to a challenge for the throne of England. It was for this reason, the prohibition on his marriage, that Clarence had followed Warwick abroad and married the Kingmaker's daughter in Calais. Edward was not going to tolerate that kind of defiance ever again; he had learnt his lesson the hard way.

The trouble began when Clarence arrested a former servant of the Duchess Isabel, rejoicing in the name Ankarette Twynho, whom he accused of having poisoned his wife. She was arrested, tried, found guilty and hanged on 15 April 1477. A month later the king appointed a commission to investigate some strange goings-on in Clarence's back yard. The duke was behaving with an alarming degree of petulance at the refusal of the king to allow him to marry Mary. He hardly attended court, refused to eat in the royal presence and sat in sullen silence during council meetings. The king suspected that treasonable plots were afoot and the commission seemed to confirm something of the kind. One of Clarence's servants, Thomas Burdett, had been visiting a magician who had been sticking pins in effigies of Edward and compassing his death thereby. Whether Edward had been feeling random sharp pains in recent days we cannot tell but he certainly took the charges and the evidence seriously, probably in the hope of teaching Clarence to step into line. Burdett and an Oxford astronomer called Dr John Stacey were convicted of treason, drawn to Tyburn and hanged. Instead of taking the hint Clarence became impossible.

While Edward was at Windsor, Clarence burst into a council meeting in Westminster and made it hear the declarations of innocence which Burdett and Stacey had made. He then stormed out again. Taken with the hasty arrest and conviction of Ms Twynho, whom jurors were now saying had been innocent, Edward considered that Clarence had violated royal authority once too often. In June 1477 he was arrested and taken to the Tower to await the verdict of Parliament, the highest court in the land.[7] Parliament duly assembled in January 1478 and was greeted by a lengthy tirade from Edward against his brother. Among the various treasonable offences listed was the putting about of stories that Edward was a bastard, and not the eldest surviving son of Richard duke of York. This story is interesting because it resurfaced in 1483, and again in recent times, but the evidence seems to show that Richard give it little credence and he would have benefited most if it were true.[8] Clarence was condemned to death and sent to the Tower again. It took Edward a further ten days to muster the courage to give the order but in February 1478, his brother was duly executed. The Croyland chronicler was too coy to give any information about the method of execution, simply recording 'the execution, whatever form it took, was carried out secretly in the Tower of London'. The Italian visitor, Dominic Mancini, in London four years later, heard that Clarence had been 'plunged into a jar of sweet wine'. He had obviously heard the general belief, recorded later by Polydore Vergil, that he had been 'drowned, as they say, in a butt of malmsey wine'.[9] Being of so high a rank Clarence would have had the honour of choosing his own method of execution and, presumably, preferred to leave this world in a catatonic state. We cannot know for certain because a further privilege granted to those with such a royal pedigree is to have the thing done quietly and not in public. There were advantages in being the brother of a king after all.

Fratricide is an unpleasant business and Edward must have been loathe to do it but was short of alternatives. Mancini, writing after the usurpation of Richard, and prejudiced against him, has some interesting views on Richard's reaction to the death of his brother. Most of the other hostile sources assume Richard had a hand in his brother's death, or at least that he was glad of it,[10] but Mancini took a different view:

> At that, Richard duke of Gloucester was so overcome with grief for his brother, that he could not dissimulate so well, but that he was overheard to say that he would one day avenge his brother's death. Thenceforth he came very rarely to the court.[11]

Mancini blames the death on the queen, Elizabeth Woodville, saying that she concluded that her own children would never come to the throne while Clarence lived. She saw him as ambitious for the throne and headstrong enough to make an attempt on it. The charges against him could have been fabricated, though Mancini seems to have found them plausible. Mancini's evidence always has to be treated with caution as he was reliant on other partisan sources for his information, but there can be no doubt that the dissatisfied and restless Clarence posed a threat to Elizabeth's son, Edward. It is not beyond the bounds of possibility that she had a view on Clarence's defiance of the king, and expressed that view to her husband. Whether Mancini was correct in assuming that Richard from henceforth bore a grudge against the queen is another matter. If he did, he did not show it in any form visible to us today. Nor can we be too sure that he spent less time at court after Clarence's demise. He appeared when he was expected to and no one commented, apart from Mancini, on his absence. He was, however, very busy in the north. Mancini noted that he was popular there through the favours and the justice which he distributed, and also that 'the good reputation of his private life and public activities powerfully attracted the esteem of strangers'.

Whatever Richard's private thoughts on the death of his brother and on Elizabeth Woodville, his conduct in the remaining five years of Edward's kingship was exemplary. His exercise of lordship in the north became well known for its probity, discretion and even-handedness. His loyalty and good service to his brother Edward was unquestioned and invaluable. The records of the city of York reveal the duke of Gloucester working solicitously on behalf of the city and receiving their thanks for it. When they found that illegal garths and weirs on the river were reducing their fish stocks and threatening the livelihoods of the citizens, they appealed to Richard for help. His council wrote to them on 15 November 1477:

According to your desires regarding Goldale garth or any others, we have moved the king's grace on the matter and he has commanded us at our next meeting to take a view and oversight of such garths and weirs, and, if they have not been allowed before justices of eyre, see that they be pulled down; the which, or any other thing we may do for the welfare of your city, we shall put us in our utmost devoir and good will...[12]

His justice was famous for its impartiality. When one of his own servants, Thomas Redeheid, assaulted a citizen of York he may have believed that his status gave him protection from prosecution. Richard sent him, in the custody of one of his household knights, to be punished by the city. The York Civic Records confirm that Redeheid and his escort duly arrived:

At the which day came into the council chamber the right worshipful Sir Ralph Assheton, knight, in the name and by the high commandment of the most high and mighty prince the duke of Gloucester, and there and then showed how that his highness was done to understand that whereon Thomas Redeheid, servant to the treasurer unto his said highness, of old rancour and evil will did countenance on Roland Pudsey, citizen of the city of York within the household of the said grace, and him showed for the offence done within this city, his grace sent in to the mayor and his brethren by the said Sir Ralph the said Thomas Redeheid to correct and punish him for his said offence and upon that commit to prison.[13]

The city was deeply grateful for the benign lordship and protection Richard gave them. In December 1476 a visit to the city was the occasion for a little celebration:

By the mayor and council it was wholly agreed and assented that the Duke of Gloucester shall, for his great labour made to the king's good grace for the conservation of the liberties of this city, be presented at his coming to the city with six swans and six pikes...

In March 1482 the council agreed that:

...for the great labour, good and benevolent lordship that the right high and mighty prince the Duke of Gloucester has at all times done for the welfare of this city, he shall receive praise and thanks...[14]

Mancini also noted that the martial ability of Richard was famous and that 'such was his renown in warfare, that whenever a difficult and dangerous policy had to be undertaken, it would be entrusted to his discretion and generalship'.

The opportunity for Richard to demonstrate these qualities arrived in 1480 when a truce with Scotland broke down. Edward had been moving towards a rapprochement with Burgundy and Louis XI of France began reviving the 'Auld Alliance' with James III of Scotland. In the summer of 1480 the Scots carried out a large-scale raid deep inside English territory, burning Bamborough twenty miles south of the border. Richard and the earl of Northumberland called out their levies to defend the frontier but when it became apparent that this was more than the usual raiding and feuding so endemic in the border region, Richard was appointed lieutenant-general with power to raise levies in all the northern counties. James III did not particularly want a war; like many kings of Scotland, he was having difficulty controlling his aggressive nobles. He tried to discuss matters with Edward but his overtures were intemperately brushed aside. Edward, it seems, was keen to wage war and resolved to go to Scotland at the head of an army in person the following year. During the best part of 1481, however, he lingered in the south, uncertain of whether he could afford to leave London at a time when he was awaiting critical events on the Continent with a possible meeting between himself and the new ruler of Burgundy, Maximilian of Austria. To complicate matters further, Louis XI had sent an embassy to London in August with a substantial sum of money. Edward did not like losing the French pension agreed at Picquigny, a loss which had been occasioned by his overtures to Burgundy. In the end he managed to get to Nottingham, but it was already October and the campaigning season was effectively over. Commanders in the north were unable to launch a campaign while the king dithered in the south.[15]

In April 1482 the situation clarified a little when James III's brother Alexander, duke of Albany, arrived in England. By deposing James in favour of Alexander, a war with Scotland would produce a secure border with a grateful monarch ensconced on the other side of it. Edward decided to go to war. The king arrived at Fotheringhay with Alexander in June 1482 where they were joined by Richard. He had just returned from an aggressive and punitive raid deep into Scotland that had cheered the English borderers and fired the hopes of the northern counties for more permanent security for their fields and their cattle. There was also the possibility of some profitable plundering. Within days of Richard's arrival at Fotheringhay, Edward had decided not to lead the expedition in person but to give command of the entire conduct of the war to his brother. Although he set up an elaborate courier system to keep abreast of developments, Edward shifted a major responsibility on to the shoulders of his brother. One of a medieval king's primary functions was now devolved to Richard. There is little reason to doubt that Edward had intended to lead the expedition himself but in the event he returned south and contented himself with watching the fleet being fitted out in Dover. It would have been a boon to have had an English chronicler like Philippe de Commynes present at Fotheringhay in early June 1482 carefully observing and recording the conversation between King Edward and his brother Richard in the great hall. What a pity that politicians in the fifteenth century were not so keen to publish their diaries as they are today.

The ten-year age gap between the two royal brothers may have been noted had there been a scribbler there to note it. Edward was probably not well and may have had the bitter disappointment of realising that he could not withstand the physical hardships warfare demanded. The arrival of Richard, successful, confident and eager to get back to Scotland to do the job properly, may have been a turning-point in Edward's life. He could not contemplate disappointing his brother yet again. In France in 1475 Richard had expressed his disapproval of the pusillanimous outcome but had gone on to serve the king admirably. The way he ruled the north was a model for all magnates to follow; he was effective, powerful and admired. Edward, for his part, needed to prove his military abilities to no one. He had done that many times over. His victory at Tewkesbury had occurred only eleven years before and had left a lasting impression of decisive and courageous leadership in battle. But those eleven years seem to have taken their toll. Perhaps the foreign reports about his portly incapacity and love of ease were not as wide of the mark as he liked to think. In any case here was Richard in the prime of life and raring to go. It made sense to hand over command.

The royal proclamation issued immediately after the meeting, on 12 June 1482, makes it clear just how much trust Edward had in Richard and how much power he was willing to allow him. The document begins by declaring that James, King of Scotland, has broken a treaty and behaved with 'inveterate hostility and obdurate malice':

> We therefore meaning to oppose his malice and such great injury, trusting with full powers our illustrious brother, Richard Duke of Gloucester, in whom not only for his nearness and fidelity of relationship, but for his proved skill in military matters and his other virtues, we name, depute and ordain him our Lieutenant General in our absence, to fight, overcome and expel the said King of Scotland our chief enemy and his subjects, adherents and allies, however great the fight may be, giving and allowing to our same Brother, our Lieutenant, our power and full authority to summon and levy in order to serve us, all and singular our subjects and liegemen both of our Marches towards Scotland and in the Counties adjoining those Marches, of whatever state, rank or condition they are.[16]

Edward continued the proclamation by giving Richard authority to wage 'a bitter struggle' in Scotland and to defend the realm of England 'under his own supervision, just as we would do if acting in person'.

Richard advanced into Scotland, a few weeks later, at the head of a massive army – perhaps as many as 20,000 men. The speed and size of the invasion, combined with the reputation of Richard as an able commander, caused the Scottish army to seize their own king and to withdraw. Richard approached Berwick whereupon the city that Margaret of Anjou had handed over to the Scots more than twenty years before opened its gates without a shot being fired. The citadel held out under the leadership of a few diehards but Richard wasted no time on it. He moved on towards Edinburgh pillaging and devastating the country in Roxburghshire and Berwickshire as he went. The Scottish lords had withdrawn from the capital and were keen to negotiate. Richard entered Edinburgh unopposed and set about establishing the most favourable peace terms he could. Job done, he returned to Berwick, reduced the citadel after a brief siege, disbanded his army and returned to England leaving just 1,700 men to garrison Berwick.

There was little more that he could do but he probably felt slightly frustrated at the lack of a decisive opportunity to strike a permanent blow. With such political turmoil in Scotland he was never confronted by a united enemy. Remaining in force in Edinburgh would merely have provided the Scots with the focus their resistance currently lacked and dragged his men into a costly and unwinnable war of attrition. Richard had performed the task he had been given in a swift and efficient manner. Scotland did not arouse his enmity in the way France did. He had been given a taste of what he might have been capable of doing against the French if he had been given the chance. Edward was certainly pleased with his brother's achievements, writing to the Pope, Sixtus IV:

> Thank God, the giver of all good gifts, for the support received from our most loving brother, whose success is so proven that he alone would suffice to chastise the whole kingdom of Scotland.[17]

In January 1483 Edward made Richard's wartime wardenship of the west march permanent and hereditary with a grant of land in Cumberland and a massive annuity to go with it. Richard was also granted all the lands he could 'get and achieve' in Scotland on any future campaigns and to hold them with royal power. This was to be his county palatine with 'as large power, authority, jurisdiction, liberty and franchise' as was possessed by other palatinates. This was the first such creation since the county of Lancashire had been made a palatinate and given to Henry III's son in 1351. The ruler of such a region could issue his own coins, hold his own courts, raise his own taxes and generally behave as a sovereign within his territory, every inch a king.[18] If Edward's physical powers were waning, his brother was experiencing a new freedom and authority which confirmed his position of pre-eminence in the north. Edward had relied heavily on him in the tricky business of war with Scotland and had found him to be as trustworthy and reliable as he had always been.

The future for Richard, under the authority and with the respect of the king, seemed bright. His problems with Stanley had not disappeared but his position in the north was too secure for Stanley to challenge him. Only a major upheaval of an unimaginable kind could alter that. There had been something of a squabble outside Berwick on the first campaign into Scotland in 1481 when Stanley had complained that Richard had left him dangerously exposed. In the upshot, the success of the second campaign smoothed the ruffled feathers. Perhaps Stanley believed that Richard had deliberately left him in a dangerous situation but this could never be proved. They had learnt to cooperate under the king's authority but they had not learnt to love each other. Stanley, Richard and his other lieutenant on the campaign, the earl of Northumberland, all created knights on the field of battle in Scotland. It would have been no surprise to Stanley when he heard that two of those dubbed by Richard were Robert Harrington and Charles Pilkington. They were made knights banneret, a rank of knighthood only granted for valour in the face of the enemy. Richard dubbed forty-nine knights and knights banneret on the 1482 campaign, nearly all northerners, and all destined to serve in his household in the coming months.

While he was consolidating his already strong ties with these northern families, Richard was also limiting Stanley's geographical sphere of influence and frustrating his territorial ambitions. Part of the generous grant to Richard after the Scottish campaign had been all the royal lands in Cumberland. He had the right to appoint the escheator in the county and to distribute the lands and offices that came into his hands by right of the office from confiscations, expiry of leases and lack of surviving heirs. His power in Cumberland effectively ended any hopes Stanley may have harboured of extending his influence from north Wales to Scotland. He still possessed no title which might bring with it hereditary lordships and a higher rank with which to expand his domain. He had served in Edward's inner circle but had not profited as much as he might have hoped. Perhaps it had all been to keep him close at hand and out of trouble. He had left his main gentry rivals far behind, it was true, but as a body, with Richard duke of Gloucester as their champion, they could still thwart his ambitions and undermine his pretensions.

None of the commanders on the Scottish campaign, Stanley, Northumberland and Richard, could have imagined that just three years later they would face battle again in very different circumstances. None of them could have imagined, least of all Richard duke of Gloucester, that one of them would betray their lieutenant-general and compass his death in a battle on English soil. But then none of them could have imagined that Richard would become king. Within months of the grant which made Richard viceroy in the north and opened up a bright future for him and his retainers, his brother Edward died and everything was thrown into confusion and turmoil.

# NINE

# THE DEATH OF CHIVALRY

Edward IV died on 9 April 1483 just three weeks short of his forty-first birthday. The Croyland chronicler, who had worked at Edward's court, was as surprised as anyone by the suddenness and mortality of Edward's final illness. He noted Edward's grossness, his addiction to 'conviviality, vanity, drunkenness, extravagance and passion', all of which no doubt contributed to an early death, but he was nevertheless puzzled as to why the king 'though he was not affected by old age nor by any known type of disease which would not have seemed easy to cure in a lesser person' should have died.' The death shook to its foundations the stable political structure Edward had managed to create. He had been ill for about ten days and had been alert enough to realise he was dying and to add codicils to his will. That will has not survived and we therefore do not know how he thought the government would be handled after his death. His eldest son Edward was only twelve years old, surely too young to reign by himself.

There were three possibilities in this situation, all of them valid but none of them desirable; they were methods for dealing with an emergency. The first was to appoint a protector who would rule in the young king's name and administer the kingdom on his behalf until such time as the king was old enough to rule himself. The second was to appoint a council of the most influential men to rule in the boy's name. The third was to crown the boy immediately and allow him to succeed as if he were an adult. There were other alternatives that could be devised by combining elements of any or all of these procedures, such as allowing a protector or regent to have the primacy within a council, but any method would be novel in some way because no historic precedent could entirely fit the new situation. Crisis management was the name of the game and compromise the best hope. Edward V was precisely the wrong age when his father died. If he had been younger, then a period of minority rule would have been inevitable and the most powerful in the land might have been able to plan for the future. If he had been older, then immediate coronation and direct rule by the new monarch would have been acceptable and expected. At twelve he fell between all stools. A minority government would know it had power for but a short time before possible reprisals, condemnation and retribution might catch up with it. Direct rule would expose the young king to undue influence and opportunism. Factions would quickly form with the aim of defending their own interests, destroying their enemies and directing the government according to their own advantage. In the implementation of any of the scenarios there was also the unknown quantity of the mind and attitude of the boy himself. No one could tell what pressure this might bring to bear on any temporary legal construction.

There were precedents but none of them was particularly helpful. Henry III, the son of King John, had been only nine at his accession but had been quickly crowned. He had nevertheless ruled under a regency, and, though he had been crowned again when he was sixteen, did not begin his personal rule until he was twenty. Richard II had also been crowned immediately, at the tender age of ten, but had ruled under a minority council until he was fifteen. Both these rulers had been subject to the influence of favourites and ended their reigns amid turmoil and rebellion. Henry VI, the most recent case, was another example of the dangers of young rule. He was only seven when his personal rule was said to have begun but this had the effect of inducing him to rule like a seven-year-old for the rest of the reign. He reigned under a protectorship divided between his uncles. This worked quite well as it happened, but inevitably squabbles arose between the protectors. One of them, ominously named the duke of Gloucester, was executed in due course by a rival faction. Despite the inevitable problems, it was clearly helpful to have the backing of a leading magnate, close to the regime, with a reputation for justice and impartiality. In Henry III's case this had been William Marshal and in Henry VI's, John, duke of Bedford. Richard was the obvious candidate for the role in the case of Edward V. In fact it would have been a travesty to proceed, even via a council, without first seeking his advice and approval.

The two chroniclers closest to the drama enable us to construct a timetable of events but leave so many questions unanswered that it is possible to construct many different and equally plausible narratives. The Croyland chronicler seems to imply that Edward IV on his death bed envisaged rule by a council, and possibly a quick coronation if they agreed to it. After describing Edward adding codicils to the will, without, of course, telling us what they might be, he says that 'the counsellors of the dead king, who were then attending the queen at Westminster, had fixed upon a day on which Edward, the king's eldest son, who at this time was in Wales, should hasten to London to receive the insignia of the coronation'. Either these 'counsellors' had promptly ignored the dead king's wishes, which is always a possibility of course, or they had got it into their heads that the deceased intended his son to be crowned fairly quickly. The chronicler then exposes the struggle for power that was an inevitable consequence of the untimely death. These unnamed counsellors had a difference of opinion which was bound to lead to real trouble. All who were present, the chronicler tells us, 'keenly desired that this prince should succeed his father in all his glory'. Nevertheless:

> The more foresighted members of the Council, however, thought that the uncles and brothers on the mother's side should be absolutely forbidden to have control of the person of the young man until he came of age.[2]

The chronicler then reveals that the argument was caused by the acrimony that existed between Hastings and the Woodville family. Hastings was keen, he tells us, for Richard to get to the capital from Yorkshire from whence he was marching with the duke of Buckingham. These were the men 'in whom he had the greatest trust'. If these councillors were correct in believing Edward IV wanted an early coronation for his son it was clear, even before Richard arrived on the scene, that such a move would be seen as a threat to the interests of Hastings, and other 'foresighted' members of the council. Once Edward V was crowned he would be a pawn in the hands of his mother's family, and there were plenty of powerful men who had an interest in preventing that from happening.

Two of them, the dukes of Gloucester and Buckingham, were on their way to London. Dominic Mancini had a view on Richard's role in these difficult and dangerous times. Mancini was an Italian visitor to London who spoke little English and gleaned his information from Edward V's doctor, John Argentine, who happened to be Italian. Argentine was obviously as close to events as it was possible to be but his perspective as a member of the young Edward's household is a narrow one. Mancini returned to Italy in July 1483 and began writing his memoir after Richard had usurped the throne. This caused him to read back into previous events with the dubitable benefit of hindsight. He was, nevertheless, very well informed and wrote with an intelligence and polish that reminds us that while he was receiving the benefits of an Italian Renaissance education, the English were still scribbling in monasteries. Mancini believed that the ailing Edward had appointed Richard duke of Gloucester as the protector during a minority but that the queen and her family were determined to stop this happening because they wanted to prevent Richard from gaining power. Mancini believed that Richard hated the queen for compassing the death of Clarence and she feared that he would usurp the throne to get his revenge. There are many problems associated with this interpretation, not the least of which is the speed with which the council are supposed to have discarded the will of the dead king.[3] In both the writers' accounts it is evident that members of the council wanted to crown Edward V without consulting Richard. Very few people outside the narrow confines of the Woodville circle would have considered that a proper way to proceed. To most it would have been unthinkable. Richard was powerful, trusted and a senior member of the royal family. To act in this emergency without his counsel was to court trouble and push him into opposition. There is little doubt that the marquis of Dorset, the queen's eldest son by her first marriage, was doing precisely that. Worried that Richard might gain control of the government when he arrived in London, he pressed for an immediate coronation with the remark, 'We are so important, that even without the king's uncle we can make and enforce these decisions.'[4]

Whatever the intricacies of these perspectives and their relative merits, the fact was that Edward V was on his way from Ludlow, accompanied by his uncle Earl Rivers, and Richard was on his way from York, where he had attended a funeral ceremony for his brother. Richard had been unable to get to Windsor for the actual funeral, held in the beautiful new chapel of St George built for Edward himself, because it had all happened so suddenly. He had held his own service in York Minster and had begun to march south with a relatively modest escort, all in mourning. En route he had been joined by Henry Stafford, duke of Buckingham, who now appeared on the grand stage of history having lurked unnoticed in the wings for much of Edward's reign. Buckingham was a dangerous character to throw into the mix. He detested the Woodville clan with a vengeance, having been forced to marry the queen's sister, Catherine, when he was twelve and she twenty-four. He was a royal duke descended from Thomas of Woodstock, the youngest son of Edward III, and he felt, probably rightly, that Edward had used him to propel yet another grasping low-born Woodville up the evolutionary ladder. Edward had not only forced Buckingham to marry beneath him, thus preventing him from marrying a wealthy heiress or a foreign princess, but had actively blocked his right to inherit the Bohun estates which should have fallen to him when Henry VI and his son were killed.[5] Hastings, that ubiquitous chamberlain ever at Edward's side, had been expanding his influence in precisely the areas, the north midlands for instance, that Buckingham felt belonged to him. Henry Stafford had also been keen to win something for himself in France in 1475 and had been one of those who had returned in disgust without waiting to be plied with the wine of Amiens.[6] All this added up to a potent combination of frustrated ambition and burning resentment. Richard was glad of the sudden arrival of Buckingham and his retainers. He no doubt felt isolated and in need of support. Buckingham was a duke of royal blood with what appeared to be a similar outlook on life to Richard. His dislike of Hastings and the Woodvilles may or may not have been shared by Richard but it might well have influenced the course of events. Buckingham had felt excluded by newcomers of inferior rank and we know that Richard had a view about the importance of lineage. It would be wrong to credit Buckingham with having the decisive voice in the revolutionary direction events were about to take, but it would also be a mistake to discount his influence altogether.

The young King Edward, with an escort limited to 2,000 men, reached Stony Stratford in north Buckinghamshire with his mother's brother, Anthony Earl Rivers, his half-brother Richard Lord Grey and the treasurer of his household Sir Thomas Vaughan. Here they paused, having received a communication from Richard informing them that he was at Northampton, further north, where he had been joined by the duke of Buckingham. Rivers and Grey rode back to Northampton to greet the dukes and the four spent the evening at an inn at Grafton, nine miles from Northampton, between the two camps. Earl Rivers would have made a convivial companion for the evening. He was an urbane, literate and highly experienced soldier, diplomat and courtier. His two great interests were going on pilgrimages and jousting in tournaments. He was the epitome of pious chivalry and just the sort of fellow with whom one might expect Richard duke of Gloucester to enjoy a meal. Edward IV had placed such trust in his probity, intellectual acumen and sound policy that he had made him governor to the heir to the throne. Rivers was described by Mancini as a 'kind, serious and just man' and Sir Thomas More described him as an 'honourable man, as valiant of hand as politic in council'. There were, however, a few defects on his curriculum vitae which may have been exposed in his interview with Richard. He was a highly astute politician who had spent the time he had been with Edward, prince of Wales, shoring up a potentially powerful position as controller of the next king's person and in dispensing with patronage in Wales as if he was the prince himself. There was one other factor that was likely to cause friction and that was his kinship with the queen and his role as senior member of the Woodville clan. Given Buckingham's pathological detestation of anything and everything Woodville, the pleasantries exchanged on the evening of 29 April 1483 must have required all the acting skills of an accomplished thespian. There is no evidence that Rivers expected the thunderbolt that was about to strike him. He and his nephew left the party and rode back to Stony Stratford to spend the night in the young king's entourage.

Early the next morning Richard and Buckingham rode into Stony Stratford with a 'large body of soldiers' and arrested Rivers, Grey and Vaughan. They removed the king's guard, posted their own watches on the roads and went in to meet the new sovereign. Richard knelt in obeisance, offering his profound condolences for the death of the king's father and saluted Edward V as his lord and king. He then explained as best he could the reasons for the sudden changes in personnel which the boy was currently experiencing. Judging by Mancini's account Richard was not very good at softening blows and couching his meaning in tolerable tones. He explained that he held the men he had arrested responsible for the death of Edward IV. They were the 'companions and servants of his vices, and had ruined his health'. Lest these men should attempt to play the same game with the new king, they had been removed because 'such a child would be incapable of governing so great a realm by means of puny men'. Richard continued by accusing the detainees of conspiring against him and attempting to prevent him from occupying the office of regent that had been conferred upon him by his brother. He then offered himself as the protector of the king's person and laid out his credentials as the most experienced in the discharge of government business and the most popular candidate. Edward was not being offered a menu of options but a *fait accompli* made necessary by the threat to national security posed by undesirable councillors.

Despite the blunt and uncompromising tone of this address the boy-king ventured to offer his views on the situation and replied to his uncle Richard:

> ...he merely had those ministers whom his father had given him; relying on his father's prudence, he believed that good and faithful ones had been given him. He had seen nothing evil in them and wished to keep them unless otherwise proved to be evil. As for the government of the kingdom, he had complete confidence in the peers of the realm and the queen, so that this care but little concerned his former ministers.[7]

These are the only recorded words Edward has left to the world and they proved to be his death sentence. Here was the stark proof that the boy had his own views, would adhere to them and that they encompassed the retention of the Woodville faction. Of course they did: he was a Woodville himself and had been brought up with them, had been surrounded by them, and, it would be fair to suggest, loved them most dearly. They were his family. If Richard expected the youth before him to renounce his upbringing and his affection for those closest to him on the grounds that the boy was now king and therefore above faction and party-politics, his optimism must have vanished rather rapidly on hearing this proud and defiant speech. It had suddenly become clear that the unstable variable in the constitutional solutions debated in the council in London, the strength of the views of the minor himself, would play a part immediately.

Mancini does not report Richard's reaction to this expression of the sovereign's will: perhaps there was no perceivable response. Buckingham, an altogether different character, reacted with undisguised anger:

> On hearing the queen's name the duke of Buckingham, who loathed her race, then answered, it was not the business of women but of men to govern kingdoms, and so if he cherished any confidence in her he had better relinquish it. Let him place all his hope in his barons, who excelled in nobility and power.

No one can doubt that, whether or not Mancini has accurately represented the encounter, these were the views of the two dukes and also the most likely response from Edward V. The Croyland chronicler agrees with the narrative for the most part, emphasising Richard's deference to the new king and seeing this as part of the 'conspiracy'. Richard tells the king that he has arrested Edward's advisors because they had sworn to destroy 'his honour and his life'.[8] In both accounts there is no overt mention of any plot to dethrone the boy and he was taken to London 'in regal style' having had all his attendants dismissed and sent home. The legal formalities were still honoured and, while the hasty coronation planned for 4 May was postponed until 22 June, a smooth transition of power might yet be possible.

The trouble was that the conversations at Stony Stratford had closed the door on any prospect of the peaceful accession of Edward V. It is inconceivable that after this meeting, Buckingham, at least, was not planning to sweep the board clean of the Woodvilles and this Woodville king. If he had blurted out his views on the queen on the spur of the moment and had not meant to alarm or offend his young sovereign, the damage had been manifestly and irreparably done. There could be no going back. What retribution might Buckingham reap in the not-too-distant future for insulting the king's mother and all her family? Richard, even if he had been more temperate and straightforward in his remarks to the young king, was in the same boat as Buckingham. The twelve-year-old had objected to the removal of his chief officers. He was the son of the master of a mighty kingdom and would expect to rule in his own right in three years at the outset. That was not a long time in which to forget the astounding conduct of these hostile lords. If Richard hoped to persuade Edward to rapidly outgrow his Woodville nurture, spring from the nest and begin to soar into the kind of kingship he valued, he hoped for too much. Quite when this realisation must have dawned it is difficult to tell but for a man of his intelligence, and his sensitivity to the realities of power, it could not have been too long after the fateful appointment at Stony Stratford.

On hearing the news of the arrests of her brother and son, Rivers and Grey, the queen fled into the sanctuary of Westminster Abbey with all the children she had with her, including the marquis of Dorset, Grey's brother, who was soon to escape abroad. The queen also brought her five daughters with her as well as Prince Richard, the younger brother of Edward V, and all their attendants. This was quite a crowd but there can be no doubt that the threat to herself and all her kin was real enough.[9] Rivers, Grey and Vaughan were imprisoned at Pontefract in Yorkshire and they were executed less than two months later on charges of treason. Thomas Vaughan cuts a particularly pathetic figure in this grim denouement. He was an elderly man who had served as treasurer to the young Edward V's household for many years. The warrant for his execution emanated from London after Richard had made it manifest that he had decided to take the throne for himself. Anyone associated with Edward V was in danger then, and likely to be removed from office or worse. It is difficult to imagine what possible harm the old treasurer could have committed to deserve a traitor's death. The proceedings provoked the indictment of the cloth merchant Robert Fabyan who opined that the deed smacked 'more of will than justice'.[10] There is more than a hint of a desire to expunge the remnants of Edward's associates as if they were some sort of malignant disease. Their sympathy for Edward was guaranteed and would never end except in their own deaths: perhaps this was what needed to be eradicated. The body politic was being disinfected. While attempting to rationalise these extraordinary events it is worth sparing a thought for poor old Thomas Vaughan. By any standards he was entirely blameless and totally undeserving of the fate he endured. There is also the disconcerting fact that Richard attempted to have the Pontefract Three executed as soon as he reached London at the beginning of May, but the council turned down the request at that stage. The only rational conclusion that can be drawn from the evidence is that Richard believed they really had been involved in a plot to crown Edward speedily and therefore to prevent him from exercising an oversight. Richard knew from the previous year's campaign in Scotland what trust the old king had placed in him. It had taken many years of painstaking work attending to the business of governing a large region on behalf of his brother to earn that level of trust and respect. The duke of Gloucester did not expect to be ignored when his brother died. Nor could he possibly tolerate a diminution of his status if that reduction was to occasion a return to poor governance. As soon as he got to London, with the young king in tow, he established a protectorate and re-scheduled the coronation. At this point in the saga he had acted entirely predictably and within his rights. Within six weeks all that had changed.

Richard, Buckingham and Edward V arrived in London on 4 May to be received 'in regal style'. Edward was installed in the bishop's palace at St Paul's and all the lords temporal and spiritual together with the mayor and the aldermen of the city of London took the oath of fealty to the new king. A council was now held, lasting several days, in which there was a discussion about settling the king in a more spacious place. The Croyland chronicler informs us that the duke of Buckingham suggested the Tower of London, and this proposal was accepted by all. The council then proceeded to formally grant Richard the office and title of Protector. It was now about 10 May and all was as it should be. Richard had been elevated to a position that few could doubt was both appropriate to his station and necessary for the realm. As Croyland put it, 'He exercised this authority with the consent and the goodwill of all the lords, commanding and forbidding in everything like another king, as occasion demanded.'[11] The rescheduled coronation of Edward V was to take place on 22 June. Things were not quite as simple as this account suggests, however. For a start the queen was still in sanctuary at Westminster with her supporters, and the young duke of York, and this was a situation that could not be allowed to continue. She could become the focus of serious dissension and plotting, particularly given the hostility to the current arrangements, and the personnel involved in them, that her occupation of the abbey implied. What is more, Hastings was so jubilant about the removal of her influence and the freedom he could now enjoy that he had made her fearful for her safety. As Croyland observed:

> Lord Hastings (who seemed to serve these dukes in every way and to have deserved favour of them), bursting with joy over this new world, was asserting that nothing had so far been done except to transfer the government of the kingdom from two blood-relatives of the queen to two nobles of the blood royal, moreover he asserted that this had been accomplished without any killing and with only so much bloodshed in the affair as might have come from a cut finger.[12]

These are the last recorded thoughts of Edward's chamberlain and friend. Like Anthony Earl Rivers he had no inkling of the dreadful calamity about to befall him. The real crisis that had developed in the few weeks between Richard's installation as protector and the date set for the coronation was that there were now three irreconcilable factions in London. The first centred on the queen and her supporters. Their trump card was the forthcoming coronation of her son as king. She would have to be 'released' in time to participate in the ceremonies. Her influence over her son could be paramount and neutralise any security Richard had procured for himself. Once Edward was king, the authority of the protector would be entirely a matter for negotiation. The king's wishes could not be ignored and providing him with councillors and advisers carefully screened and selected by the Protector would no longer be a viable option. The coronation itself had a universally acknowledged significance that would give a sanction to his express commands. Once Edward was anointed with holy oil and crowned in Westminster Abbey any councillor would have countless instruments of royal authority available to him with which to circumvent, nullify or even defy the protector's will.

The second faction centred on Hastings. He was opposed to the Woodvilles and could be relied upon to damage their interests and minimise their power, but this was easier said than done. In fact it would be impossible to achieve without extending Richard's protectorate indefinitely. Hastings had obviously not thought this through very carefully. Richard would have to make way for King Edward V at some stage and Hastings would be high on the list of those the new king would be keen to see the back of. He, like Buckingham, and indeed Richard, had committed too many wrongs against the king's family to go unpunished. Yet Hastings had little to gain from Richard's prolonged spell in power, particularly if Buckingham was going to be rewarded with the estates he so coveted in the north Midlands.

The third faction was grouped around Richard himself. His options were limited and diminishing by the day. Crowning the young king could not be postponed for very much longer and the difficulties he might then face from both the queen and her son could be insurmountable. The position of power and trust he had developed under Edward IV would count for nothing in a very short space of time. There were already plenty of causes ready to be pleaded against him. Would the king's uncle, Rivers, and his half-brother, Grey, meekly walk out of Pontefract jail and into the new king's council chamber without a murmur against the man who had imprisoned them and attempted to have them executed? There was an added complication in that Richard owed a large portion of his Neville lands by an act of Parliament that granted them to him for as long as George Neville, the son of John Marquis Montagu, or his male heirs, lived. By a remarkable and unfortunate coincidence George died without male heir on 4 May. The true inheritor and possessor of these Neville lands was now the fourteen-year-old Richard Lord Latimer. In the normal course of events it should have been possible to overcome this difficulty by further acts of Parliament or payment of compensation to the new heir, but Richard Lord Latimer had powerful protectors in the form of his guardian, the archbishop of Canterbury Thomas Bourchier, and the Archbishop's brother, the earl of Essex. If Richard duke of Gloucester lost his political hegemony at court he could also lose a great deal else.[13]

While these thoughts were circulating wildly in Richard's mind, another thought may have occurred to him. What were the options available to Hastings? It was all very well crowing about the suffering and exclusion of the Woodvilles, but Hastings was depending on a new political landscape opening up under Edward V. He had served the young Edward's father in ways no other person had been able to emulate. He was the most loyal of all Edward's servants and his authority within the royal household was paramount. His expectation, in a rather naïve way, must now be to recreate that position in the household of the new king. He presumably expected his role as chamberlain to continue and the network of royal officials beneath him to operate as before. He would need to normalise his relations with the king's family, despite their residual enmity, as he had managed to do during the reign of Edward IV. While this reflection was receiving Richard's consideration, alarm bells may have begun to ring.

It was only a matter of time before similar thoughts occurred to Hastings. If he looked to the future, as surely he must, he was better placed than Richard to protect himself from a giddy fall once Edward ruled in his own right. The solution was simple. Hastings had done nothing, as far as Edward knew, to offend the king or damage his rights. He was and always had been a staunch supporter of Edward IV and would be an invaluable assistant to a young king reliant on such a fund of knowledge and experience. All that was necessary was for Hastings to reach an accommodation with the queen. Hastings had had nothing to do with any of the arrests of her kin and could make the queen in her present plight feel obliged to him if he secured her interests. It was true that his feud with the queen's eldest son, the marquis of Dorset, had reached alarming proportions but Dorset would be far safer with Hastings back in harness than he would be with Richard running the show. Hastings had no ambition to rule the king, merely to serve him. Whether or not these thoughts passed through the minds of Richard and Hastings as the days passed and the preparations for the coronation proceeded apace, there was an inherent conflict of interest between the two men. Hastings stood little to gain from an extension of the protectorate because his authority had always depended on his service in the royal household. He had less to fear from the re-establishment of that household than he had if it was to be disbanded or reconstituted. Richard, on the other hand, would only be secure as a Protector with guaranteed authority. An alliance between Hastings and the queen would be the end of him.

On 10 June the tension finally reached breaking point. Richard sent one of his most trusted northern retainers, Richard Ratcliffe, to the city of York with a letter to be delivered to the mayor:

The Duke of Gloucester, brother and uncle of Kings, protector, defender, great Chamberlain, Constable and Admiral of England. Right trusty and well beloved, we greet you well, and as you love the weal of us, and the weal and surety of your own self, we heartily pray you to come to us in London in all the diligence you possibly can, with as many as you can make defensibly arrayed, there to aid and assist us against the queen, her blood adherents and affinity, who have intended and daily do intend, to murder and utterly destroy us and our cousin, the Duke of Buckingham, and the old royal blood of this realm, and as it is openly known, by their subtle and damnable ways forecast the same, and also the final destruction and disinheritance of you and all other the inheritors and men in honour, as well of the north parts as other countries, that belong to us...[14]

By the time this letter reached York, Richard had removed Hastings from the equation. On 13 June Richard had arranged for the council to be split to conduct two separate meetings, one at Westminster, under the chairmanship of the chancellor, and the other in the Tower under Richard's auspices. As the meeting in the Tower got under way, Richard suddenly accused Hastings of plotting with the queen. At a signal from the protector, armed men then rushed into the council chamber and arrested Hastings without waiting to hear his reply. He was dragged out of the Tower, denied even the pretence of a trial, and beheaded on Tower Hill. He had been taken by complete surprise. Richard, it would seem, would not be outmanoeuvred by anybody.

It is impossible to tell whether Hastings was guilty of the offence with which he was charged. Any extension of Richard's protectorate would threaten his landed interests in favour of Buckingham and also diminish the role of Hastings as the household supremo. It is possible that he had begun to negotiate with the queen. Any approach from him would have been a great advantage to her. There are other possibilities. Richard's critics have pointed out that an extension of the protectorate and a postponement of the coronation, the only surety for a man whose power would inevitably be threatened by the accession of Edward V, would inevitably result in usurpation. If usurpation was the name of the game then Hastings would have to go because he would never agree to the overthrow of Edward V. His loyalty to Edward IV extended to his son and heir. The call to York for troops was a prerequisite of the coup that had already begun. Force might be needed and London and the council would have to be subdued. In other words Richard had decided to seize the throne on 10 June at the latest. This version of events requires the letter to York to be part of a dissembling scheme to outflank potential opposition. There can be no doubt that if the letter is taken at face value and Richard was genuinely fearful of the queen 'and her blood adherents', then an explosion of some kind was going to happen soon. There are those who believe Richard simply panicked and in desperation killed Hastings and grabbed the safety of the throne. Certainly his actions on 13 June in the council meeting in the Tower have provided his detractors with ample material. Hastings was not guilty of any crime and was executed without trial. If Richard was planning on taking the throne on 13 June then just when might that possibility have shaped his resolve? At Stony Stratford he had seized the boy-king against his wishes. That could be seen as the beginning or not. Perhaps the evil creature created for the Elizabethan stage by Shakespeare is the real Richard. If he plotted to take the throne after Edward IV's death then perhaps he had always coveted it.

It is precisely this picture of Richard, generated by the Tudor propaganda machine, cultivated by Polydore Vergil and Sir Thomas More, which has created the gulf that currently exists between 'Ricardians' and many professional historians. For Ricardians the character of Richard, his previous life of service and good lordship and the morality of his private life, make it impossible to accept that he suddenly became the evil nephew-murdering villain of legend. For many historians the facts bear this lurid interpretation reasonably well and the only ingredients which have to be surmised are the extent of Richard's ambition, the effect on him of the proximity of absolute power and the timing. For the time being let us keep to the firm ground of solid consensus. Richard's actions in the middle of June 1483 would have been unthinkable before his brother's death in April. What happened after that was the consequence of the age of Edward's elder son. Whatever ambition Richard nurtured for kingship before his brother's death would have been irrelevant within a few years if Edward IV had continued to live as expected. The death of the king at the age of forty threw up dangers, both real and imagined. The arrest of Rivers, Grey and Vaughan changed an already volatile situation so that now there were two possibilities: the succession of a minor free from the influence of a partisan faction or a counter-attack by that faction. When it became clear that the young king was going to remain very much part of the court establishment, he was doomed. There could be no going back for Richard. Throughout the whole drama there was one constant theme and that was Richard's determination to prevent kingship from becoming weak, corrupt or subject to manipulation. Perhaps forty years of that was enough for one century. In a rather unexpected way he achieved that.

The death of Hastings may or may not have been the consequence of a conspiracy against the Protector or a response to a rearguard action by the Edwardian court but it was illegal, brutal and dangerous. Richard would have to become king himself after the murder of Edward IV's most loyal household servant or face retribution sooner or later. Again it is difficult to be certain whether Richard believed that Hastings was plotting with the queen or not but the chamberlain's unquestioned loyalty to Edward V would give him common cause with her and if he wasn't plotting in early June then he would be in due course. Similarly it is not possible to deduce whether Hastings' fate was a consequence of Richard's decision to take the throne or a proximate cause of it but either way the usurpation of the throne and the setting aside of the princes was now on.

Hastings was not the only man arrested in the council chamber at the Tower that day. John Morton, the bishop of Ely, and Thomas Rotherham, archbishop of York, were also arrested, stripped of their royal posts and confined to secure quarters in the Tower. Both these men had strong links with the queen and their arrest would suggest that some communication had occurred with the Woodville party. If Richard can be accused of paranoia it should also be noted that he was very vulnerable to a swift reaction that many people would have both welcomed and justified. One other man was also arrested in that eventful council meeting on 13 June, and he was none other than Thomas lord Stanley. The arrests were effected by stationing armed men outside the council chamber, under the leadership of Thomas Howard, the son of John Howard, and two well-known northerners. At a given signal these men burst in and pounced on their victims. The two men from the north country busy by Richard's side, as they were to be for the next two years, were Charles Pilkington and Robert Harrington. Stanley was slightly wounded in the fracas, either trying to defend himself or being pressed too hard by his assailants. With what we know about the history of these men it would seem that Stanley was lucky to escape with his life. How opportune the occasion must have appeared to men with so much to gain from Stanley's removal. Perhaps a sword did accidentally slip during the arrest. Robert had still not got his rightful authority in the bailiwicks of Blackburn and Amounderness because of Stanley's obduracy, and Charles' brother was the other loser in that affair. If Harrington and Pilkington had got as close as this at Bosworth, Stanley would surely not have lived to tell the tale. Stanley, as ever, not only escaped summary retribution but also escaped any other form of punishment for whatever it was he was supposed to have been doing. It was not long before he was back in harness proving himself to be indispensable to yet another king.

Events now moved speedily towards usurpation. On 16 June the precincts of Westminster Abbey were surrounded by armed men and the queen induced, through the good offices of the aged Thomas Bourchier, archbishop of Canterbury, to hand over the younger son of Edward, Richard duke of York. She was told that the coronation of Edward V would not be complete without the presence of the other prince. On the same day parliament was cancelled and preparations for the coronation postponed. There were now two princes in the Tower. On 22 June a certain Dr Ralph Shaw preached a sermon at St Paul's cross, in the presence of Richard and other leading nobles, declaring that Edward IV had been illegitimate and therefore Edward V was not the rightful king. This sermon was not particularly well received by the populace and the declaration turned out to be a poor career move for the learned theologian. The warrant for the execution of the Pontefract Three was now issued while Buckingham was busy entertaining the mayor and aldermen of the city of London in the Guildhall with a speech about the entitlement of Richard duke of Gloucester to become king. He repeated the performance to the lords and gentry the next day and the result was the sending of a petition from lords and commons to Richard, now residing in Baynards Castle, on 25 June. The bishop of Bath and Wells, Robert Stillington, had managed to come up with a better legal argument than Shaw's rather speculative affair, and declared that the princes were indeed illegitimate, not because their father was, but because their father's marriage to Elizabeth Woodville was invalid. The story went that Edward had been pre-contracted to another woman, Lady Eleanor Butler, at the time of his clandestine marriage to Elizabeth Woodville and that this contract barred him from marrying another woman. The pre-contract had been witnessed by only one man, apparently, and that happened to be Bishop Stillington. This was the main gist of the argument laid out in the petition sent to Richard on 25 June.

The argument was, of course, pathetic. Eleanor Butler had died in 1468 so she couldn't verify the details, but even if she could, Edward's marriage of almost twenty years to Elizabeth Woodville had been recognised by both church and state and could not be undone by parliament. An ecclesiastical court, the only court with the jurisdiction to rule on the matter, would have thrown the petition out in three minutes. Stillington would have had to provide evidence and witnesses and he had neither. The two princes were born after Eleanor Butler's death so Edward would have been free to marry Elizabeth Woodville in order to legitimise his male offspring if anyone had claimed at any point that he was not properly married. They didn't, despite the opposition and the subsequent furore that the marriage to Elizabeth Woodville had created. Presumably the story that Edward IV was illegitimate had been quietly shelved because Richard was actually staying in his mother's house at this time. The Duchess Cecily may have had a view on whether she had committed the sin of adultery while her husband's back was turned during his French campaign in Rouen in 1442. Indeed it is a great shame that we do not have any of her views on these critical matters. It would be interesting to know what she and Richard talked about at Baynards Castle in June 1483. Perhaps they discussed her grandchildren, Richard and Edward, playing in the gardens of the Tower of London, or there again perhaps the conversation turned to the memory of Richard's father. We will never know.

The petition was duly presented by the duke of Buckingham, playing a leading role, some would say a decisive role, in these events. The lords and commons, whoever they happened to be at this time, parliament having been cancelled, declared that Richard was 'the very inheritor of the said Crown and

Dignity Royal, and as in right King of England, by way of inheritance'. The next day, 26 June, Richard rode to Westminster Hall and sat in the seat reserved for the king in the court of King's Bench where he formally accepted the offer of the throne. As the Croyland chronicler put it, 'he thrust himself into the marble chair' having a 'pretext' for this 'intrusion'. On the 2 July the army arrived from the north and on 6 July Richard finally gained the security of the throne. As Croyland eloquently put it:

> ...the cardinal, Thomas, archbishop of Canterbury, was summoned and on 6 July fol-
> lowing Richard of Gloucester received the gift of the royal unction and the crowning
> in the conventual church of St Peter at Westminster [Abbey] and at the same time
> and in the same place his wife, Queen Anne, received her crown. From that day,
> while he lived, this man was called King Richard, the third after the Conquest.[15]

After accepting the offer of the crown on 26 June, and before the coronation on 6 July, Richard promoted John Howard, so helpful in the Tower opera-tion on 13 June, to the dukedom of Norfolk. This had already been given to the younger of the princes in the Tower, but no matter. It is one of the first documents to be produced by Richard as king and the charter, dated 28 June, is unusual in that it spends less time enumerating the qualities of the grantee, John Howard, which is what one would expect from such a document, and more speaking about Richard's authority:

> The king to the archbishops, Etc. Whereas the radiance of the eternal king through
> whom all kings reign and princes have dominion, the ray of his light and glory in
> many and divers ways shines upon all his creatures and marks out those who share
> in his goodness, and whereas We, who under his providential design rule and govern
> his people, endeavour by his grace to conform our will and acts to his will, we have
> deemed it right and consider it fit by natural and prudent reason to walk in his ways
> and, insofar as it is granted to us from above, to mark his footsteps, therefore, led by
> his example, we have determined by the grace and liberality of our royal majesty to
> illumine those noble and distinguished men who are most deserving of the public
> weal, and hence we have determined to raise the outstanding nobility of our most
> dear cousin John Howard...[16]

Richard seems rather keen to emphasise the source and fount of the power he has recently acquired. It is by 'providential design' that he now rules the kingdom of England and he is proceeding in his task by 'natural and prudent reason'. He is ennobling John Howard through the 'grace and liberality' of his royal majesty, in exactly the same way that God has illumined him. If this gives a hint of Richard's true beliefs, and public pronouncements are hardly evidence of that, it accords well with the letter to the city of York asking for troops on 10 June. We recall on that occasion that Richard had told the city that the queen and all her 'blood adherents' were intent on destroying the 'old royal blood of the realm'. This talk of blood is rather significant. The queen, he alleges in the letter to York, has used 'subtle and damnable ways' to seek the 'final destruction and disinheritance of you and all other the inheritors and men of honour'. The 'providential design' which illumines noble and distinguished men, also determines noble birth and the blood lines through which these are passed. Reason and grace are the characteristics of nobility, but these can be perverted by corruption and 'subtle and damnable' means.

Both these documents may be the products of a scheme of propaganda to mask the blatant and shocking seizure of the crown which lies behind them. But this dismissive conclusion is far too simplistic and ignores too much. They both embody concepts and a world view which chimes perfectly with what we know of Richard already. He has of course been accused of deliberate deception and even of self-delusion, both natural assumptions in the context of the dramatic events of June 1483, but again, these convenient charges do not quite fit the bill: they ignore the whole life-story behind Richard's thinking. They create a character to fit the events without considering how the pertinent features of the character he had already exhibited might have shaped his conduct during the crisis.

In Richard's one and only Parliament held in January 1484, his title to the throne was confirmed in the usual way by an act which rendered it legal. The act is interesting because it purports to incorporate the text of the petition presented to Richard by Buckingham in Baynards Castle. More than any other source it gives us an insight into the attitude of those keen to justify the usurpation, and, in as much as it must have been sanctioned and approved by him, of Richard himself. It begins by recalling a distant past in which an idyllic peace was enjoyed by all the people under the just rule of a king chosen by God and following His will:

> ...heretofore in time past this land many years stood in great prosperity, honour and tranquillity, which was caused, forsomuch as the kings then reigning used and followed the advice and counsel of certain lords spiritual and temporal, and other persons of approved sadness, prudence, policy and experience, dreading God, and having tender zeal and affection to indifferent ministration of justice, and to the common and politic weal of the land.[17]

Those perfect conditions in which 'our Lord God was dread, loved and honoured' brought peace and tranquillity, and among neighbours 'concord and charity'. The prosperity was shared by all including merchants, artificers and other poor people 'labouring for their living in diverse occupations' who 'had competent gain to the sustenation of them and their households, living without miserable and intolerable poverty'. What had brought this paradise to an end was that those who had the rule and governance of the land 'delighting in adulation and flattery and led by sensuality and concupiscence, followed the counsel of persons insolent, vicious and of inordinate avarice, despising the counsel of good, virtuous and prudent persons'. The result was that prosperity daily decreased 'felicity was turned into misery, and prosperity into adversity, and the order of policy, and of the law of God and man, confounded'. Rather than the appalling misgovernance of Henry VI, this description seems to have been levelled at that of Richard's brother, Edward IV, and certainly hints that the accession of his son would lead to ruin:

> ...whereby it is likely this realm to fall into extreme misery and desolation, which God defend, without due provision of convenable remedy be had in this behalf in all godly haste.

The Act then goes on to impugn the 'ungracious pretenced marriage' of Edward IV and Elizabeth Woodville 'late naming herself and many years heretofore Queen of England'. As a consequence of this unholy matrimony:

> ...the order of all politic rule was perverted, the laws of God and God's church, and also the laws of nature and of England, and also the laudable customs and liberties of the same, wherein every Englishman is inheritor, broken, subverted and condemned, against all reason and justice.

The people who particularly suffered from the ensuing 'inconvenients and mischiefs', the murders, extortions and oppressions, were the 'poor and impotent people' so that:

> ...no man was sure of his life, land, nor livelihood, nor of his wife, daughter, servant, every good maiden and woman standing in dread to be ravished and defouled.

The document moves on to remember the civil war which erupted during Edward's reign, the discords and the effusion of Christian blood which followed from these 'inward battles' and 'the destruction of the noble blood of this land'. Once again we find the audience being reminded of that precious blood. It was the perversion of that blood, and the subversion of God's laws and the laws of nature which resulted from it, that caused the whole land and its people to suffer. Richard, through his clerks, seems to be remembering the period between 1469 and 1471 in which the seventeen-year-old found himself flung into dangerous conflicts, exile and two tremendous battles. That experience of bloody revolution and the thousands who suffered from it had strengthened his resolve to ensure that it never happened again. The remedy lay in the fact that Richard was 'the undoubted son and heir of Richard late Duke of York, very inheritor to the said crown and dignity royal and is in right King of England by way of inheritance'. Further 'there is no other person living…that by right may claim the said crown and dignity royal by way of inheritance'. Richard had donned the mantle of his father. The 'old royal blood' had descended to him by true inheritance and all that was now needed was God's will to be made manifest in virtue and justice. The Act reveals that Richard no longer saw himself as the successor of Edward IV, but of his father. Buckingham's rebellion may have led him to realise that he would not be accepted as the continuity candidate by the old regime.

Richard's record bears ample testimony to his concern for justice, the interests of the common people and the virtue of his private and public life. In the Parliament that produced the declaration of his title he passed several laws that remedied abuses and corrected legal defects and these undoubtedly benefited many of his subjects. The despised 'benevolences' by which Edward had extracted money from the rich were made illegal. Ordinary persons who were arrested on suspicion of causing crimes were to be allowed bail to prevent their more powerful enemies bringing malicious prosecutions and then seizing the property of the incarcerated defendant. Stanley had attempted to do precisely this against James Harrington twenty years before. Another law remedied a defect which Stanley had also exploited all those years ago. It was now forbidden to empanel a jury by means of the 'sheriff's tourn'. Again, this is precisely what Thomas lord Stanley did in order to maliciously prosecute the Harringtons and their supporters. In October 1483, after the collapse of a major rebellion, Richard issued a proclamation in Kent outlining the measures he proposed to employ to improve justice:

> The king's highness is fully determined to see due administration of justice throughout this his realm to be had, and to reform, punish and subdue all extortions and oppressions in the same. And for that cause will that at his now coming into this his said County Kent that every person dwelling within the same that find him grieved, oppressed or unlawfully wronged do make a bill of his complaint and put it to his highness and he shall be heard and without delay have such convenient remedy as shall accord with his laws. For his grace is utterly determined all his true subjects shall live in rest and quiet and peaceably enjoy their lands, livelihoods and goods according to the laws of the land which they be naturally born to inherit.[18]

Of course these pronouncements made for good public relations and were also propaganda tools, particularly at this early and troubled period in the reign, but that doesn't preclude the possibility that Richard believed in the sentiments they expressed. His 'progress' through his newly acquired kingdom at the beginning of the reign might also be seen in this light. He showed himself to his new subjects and showered them with gifts and marks of his royal favour. The itinerary inevitably led to York where he must have been mightily relieved to be on home turf, free from the swirling vapours of political intrigue in the south and back among his friends and supporters. John Kendall, his new secretary, wrote to the city of York from Nottingham confirming the king's interest in giving poor people justice and preparing the city for his visit. Kendall was himself a citizen of York and was therefore particularly keen for the city to show 'the southern lords' what they could do and how much they valued the lordship of Richard. There can be little doubt that both Richard and the city of York looked forward to the occasion with eager anticipation:

> ...the king's grace is in good health, and in likewise the queen's grace, and in all their progress have been worshipfully received with pageants; and his lords and judges sitting in every place, determining the complaints of poor folk with due punishment of offenders against his laws...I truly know the king's mind and entire affection that his grace bears towards you and your worshipful city, for your many kind and loving deservings shown to his grace heretofore, which his grace will never forget, and intends therefore so to do unto you that all the kings that ever reigned over you did never so much, doubt not hereof... (19)

The city did the new king proud with feasts and pageants accompanied by gifts to the king and queen, many of which he returned, aware that their value would rob the townsfolk of much needed revenue. He repaid their goodwill by repeating the coronation in York Minster, an extraordinary and singular expression of his respect for York, and further honouring the citizens by choosing to use the ceremony to give his only son, the seven-year-old Edward, the title and insignia of Prince of Wales. He also made substantial grants of money to repair decay in the city, relieve poverty and for the uses of the mayor and commonalty 'yearly for ever'. The city council recorded their amazement that these generous annuities were given 'without any petition or asking of anything'. The celebrations were marred only by the absence of Archbishop Thomas Rotherham, recently released from his confinement, who could not stomach the general rejoicing around him. One prelate only too keen to be by Richard's side during all this excitement was Thomas Langton who had every reason to be happy with the new regime, having just been made bishop of St David's. He wrote to his friend, the prior of Canterbury, describing the experience of accompanying the king on his progress to the north:

He contents the people where he goes best that ever did Prince, for many a poor
man that hath suffered wrong many days hath been relieved and helped by him and
his commands in his progress. And in many great cities and towns were great sums of
money given him which he refused. On my troth I liked never the conditions of any
prince so well as his; God hath sent him to us for the weal of us all.[20]

Again there is evidence in Langton's letter of Richard's concern for the poor
and his determination to ensure they received justice and relief from oppression. One man who had been on Richard's ducal council in York and now
joined the king's council as its clerk, was John Harrington. He was a kinsman of James and Robert Harrington and was given special responsibilities for
liaising between the council of York and the king's council.[21] He had received
the training of a lawyer and Richard gave him responsibility for hearing the
complaints of the poor and dispensing speedy justice to them. A grant dated
27 December 1483 is made 'for life to the king's servitor John Harrington,
for good service before the laws and others of the council and elsewhere and
especially the custody, registration and expedition of bills, requests and sup-
plications of poor persons, of an annuity of £20'.[22]

John Harrington was a member of an impoverished cadet branch of the
Harrington family but Robert Harrington readily acknowledged their kinship and John was thus able to advance in the service of the vicar-general of
the archdiocese of York and other important members of the upper gentry
who were associates of the Harrington brothers. His work in the court of
Requests was to continue after Bosworth, though not under his direction, and
has an important place in legal history. It may also be one of the few lasting
memorials to Richard's concern for justice for the common people.

Another John Harrington was also at court. He was the illegitimate son of James
Harrington, described as 'an esquire of the body'. He has an unfortunate place in
the history of the feud between the Stanleys and the Harringtons. After the death
at Bosworth of James Harrington, his heir was his only son John. Illegitimacy
was not a great obstacle in the inheritance of a family's estates if there were no
legitimate heirs and as long as legal steps had been taken to secure the appropriate
rights. When John Pilkington had died in 1479 he had made provision for both
his legitimate son, Edward, and his illegitimate son, Robert. When Edward died in
1486 Robert was recognised as the sole heir. Similarly when Charles Pilkington,
faithful servant of Richard and knight of the Body, died in the late spring of 1485,
Richard recognised his illegitimate son, Edward, as the legal heir. There should,
therefore, have been little difficulty involved in legitimising John's claim to be the
heir of James Harrington, especially given the considerable marks of favour and
mutual respect which characterised the relationship between his family and the

king. Despite the fact that after the battle of Bosworth Field James was attainted and all his lands forfeit, the residual claim to the title of the forfeited lands would remain as long as his son John survived. Acts of attainder could, and frequently were, reversed. This fact put poor John in mortal danger from a member of the Stanley clan who just happened to be living at Hornby Castle. This was Edward Stanley who had been married to Ann Harrington after Thomas lord Stanley had managed to get custody of both she and her sister.

Edward Stanley, son of Thomas lord Stanley, had managed to inhabit the castle of Hornby when James Harrington had finally been removed in 1475, but his wife Ann, the daughter of the John Harrington killed with his father at the battle of Wakefield, did not live for very much longer and they had no children. Perhaps the air at Hornby did not suit her as much as it might, or perhaps her conjugal relations were affected by the bitter struggle between her own family and his. Whatever the reason, her childlessness caused Edward Stanley some anxiety. Her right to inherit Hornby had passed to him when he married her. It would have devolved upon their children but his own rights were now negotiable. The inheritance ought to have provided Ann's other sister, Elizabeth, with a division of the estate. Edward Stanley certainly had not allowed this to happen and would continue to do everything he could to prevent it. He wanted to keep Hornby. His father, Thomas lord Stanley, had fought long and hard to obtain the property and he too valued it so highly that to relinquish it, especially to a Harrington, was unthinkable.

During the reign of Richard III the unthinkable had begun to be thinkable. There is evidence that Richard, with the power at last to right a wrong, had begun to look into the legal ownership of Hornby, now that Ann was dead. Shortly after the battle of Bosworth, Ann's sister, Elizabeth, received a letter from the parson of Slaydburn in Lancashire. She had written to him expressing a number of concerns, one of which involved her rights over Hornby. The parson assured her that contrary to the story being put about by Edward Stanley, King Edward had not given her portion of the inheritance to James Harrington. This legal fiction would have suited Edward perfectly because it would have enabled him to claim the ownership of Hornby by right of James Harrington's attainder. If James had had the right to Hornby instead of Elizabeth, then when he was killed with Richard at Bosworth, the castle could be granted to Edward Stanley, the current occupier, as a forfeiture of the crown. All Harrington rights in the property would be expunged and the ownership of Edward Stanley, by right of his deceased wife, confirmed. It is ironic that this Stanley, after all that his father had gone through to obtain the castle of Hornby from its rightful owners, should now be keen to show that James Harrington owned it after all. That was precisely what he now claimed.

The parson's letter reveals something else about that pleasant spot on the River Lune. He makes it clear that Richard III was preparing to reopen the whole question of the Hornby inheritance:

> ...it was so laboured that King Richard commanded a Note to be Drawn and caused the Chancellor of the Duchy to examine the true valour of all the manors and livelihood the which your father was lawfully possessed and died seised of, and yet this notwithstanding, King Richard never made award betwixt you and your uncles.[23]

Richard had unfinished business in Lancashire and the Stanleys probably knew it. In the end the matter was conveniently resolved for them, with a helping hand from their armed retinues, at Bosworth. In the spring of 1485, months before Richard's final battle, James Harrington, who had been ever busy by Richard's side throughout the short reign, was appointed chief forester of Bowland. He had been Richard's deputy there and the appointment would have made little practical difference, but it was confirmation, if it were needed, that the Harringtons had a new champion and that he was willing to promote their cause.

There is an unpleasant sequel to the Hornby affair. Edward Stanley, later to become Lord Monteagle under Henry VIII, did not feel secure in his castle home, despite the death and attainders of James Harrington and his brother Robert. Within two years of the battle of Bosworth, John Harrington, the heir of James, had been poisoned. Elizabeth, the surviving Harrington sister, had written to her husband, Richard Beaumont, whom she had married after the death of her first husband, John Stanley, asking him as a matter of urgency to get as much evidence as he could from John Harrington's servant. She wrote that Sir James Harrington, Robert's son who became dean of York Minster, was coming to her with the evidence which he had managed to obtain and Elizabeth told her husband, 'Sir James and the parson of Slaydburn think that my cousin John was poisoned and that his servant was hired to do it by my brother [in-law] Sir Edward and if it so be then he forfeit all.' She believed that if it could be proved that Edward Stanley had murdered John Harrington then he would have to forfeit Hornby as a convicted felon. Whether or not she was right to think so is unclear, but we can still hear across the years that separate us from them the fervent desire of the Harringtons to get Hornby back from the Stanleys. We can also get a glimpse of the depths to which the Stanleys were prepared to sink in order to hang on to it. Poor old John was killed because he was the sole surviving male heir of James Harrington. A fragment of a witness statement to an inquisition post mortem seems to confirm John Harrington's fate: it simply reads 'poisoned at the Temple 2 Henry VII'.[24] This provides the date as the second year of the reign of Henry VII, that is

1487. Robert Harrington's son, another Sir James, managed to live long after Bosworth in a degree of poverty and clerical service that may have protected him. A distant cousin of his, also called James, from the cadet branch of the Harrington family (James and Robert Harrington's great-uncle was his great-great-grandfather) was granted the Harrington estates of Farleton in Lonsdale, Farleton in Kendal and Brierely in Yorkshire, by Henry VIII in 1521. Hornby was retained by the Stanleys, of course. The doubt about its ownership had to be settled by a special grant made by Henry Tudor after Thomas lord Stanley had intervened on behalf of his son. Henry VIII excluded Hornby from his grant to the James Harrington of 1521 but provided for this estate to revert to the Harringtons if Edward Stanley died without male heirs. Edward left a son, Thomas, when he died in 1523 and that faint glimmer of hope that Hornby would revert to the Harringtons was lost for ever.[25]

While Richard was busy in the north being entertained and distributing good will, justice and royal largesse, the neglected south began to grow restless and eventually began to rebel. An attempt was made at the end of July to rescue the princes from the Tower and to get the daughters of Edward IV out of the sanctuary of Westminster to some secret hiding place. Edward's gentry household retainers, largely living on estates in the south, remained loyal to his son, Edward V, and did not share Richard's fears about his rule. The succession of Edward IV's son would ensure their own continuation in place, office and courtly connections. The attempted rescue of the princes was thwarted but it may have sealed their fate. Once Richard had taken the throne they were as good as dead in any case. He considered them to be the product of a corrupt union, one which could pollute the blood royal and had to be quarantined. If there was any possibility that the princes would become the focal point of treason and rebellion, that their polluted blood might infect the realm and pervert the providential design of the creator to the great harm of all people, then the solution was fairly obvious. By the end of July 1483 he must have reached that resolution although there is enough evidence to show that the murders were not carried out immediately, and they may not have occurred until September. The difficulty was that by keeping them alive he was providing an incentive to their would-be rescuers, but by killing them he would be providing his enemies with ammunition to use against him. Propagating news of their deaths would have been a spectacular public relations disaster. Richard was intelligent enough to realise that his own beliefs about them were not shared by all. If he had lived for five hundred years or so he would have seen that very few shared his convictions. The princes would have to be killed and they would have to be killed in secret. That job was very well done. So well done that there are plenty of people around today who argue that it didn't happen at all. Richard was far too noble to do such a barbaric thing, they say, and those that believe otherwise will burn in hell. This is a quasi-religious phenomenon, a cult of adulation that brooks no heresy.[26]

It is also based on a thorough misunderstanding of the medieval aristocratic mind. Richard seized the throne by killing four adults and two boys. That is not a bad bodycount when set against the thousands killed during his brother's bid for the throne, or his father's failed bid, which cost him his own life along with thousands more. It may have seemed to Richard that the death of the princes was very little collateral damage when set against the possibility of war. That possibility was very real. The last time a young man had sat on the throne of England, accompanied by a determined woman and friendly courtiers, war had become a fact of life. When Edward, the son of Henry VI, had been killed at Tewkesbury, whoever did that deed killed the young innocent heir to the throne. No one had batted an eyelid, except perhaps his grief-stricken mother now in retirement in her native France. If Edward V had succeeded peacefully it would surely have only been a matter of time before his family had sought to reduce Richard's power. That eventuality would, in turn, have caused civil war to break out again. Richard and his retainers would then have resembled his father, Richard duke of York, taking up arms to protect his rightful inheritance, to rid the court of factions, to secure honourable policies at home and abroad. Not all that again, surely. A few swift and well-chosen executions would save the country from the descent back into the abyss of uncertainty and bloodshed. When civil war broke out it was the poor people who suffered the most in the lawlessness and loss of livelihood that came with it. Richard saw the necessity for usurpation in rescuing himself, but also in saving the country as a whole from a return to the horrors of the past.

This is only one interpretation of Richard and there will always be many others. He was a complex man with vision, courage and a sense of destiny. He was a product of trauma and turmoil, danger and exile. He was also highly ambitious and ruthless. How else could he rule the turbulent regions of the north and subject them to peace and law? It could not have been done by holding tea parties and outreach workshops offering counselling to the disaffected cattle-rustlers on the borders. Even if it is argued that Richard was not directly responsible for the deaths of the princes, that Buckingham, or someone else with a motive, killed them, the fact will always remain that they died on his watch. He was responsible for their safety, for their security, for their lives. The evidence put forward to promulgate the theory that they survived his reign is derisory at best and laughable for the most part. It is certainly true, and has provided a crumb of comfort for those keen to exonerate him, that if they had survived Richard's reign, Henry Tudor would have put them to death in record time. Henry inherited a boy locked up in the Tower, Edward, earl of Warwick, Clarence's son. He was executed in 1499, still only twenty-eight and having spent more than half his life as a prisoner. Summary executions are always easier in the aftermath of a battle and Henry put many of Richard's supporters to death to secure his own throne, within days of victory at Bosworth. Richard's problem is that the princes in the Tower, whatever his views on their bastardy or the dangers of their survival, were wholly innocent of any crime, real or imagined. Richard is the only king to have taken the throne from another king without accusing him of any wrongdoing. For all Henry VI's simplicity and piety he could still be accused of misrule. Edward V had not had time to misrule. No other boy-king had been deposed: it was customary to wait until they had proved themselves to be incompetent before making the attempt, as in the cases of Henry III and Richard II, not to mention Henry VI again. If Richard had not lost at Bosworth his reign may have vindicated him in the eyes of posterity, but we cannot tell. He lost, and the removal of Edward V, by whatever means, was cruelly exposed for ever.

Richard may have anticipated some reaction to the usurpation but he was shocked to the core when he heard that Henry Stafford, duke of Buckingham, had put himself at the head of the rebellion. On 12 October Richard wrote to the Chancellor, John Russell, bishop of Lincoln, requesting that the Great Seal be brought to Lincoln as soon as possible. The seal authenticated royal documents and Richard wanted to prevent it falling into Buckingham's hands. At the bottom of the warrant Richard wrote in his own hand:

> We would most gladly you came yourself if that you may, and if you may not we pray you not to fail but to accomplish in all diligence our said commandment to send our seal incontinent upon the sight hereof as we trust you with such as we trust, and the officers pertaining to attend with it, praying you to ascertain us of your news. Here, loved be God, is all well and truly determined and for to resist the duke of Buckingham the most untrue creature living, whom with God's grace we shall not be long until that we will be in that parts and subdue his malice. We assure you that never was false traitor better provided for, as this bearer, Gloucester, can show.[27]

What Buckingham's motives were in rebelling remains a mystery. He may initially have aimed at the throne itself as he had a distant claim, but soon began to champion the claims of Henry Tudor who set sail from Brittany with a small fleet. Buckingham had set out with the king on his progress and had been with him as far as Gloucester before excusing himself and disappearing onto his Welsh estates. Margaret Beaufort, now the wife of Thomas lord Stanley, had persuaded him to support the slightly stronger claim of her son,

Henry Tudor. Buckingham must have known at this point, in early October at the latest, that the princes were dead. There would have been no point otherwise in supporting Tudor. Even more telling on that thorny subject is the fact that Elizabeth Woodville herself was found to be part of the conspiracy, having promised to support Margaret Beaufort's efforts by allowing Henry Tudor to marry Elizabeth, her daughter. She would not have countenanced this scheme if she had believed there was any hope that her sons were alive. The rebellion collapsed in the face of swift military action by Richard. Buckingham was betrayed by one of his servants and handed over to the king. Richard did not even grant him an interview before having him executed. Perhaps the whole thing proved Edward was right to keep the duke of Buckingham in the shadows. He had gained a great deal from supporting Richard's accession, as much as he could have expected, and yet he was not satisfied. With the collapse of the rebellion the little fleet carrying Henry Tudor across the Channel, having arrived off the Plymouth coast, hoisted sail and returned to Brittany. He was to try again in two years time with greater success.

While all this was going on Thomas lord Stanley and his brother William were at the king's side. Richard had returned Stanley to his former post as steward of the household after his unfortunate scare in the Tower. Perhaps Richard saw the sense in his brother's approach to the Stanleys: keep them away from their estates and always within sight. He had borne the great mace at Richard's coronation and been elected to the Order of the Garter in the place of Hastings. After the collapse of Buckingham's rebellion. Thomas was appointed Constable of England in his stead and richly rewarded for his loyalty with the confiscated estates of the rebels. Nevertheless all was not as straightforward as might at first appear. One of the leading conspirators in the rebellion, Margaret Beaufort, was Stanley's wife. Stanley may not have joined the rebellion on this occasion simply because he was with the king and could not depart easily. Suspicion must have hung thickly in the air. Stanley only saved Margaret Beaufort from attainder by making a solemn pledge to keep her in custody and prevent her from behaving in a treasonable way in the future. Richard may have tried to handle Stanley in the way his brother had, giving him ample rewards and important honours but never allowing him a title or a major extension of his regional influence, but it was difficult to conceal his manifest dislike of him and his legitimate distrust.

When Henry Tudor tried his luck again in 1485 he was able to march through Stanley country without facing any opposition. He chose to land in Wales, at Milford Haven in Pembrokeshire, and to march to Shrewsbury. This was the region in which William Stanley as chamberlain of Chester and north Wales was in charge of security. Tudor marched through the region unopposed. Thomas lord Stanley had asked leave of Richard to return to Lathom in the north-west just before Tudor's invasion. Richard had been so suspicious of this request that he had asked for Stanley's son, George, Lord Strange, to take his place at court. No one could be in any doubt about the implication behind the king's request. George was to be insurance for the good behaviour of his father. Once informed of the invasion and its easy progress, Richard ordered Thomas to join him immediately. Stanley replied that he was unwell and could not comply with the request. He was suffering from 'the sweating sickness', according to the Croyland chronicler. Even before the protagonists reached the field of battle in August 1485, Richard had plenty of evidence of Stanley's complicity in the rebellion. George Stanley had tried to escape from court and under interrogation revealed that he, his uncle William Stanley and William's son John, Lord Savage, were in league with Henry Tudor. Richard promptly declared Sir William and his son traitors. When Richard arrived at Bosworth he already knew what to expect from the Stanleys. William Stanley was a declared traitor and Thomas was the stepfather of Henry Tudor.

Richard was at Nottingham when he heard of Henry Tudor's invasion. It was here in April 1484 that Richard and his wife Anne had suffered from hearing the terrible news of the loss of their only son, Edward. He had died at Middleham after a short illness. The Croyland chronicler explained that on this boy 'all hope of the royal succession rested' and when they received the news they were 'almost out of their minds for a long time when faced with the sudden grief'.[28] Anne herself was to die in March the following year and the thirty-two-year-old Richard was rather short of home comforts when he arrived at Bosworth. One consequence of the death of his son was to make his nephew his heir. John de la Pole, earl of Lincoln, was the son of Richard's sister Elizabeth. In July 1484 Richard appointed John as leader of the council of the north. The council and the role of leader were very much Richard's own creations, endorsed by Edward IV. When Richard had taken the throne, Henry Percy, earl of Northumberland hoped to regain some of his lost influence in the north. Richard, as king, would not be able to maintain the presence in the region that had previously allowed him to become so powerful there. We can get a sense of the disappointment felt by Percy when he realised that the council was going to be continued, but he must have hoped that there was still the possibility that he could take over Richard's leadership of it. When John de la Pole was given that role it was a bitter blow to Percy. The council was to be used much as it had been before, as an extension of the royal writ into areas Percy felt should have been his alone.

We can now see that when Richard faced Henry Tudor at Bosworth he knew that he could only really rely on John Howard, duke of Norfolk from among the nobility. All the remainder of his hopes rested in the collective strength of his northern affinity, the men who had filled so many positions in the south after Buckingham's rebellion. Men such as Richard Ratcliffe, John Lord Scrope, Ralph Assheton and John Saville, who were all Yorkshiremen and who had become the constables, sheriffs, commissioners, justices of the peace and stewards across wide areas of the south and west of England. Other retainers such as the Huddlestons, the Harringtons, and the Pilkingtons were ruling the north in the king's name as surely as if Richard had been there himself acting as the leading magnate as before. In a sense Richard was ahead of his time in taking royal power directly into the localities via these gentry adherents and not through a dominant lord. His problem was that the effectiveness of this system in the north had not been replicated elsewhere. When Richard realised that he could not rely on the loyalty of his brother's retainers, he tried to fill the gap with his own affinity from the north. This was only partially successful and gave men like Ratcliffe, Brackenbury, Assheton and Catesby so much power that it was bound to cause resentment. In due course these initial difficulties might have been overcome, but Bosworth put paid to that.

As Richard arrived at Sutton Cheney near Market Bosworth to meet Henry Tudor and his motley band of rebels, he knew full well that Henry Percy, earl of Northumberland could not be fully relied upon. No one knows why the earl failed to engage his substantial forces at Bosworth. The people of Yorkshire thought they knew, and lynched him when he made his first visit to their county to collect taxes in 1489. Feelings there were still pretty raw four years after Bosworth. Richard also knew that to rely on the Stanleys would be suicide. There was not a battle that Thomas and his brother William had attended in which they had not been willing to switch sides to suit themselves. Here was another opportunity to profit just like old times. For his betrayal of Richard at Bosworth, Thomas lord Stanley was made earl of Derby. This Derby, not the Derby of Derbyshire but the ancient hundred known as South Derby in Lancashire, was the heart of Stanley's power in the north-west. It had been a long journey but he had finally got the title he so coveted. His father had been a member of the gentry only thirty years before Bosworth but the Wars of the Roses had been good times for the Stanleys. Henry Tudor correctly calculated that Stanley would support his mother, Margaret Beaufort, Stanley's wife, in her determination to get Henry crowned. Margaret had been only thirteen years old when she had given birth to Henry and her husband had died before the birth. She and Henry were very close; her life was predicated on his advancement. No husband of hers could fail to be aware of the Tudor imperative. Richard knew that the Stanleys were treacherous and dangerous.

Knowing all this would not have dismayed Richard unduly. He had with him a formidable fighting force, the very elite of the knights of the realm. These men, veterans of the battles of Barnet, Tewkesbury and Berwick where they had fought by his side, were welded together in a brotherhood of arms that reeked of confidence and violent power. As Richard watched the vanguard under John Howard, duke of Norfolk, come under intense pressure from the earl of Oxford, he would nevertheless have felt a certain pride in this group of knights around him. Here was Thomas Dacre whose grandfather had fought at Agincourt. He was a cousin of James and Robert Harrington and father-in-law of Richard Huddleston. Here was John Huddleston whose father had fought at Agincourt. He was also a cousin of the Harrington brothers. Next to them was Thomas Pilkington whose uncle and great-uncle had both fought at Agincourt. His cousin was brother-in-law of Robert Harrington. And by the king's side was James Harrington himself, possibly carrying, as his grandfather had done for Henry V at Agincourt, the royal banner of England and ready to do battle against the king's enemies and to win or die. This close-knit band of household knights was a body of men wholly wedded to the service of their good lord. There was nothing they would not do for him, nothing they would not venture in his name and no hardship they would not endure for his greater honour. Richard had inherited a concept of chivalry and chivalric behaviour from his father and it had been nurtured in adversity. He had been king for just over two years and that cherished dream of vindication in battle against the French had not been even a remote possibility. He had been unable to contemplate a foreign war while he had been tied down here in England ensuring that his rule was established and accepted. In a way Bosworth was something of an opportunity. Henry Tudor was all but French, having spent most of his time there, and he was supported by the king of France, both morally and materially with soldiers and weapons.

Even when John Howard fell in the heat of battle and it became clear that the earl of Oxford would defeat the vanguard, Richard must have felt that the knights about him could turn the tide. It was simply a matter of when and where to launch them. The loss of the duke of Norfolk was a blow, certainly, and it was also a reminder of the sort of loyalty Richard may have been able to create among the higher nobility, as he had done with the northern gentry, if he had been given time. A Tudor historian wrote of John Howard:

> He regarded more his oath, his honour and his promise made to king Richard like a gentleman and a faithful subject to his Prince, and absented not himself from his master, but as he faithfully lived under him, so he manfully died with him, to his greater honour and laud.[29]

The same could be said of the knights Richard now readied for battle. Few kings of England could have felt more confident in the loyalty and bravery of this contingent of soldiers. As Richard spotted the opportunity he had been waiting for and saw an isolated Henry Tudor attempting to cross towards the Stanleys, he would have felt proud of this troop. The bond between the king and this group going forward into battle was a complete thing, almost a spiritual one, and something this king had longed for. To reach Henry Tudor it would be necessary to cross in front of William Stanley's forces with Thomas, hanging back as usual, behind him. The group that was about to charge in front of the Stanleys contained precisely the men whose fortunes had risen in recent times and whose influence threatened them. Watching as the king swept down towards them with James Harrington and his friends beside him, the Stanleys beheld their enemies, not their compatriots.

Battles are always risky but the king would have had some confidence in the strength of a charge of knights at speed, with all the experience and force that this would bring to bear at the very heart of the enemy. It was a calculated risk but an intelligent one too. It was also an impelling prospect. As the king lowered his visor, the golden crown specially designed to encircle his helm glittering for all to see, and as James Harrington and his friends closed ranks around him, Richard, for all the confusion, screams and bloody violence before him, may have felt a certain peace. The chivalric code his father aspired to and the bonds it had forged between Richard and his trusty retainers had a life at this moment and gave an energy, a purpose and a sense of the sublime to this final act. Richard III, at the head of his troops, led the last charge of knights in English history; he was the last king of England to truly lead troops in battle. His act was an echo from another age. That heroic glory experienced by their ancestors at Agincourt, the story of which had so thrilled them in their youths, would not be reborn here. As Richard bravely battled his way towards Henry Tudor and was cut down from behind by the opportunistic treachery of William Stanley, he died crying 'Treason! Treason!' Those words finally ushered in a new age and a new form of lordship. Chivalry was dead.

# NOTES

## CHAPTER ONE: THE SHADOW OF AGINCOURT

1    M. K. Jones, 'William, Lord Hastings, the Calais Garrison and the Politics of Yorkist England', *The Ricardian* XII, 153 (June 2001), p. 284.

2    B. Coward, The Stanleys: Lords Stanley and Earls of Derby, Chetham Society 3rd ser. vol. 30 (1983), p.6.

3    M. Bennett in A. Curry, ed. Agincourt: 1415 (2000), p. 35.

4    P. Bramley, The Wars of the Roses: A Field Guide and Companion (2007), p. 158.

5    K. B. McFarlane, The Nobility of Later Medieval England (1973), p. 284.

6    M. K. Jones, *Bosworth 1485: Psychology of a Battle* (2003), pp. 196-7.

7    Bede, *Ecclesiastical History of the English People*, II. 9. D. H. Farmer, ed. (1990), p.119.

8    D. Pratt, *The Political Thought of King Alfred the Great*, (2007), pp. 240-241.

9    R. Fletcher, *Bloodfeud*, (2002), p. 12.

10    N. J. Higham, *The Death of Anglo-Saxon England*, (1997), p. 27.

11    *The Battle of Maldon*, E.V. Gordon, ed. (1964), ll. 181-201.

12    See J. Riley-Smith, *Hospitallers* (1999); D. Nicolle, *Knights of Jerusalem* (2008).

13    J. Gillingham, 'War and Chivalry in the History of William the Marshal', in M. Strickland, ed. *Anglo-Norman Warfare* (1992), p. 263.

14    J. Richard, *The Crusades* (2001), p. 26.

15    N. Saul, ed. *The Age of Chivalry* (1992), p. 19.

16    A. Sutton, 'The Court and its Culture in the Reign of Richard III', in J. Gillingham, ed. *Richard III: A Medieval Kingship* (1993), p. 85.

17    I. Mortimer, *The Perfect King* (2006). Of course a 'perfect king' could not possibly have murdered his father.

18    P. W. Hammond and A. F. Sutton, eds. *Richard III: The Road to Bosworth Field* (1985), p. 220.

19    K. Dockray, *Richard III: A Source Book* (1997), p. 123.

20    K. Dockray, *Richard III: A Source Book* (1997), p. 125.

21    K. Dockray, *Richard III: A Source Book* (1997), p. 126.

22    *Crowland Chronicle Continuations*, p. 574.

23    K. Dockray, *Richard III: A Source Book* (1997), p. 126.

24    P. W. Hammomd and A. F. Sutton, eds. *Richard III: The Road to Bosworth Field* (1985), p. 223.

## CHAPTER TWO: CHILDHOOD DANGERS

1   C. Ross, *Richard III* (1981), p. 3.
2   A. Crawford, *The Yorkists* (2007), p. 24.
3   A. J. Pollard, *Late Medieval England* (2000), pp. 129-130.
4   P. A. Johnson, *Duke Richard of York* (1988), p. 85.
5   P. A. Johnson, *Duke Richard of York* (1988), p. 108.
6   P. W. Hammond and A. F. Sutton, *Richard III: The Road to Bosworth Field* (1985), p. 23.
7   C. Carpenter, *The Wars of the Roses* (1997), p. 91.
8   J. Gillingham, *The Wars of the Roses* (1981), p. 94.
9   J. Warren, *The Wars of the Roses and the Yorkist Kings* (1995), p. 53.
10  J. R. Lander, *The Wars of the Roses* (1990), p. 53.
11  P. A. Johnson, *Duke Richard of York* (1988), p. 158.
12  R. Virgoe, ed. *Illustrated Letters of the Paston Family* (1989), p. 89.
13  A. Crawford, *The Yorkists* (2007), p. 15.
14  C. Carpenter, *The Wars of the Roses* (1997), p. 142.
15  P. Bramley, *The Wars of the Roses: A Field Guide and Companion* (2007), p. 195.
16  A. J. Pollard, *Late Medieval England* (2000), pp. 154-155.
17  P. W. Hammond and A. F. Sutton, *Richard III: The Road to Bosworth Field* (1985), p. 26.
18  P. A. Johnson, *Duke Richard of York* (1988), p. 201.

## CHAPTER THREE: THE CLOAK OF ROYALTY

1   P. A. Johnson, *Duke Richard of York* (1988), p. 211.
2   P. W. Hammond and A. F. Sutton, *Richard III: The Road to Bosworth Field* (1985), p.26.
3   J. R. Lander, *The Wars of the Roses* (1990), p. 78.
4   J. R. Lander, *The Wars of the Roses* (1990), p. 79.
5   Edward Hall, *Hall's Chronicle*, H. Ellis, ed. Camden Society (1809), p. 250.
6   Polydore Vergil, *Three Books of Polydore Vergil's English History*, H. Ellis, ed. Camden Society (1844), p. 108.
7   John Stow, *Annales, or a Great Chronicle of England*, E. Howes, ed. (1631), p. 683.
8   P. Bramley, *The Wars of the Roses: A Field Guide and Companion* (2007), p. 244.
9   Gregory's Chronicle in *The Historical Collection of a Citizen of London*, J. Gairdner, ed. Camden Society (1876), p. 211.
10  C. Ross, *Richard III*, (1981), p. 5.
11  J. R. Lander, *The Wars of the Roses* (1990), p. 89.
12  J. R. Lander, *The Wars of the Roses* (1990), p. 92.
13  R. Fabyan, *The Great Chronicle of London*, A. H. Thomas and I. D. Thorney, eds. (1938), p. 194.
14  J. R. Lander, *The Wars of the Roses* (1990), p. 90.
15  A. Crawford, *The Yorkists* (2007), p. 22.
16  Prospero di Camulio, *Calendar of State Papers, Milan*, i. 58.
17  P. Bramley, *The Wars of the Roses: A Field Guide and Companion* (2007), p. 240.
18  A. J. Pollard, *The Wars of the Roses*, (1988), p. 88.
19  P. W. Hammond and A. F. Sutton, *Richard III: The Road to Bosworth Field* (1985), p. 27.
20  P. M. Kendall, *Richard III* (1955), p. 44.
21  A. J. Pollard, *Richard III and the Princes in the Tower* (1991), pp. 44-46.

## CHAPTER FOUR: ADOLESCENCE AND UNCERTAINTY

1   C. Carpenter, *The Wars of the Roses* (1997), p. 159.
2   A. Rose, *Kings in the North* (2002), p. 530.
3   J. Gillingham, *The Wars of the Roses* (1981), p. 137.
4   D. Baldwin, *Elizabeth Woodville* (2002), p. 11.
5   Philippe de Commynes, *Memoirs*, J. Calmette and G. Durville (1923), vol 1. p. 180.
6   A. Crawford, *The Yorkists* (2007), p. 23.
7   *Crowland Chronicle Continuations*, p. 448 in N. Pronay and J. Cox, eds. (1986).
8   C. Ross, *Richard III* (1981), p. 12.
9   C. Carpenter, *Wars of the Roses* (1997), p. 172.
10  *Crowland Chronicle Continuations*, p. 551.
11  T. Rymer, *Foedera*, XI, p. 565. Quoted in C. Ross, *Richard III* (1981), p. 13.
12  A. Crawford, *The Yorkists* (2002), pp. 25, 92-93.
13  *John Vale's* Book, p. 213. Quoted in C. Carpenter, *The Wars of the Roses* (1997), p. 174.
14  *Crowland Chronicle Continuations*, p.552.
15  BL, Cotton Vespasian FIII fo. 19; for discussion on Say, see R. Horrox, *Richard III* (1989), p. 32, n. 18.
16  *Crowland Chronicle Continuations*, p.552.
17  R. Horrox, *Richard III, A Study in Service* (1989), p. 34.
18  R. Somerville, *History of the Duchy of Lancaster*, vol. 1 (1953), pp. 506 – 511.
19  M. Jones, 'Richard III and the Stanleys', *Richard III and the North*, R. Horrox, ed. Studies in Regional and Local History 6 (Hull University, 1986), p. 35.
20  The National Archives, *DL* 37/30/208.

## CHAPTER FIVE: SHOULDER TO SHOULDER

1   *Calendar of State Papers, Milan*, I, 1385-1618 (1913), pp. 65-66.
2   *Croyland Chronicle Continuations*, p. 552.
3   *Chronicles of the White Rose of York*, ed. J. A. Giles (1845), pp. 239-240).
4   *Croyland Chonicle Continuations*, p. 554.
5   L. Visser-Fuchs has plausibly argued that Richard was delayed but joined Edward in due course. 'Richard was Late', *The Ricardian*, XI, 147 (Dec. 1999), pp. 616-619.
6   C. Ross, *Richard III* (1981), p. 19.
7   Warkworth's Chronicle, *Three Chronicles of the Reign of Edward IV* (1988), p. 11.
8   *Croyland Chronicle Continuations*, p. 554.
9   *Historie of the Arrivall of Edward IV in England*, ed. J. Bruce (Camden Society, 1838), pp. 5 ff.
10  Warkworth's Chronicle, *Three Chronicles of the Reign of Edward IV* (1988), p. 14.
11  A. Crawford, *The Yorkists*, (2007), p. 37.
12  J. Gillingham, *The Wars of the Roses* (1981), p. 194.
13  J. R. Lander, *The Wars of the Roses* (1990), p. 135, n.
14  *The Great Chronicle of London*, ed. A. H. Thomas and I. D. Thorney (1938), p. 215.
15  Philippe de Commynes, *Memoirs*, ed. J. Calmette and G. Durville (1923-5), vol. 1, p. 213.
16  P. Bramley, *The Wars of the Roses: a Field Guide and Companion* (2007), p.69, for example.
17  M. K. Jones, 'Richard III as a Soldier', in *Richard III: a Medieval Kingship* (1993), p. 96.

See also P. J. Watson, 'A Review of the Sources for the Battle of Barnet', *The Ricardian*, vol XII, no. 149 (June 2000), pp. 50 – 70.

18   Statutes of Queen's College Cambridge, quoted in P. W. Hammond and A. Sutton, eds. *Richard III: the Road to Bosworth Field* (1985), p. 68.

19   T. Wright, ed. *Political Poems and Songs*, Rolls Series (1861), vol. 1, p. 280.

20   *Historie of the Arrivall of Edward IV in England,* ed. J. Bruce (Camden Society, 1838), pp. 28–30.

21   J. Warkworth, *A Chronicle of the First Thirteen Years of the Reign of King Edward IV*, ed. J. O. Halliwell (Camden Society, 1839), p. 20.

22   E.g. C. Carpenter, *The Wars of the Roses*, (1997), pp. 180-181.

## CHAPTER SIX: FEUD

1   *Calendar of Patent Rolls 1461-1467*, p. 164; National Archives, *DL/10/386;* see R. Somerville, *History of the Duchy of Lancaster* (1953), vol 1. esp. pp. 230-235.

2   J. S. Roskell, *The Knights of the Shire for the County Palatine of Lancaster 1377-1460*, Chetham Society, new series, 96 (1937), p. 124; I. Grimble, *The Harrington Family* (1957), pp. 35 ff.; R. Horrox, *Oxford Dictionary of National Biography* (2004 and online edn. 2007) article 54525.

3   J. S. Roskell, *The Knights of the Shire for the County Palatine of Lancaster 1377-1460*, Chetham Society, new series, 96 (1937), p. 125;

4   B. Coward, *The Stanleys, Lord Stanley and Earls of Derby*, Chetham Society, 3rd series, 30 (1983), p. 4.

5   M. J. Bennett, *Oxford Dictionary of National Biography* (2004 and online edn. 2006), article 26278.

6   D. J. Clayton, *The Administration of the County Palatine of Chester, 1442-1485*, Chetham Society, 3rd series, 35 (1990), pp. 78, 92.

7   *Rotuli Parliamentorum*, J. Strachey, ed. (1767-77), vol. 5, p. 191.

8   Gregory's Chronicle, *Collections of a Citizen of London*, J. Gairdener, ed. Camden Society (1876), p. 210.

9   National Archives, DL 37/31/69.

10   National Archives, DL 5/1/44.

11   National Archives, DL 42/19/89.

12   R. Horrox, *Richard III: A study in service* (1989), p. 47; R. Somerville, *History of the Duchy of Lancaster* (1953), vol 1. p. 254.

13   National Archives, DL 42/19/10: 'To arm against the Scots'.

14   National Archives, DL 37/32/69.

15   National Archives, DL 37/32/61.

16   *Calendar of Patent Rolls, 1461-67*, pp. 495, 460, 541, etc.

17   *Calendar of Close Rolls, Edward IV*, vol. 1. no. 136.

18   *Calendar of Close Rolls, Edward IV*, vol. 1. no. 535.

19   *Calendar of Close Rolls, Edward IV*, vol. 1. no. 900.

20   *Calendar of Close Rolls, Edward IV*, vol. 1. no. 1155.

21   *Calendar of Patent Rolls, 1476-85*, p. 151.

## CHAPTER SEVEN: IN MEMORIAM

1   F. Sandford, *A Genealogical History of the Kings and Queens of England* (1707), pp. 391-2. Also H. K. Bonney, *Historic Notices in Reference to Fotheringhay* (1821). I am grateful to St Mary and All Saints Church, Fotheringhay, for displaying the record of the funeral.

2   J. Raine, The Statutes for the College of Middleham, *Archaeological Journal* (1857), vol. 14, pp. 160-70.

3   M. K. Jones, Richard III as a Soldier, J. Gillingham, ed. *Richard III: a Medieval Kingship* (1993), p. 94.

4   C. Ross, *Richard III* (1981), p. 142; J. Potter, *Good King Richard?* (1983), pp. 138-9

5   J. C. Wedgewood, *History of Parliament: biographies of members of the Commons 1437-1509* (1936), p. 85.

6   R. Horrox, *Oxford Dictionary of National Biography* (2004), online ed. Article no. 52792.

7   A. Sutton, 'The Court and its Culture in the Reign of Richard III', J. Gillingham, ed. *Richard III: a Medieval Kingship* (1993), p. 81.

8   R. Horrox, *Richard III: a study in service* (1989), pp. 37, 38, 41.

9   A. Sutton, 'A curious searcher of our public weal', Richard III, Piety, Chivalry and the Concept of the 'Good Prince', P. W. Hammond, ed. *Richard III: Loyalty, Lordship and Law* (1986), p. 65.

10  D. H. Farmer, *Oxford Dictionary of Saints* (1987), p. 318.

11  P. W. Hammond and A. F. Sutton, *Richard III: the road to Bosworth Field* (1985), p. 76.

12  C. Ross, *Richard III* (1981), p. 141.

13  C. Ross, *Richard III* (1981), p. 28.

14  M. Hicks, *Anne Neville* (2007), p. 132.

15  *Croyland Chronicle Continuations*, p. 557.

16  M. Hicks, 'Richard Duke of Gloucester: the Formative Years', J. Gillingham, ed. *Richard III: a Medieval Kingship* (1993), p. 30.

## CHAPTER EIGHT: THE HOPE OF GLORY

1   *Calendar of State Papers, Milan, 1385-1618*, p. 197.

2   Philippe de Commynes, *Memoirs*, J. Calmette and G. Durville, eds. p. 226.

3   C. Ross, *Edward IV* (1974), p. 226.

4   Philippe de Commynes, *Memoirs*, quoted in J. R. Lander, *The Wars of the Roses* (1990), p. 158.

5   *Croyland Chronicle Continuations*, p. 559.

6   C. Ross, *Edward IV* (1974), p. 235.

7   *Croyland Chronicle Continuations*, p. 561.

8   M. K. Jones, *Bosworth 1485* (2002), pp. 79 ff.

9   Also *The Great Chronicle of London*, all quoted in K. Dockray, *Richard III: A Source Book* (1997), pp. 26, 28.

10  Thus Sir Thomas More, *The History of King Richard III*, R. S. Sylvester, ed. (1963), pp. 8-9.

11  Mancini, quoted in P. Hammond and A. Sutton, *Richard III: The Road to Bosworth Field* (1985), p. 72.

12  K. Dockray, *Richard III: A Source Book* (1997), p.36.

13  P. Hammond and A. Sutton, *Richard III: The Road to Bosworth Field* (1985), pp. 81-82.

14 K. Dockray, *Richard III: A Source Book* (1997), pp. 36-37.
15 C. Ross, *Edward IV* (1974), pp. 283-290.
16 P. Hammond and A. Sutton, *Richard III: The Road to Bosworth Field* (1985), pp. 82-83.
17 P. Hammond and A. Sutton, *Richard III: The Road to Bosworth Field* (1985), p. 86.
18 R. Horrox, *Richard III: a study in service* (1989), p. 71; K. Dockray, *Richard III: A Source Book* (1997), p. 38.

## CHAPTER NINE: THE DEATH OF CHIVALRY

1 *Croyland Chronicle Continuations*, p. 564.
2 The translation by Pronay and Cox uses the term 'counsellors' rather than 'councillors' but the Latin makes it clear that these were the men who sat on the Council (*consiliarii* and *Consilio*).
3 R. Horrox, *Richard III: a study in service* (1989), p. 92.
4 J. R. Lander, *The Wars of the Roses* (1990), p.173; also see A. J. Pollard, *Richard III and the Princes in the Tower* (1991), p. 97.
5 C. Ross, *Richard III* (1981), p. 38.
6 M. K. Jones in J. Gillingham, ed. *Richard III: A Medieval Kingship* (1993), p. 98.
7 P. Hammond and A. Sutton, *Richard III: The Road to Bosworth Field* (1985), p 97.
8 *Croyland Chronicle Continuations*, p. 566.
9 D. Baldwin, *Elizabeth Woodville*, (2002), p. 103.
10 Robert Fabyan, *The Concordaunce of Hystoryes*, 514.
11 *Croyland Chronicle Continuations*, p. 566.
12 *Croyland Chronicle Continuations*, p. 566.
13 M. Hicks, *Anne Neville* (2007), pp. 137-141.
14 K. Dockray, *Richard III: A Source Book* (1997), p. 56; Hammond and Sutton, p. 103.
15 *Croyland Chronicle Continuations*, p. 567.
16 S. Cunningham, *Richard III: A royal enigma* (2003), p. 46.
17 *Titulus Regius*, in P. Hammond and A. Sutton, *Richard III: The Road to Bosworth Field* (1985), p. 155.
18 P. W. Hammond, in J. Gillingham, ed. *Richard III: A Medieval Kingship* (1993), p. 136.
19 K. Dockray, *Richard III: A Source Book* (1997), p. 72.
20 P. W. Hammond, in J. Gillingham, ed. *Richard III: A Medieval Kingship* (1993), p.134.
21 H. Kleineke, 'Richard III and the Origins of the Court of Requests', *The Ricardian*, XVII (2007), p. 27.
22 *Calendar of Patent Rolls 1476-85*, p. 143
23 T. D. Whitaker, *A History of the Original Parish of Whalley* (3rd ed, 1878), v. p. 509.
24 T. D. Whitaker, *A History of Richmondshire* (1823), ii. P. 261; W. Farrer and J. Brownbill, eds. *A History of the County of Lancaster* (1914), vol. 8, pp. 191-201, n.61.
25 *Letters and Patents: Henry VII*, iii, g. 2016(3); Pat. 13 Henry VIII, pt. iii, m. 22.
26 Eg. A. Carson, *Richard III: The Maligned King* (2008).
27 S. Cunningham, *Richard III: A royal enigma* (2003), p. 54.
28 *Croyland Chronicler Continuations*, p. 571.
29 Edward Hall, *Union of the Two Noble and Illustre Famelies of Lancastre and York* (1809), p. 419.

# SELECT
# BIBLIOGRAPHY

## PRIMARY SOURCES

*British Library Harleian Manuscript* 433, P. W. Hammond and R. E. Horrox, eds. (4 vols. 1979-83).

*Calendar of Close Rolls*, 1452-94.

*Calendar of Patent Rolls*, 1452-94.

Camulio, Prospero di, *Calendar of State Papers, Milan.*

*Chronicles of London*, C. L. Kingsford, ed. (1905)

*Chronicles of the White Rose of York*, J. A. Giles, ed. (1845).

Commynes, Philippe de, *Memoirs*, J. Calmette and G. Durville (1923).

*Croyland Chronicle Continuations*, N. Pronay and J. Cox, eds. (1986).

Dockray, K., *Richard III: A Source Book* (1997).

Fabyan, R., *The Great Chronicle of London*, A. H. Thomas and I. D. Thorney, eds. (1938).

Hall, E., *Hall's Chronicle*, H. Ellis, ed. Camden Society (1809).

Hammomd, P. W., and Sutton, A. F., eds. *Richard III: The Road to Bosworth Field* (1985).

*Historie of the Arrivall of Edward IV in England*, ed. J. Bruce (Camden Society, 1838).

Mancini, D., *The Usurpation of Richard III*, ed. C. A. J. Armstrong (1969).

More, T., *History of King Richard III*, ed. R. S. Sylvester (1963).

*Paston Letters and Papers of the Fifteenth Century*, N. Davis, ed. (2 vols. 1971-76).

Polydore Vergil, *Three Books of Polydore Vergil's English History*, H. Ellis, ed. Camden Society (1844).

*Rotuli Parliamentorum*, J. Strachey, ed. (1767-77).

Stow, J., *Annales, or a Great Chronicle of England*, E. Howes, ed. (1631).

The National Archives, *DL* 42, *DL* 37, *DL* 5.

Warkworth's Chronicle, *Three Chronicles of the Reign of Edward IV* (1988).

## SECONDARY SOURCES

Baldwin, D., *Elizabeth Woodville* (2002).

Bennett, M., in Curry, A., ed. *Agincourt: 1415* (2000).

Bramley, P., *The Wars of the Roses: A Field Guide and Companion* (2007).

Carpenter, C., *The Wars of the Roses* (1997).

Castor, H., *Blood & Roses: the Paston Family and the Wars of the Roses* (2004).

Clayton, D. J., *The Administration of the County Palatine of Chester,* 1442-1485, Chetham Society, 3rd series, 35 (1990).

Coward, B., *The Stanleys: Lords Stanley and Earls of Derby*, Chetham Society 3rd ser. vol. 30 (1983).

Crawford, A., *The Yorkists* (2007).

Cunningham, S., *Richard III: A Royal Enigma* (2003).

Gillingham, J., ed. *Richard III: A Medieval Kingship* (1993).

Gillingham, J., *The Wars of the Roses* (1981).

Given-Wilson, C. *The Royal Household and the Kings Affinity* (1986).

Goodman, A., *The Wars of the Roses* (1981).

Griffiths, R. A., *The Reign of King Henry VI* (1981).

Grimble, I., *The Harrington Family* (1957).

Hicks, M., *Anne Neville* (2007).

Hicks, M., *Richard III* (200).

Horrox, R. E., *Richard III: A Study in Service* (1989).

Johnson, P. A., *Duke Richard of York* (1988).

Jones, M. K., 'Richard III and the Stanleys', *Richard III and the North*, R. Horrox, ed. Studies in Regional and Local History 6 (Hull University, 1986).

Jones, M. K., *Bosworth 1485: Psychology of a Battle* (2003).

Keen, M. H., *Chivalry* (1984).

Kendall, P. M., *Richard III* (1955).

Lander, J. R., *The Wars of the Roses* (1990).

McFarlane, K. B., *The Nobility of Later Medieval England* (1973).

Pollard, A. J., *Late Medieval England* (2000).

Pollard, A. J., *Richard III and the Princes in the Tower* (1991).

Pollard, A. J., *Warwick the Kingmaker* (2007).

Potter, J. *Good King Richard?* (1983).

Rose, A., *Kings in the North* (2002).

Roskell, J. S., *The Knights of the Shire for the County Palatine of Lancaster* 1377-1460, Chetham Society, new series, 96 (1937).

Ross, C., *Edward IV* (1974).

Ross, C., *Richard III* (1981).

Saul, N., ed. *The Age of Chivalry* (1992).

Somerville, R., History of the Duchy of Lancaster (1953).

Warren, C., *The Wars of the Roses and the Yorkist Kings* (1995).

Watts, J., *Henry VI and the Politics of Kingship* (1996).

Whitaker, T. D., *A History of Richmondshire* (1823).

Whitaker, T. D., *A History of the Original Parish of Whalley* (3rd ed, 1878).

# INDEX